The Second Coming of Jesus -
Think Again

The Second Coming of Jesus -
Think Again

A Call to Biblical Theology

———••———

William H. Hogue

About the front cover:

> After this I looked, and, behold, a door was opened in heaven: and the first voice which I heard was as it were of a trumpet talking with me; which said, Come up hither, and I will shew thee things which must be hereafter. And immediately I was in the spirit; and, behold, a throne was set in heaven, and one sat on the throne.—Rev. 4:1-2

Order this book online at www.trafford.com
or email orders@trafford.com

Most Trafford titles are also available at major online book retailers.

Printed in the United States of America.

ISBN: 978-1-4669-4591-3 (sc)
ISBN: 978-1-4669-4590-6 (e)

Trafford rev. 04/12/2014

 www.trafford.com

North America & international
toll-free: 1 888 232 4444 (USA & Canada)
fax: 812 355 4082

Dedicated to:

Christ Jesus, Daniel,
The holy apostles, and to all who yearn to *understand*
What they said.

Contents

The Second Coming of Jesus - Think Again

By
William H. Hogue

ANNOUNCEMENT

In the year AD 72 Jesus Came again to rapture His elect brethren into Heaven and pour out His wrath upon the Antichrist in Asia (cf. Rev. 6:17). He then sat down with His brethren to eat and drink wine at the "marriage supper of the Lamb" (see Matt. 26:29; Rev. 19:9). Then, "according to their works," He gave them "mansions" and "cities" (Matt. 16:27; Luke 19:17, 19; John 14:2-3), at the same time exalting them on God's throne with Him in Heaven (Rev. 3:21). They then, as "New Jerusalem," descended from God out of Heaven to the "new earth, wherein dwelleth righteousness" (II Pet. 3:13; Rev. 21:1-2). Thus, their prayer "Thy kingdom come" came true *at last* (Matt. 6:10a)!

A Word about This Announcement

Dear reader, if you are a Christian today this announcement will probably strike you as way out of line, possibly even as *anti-Christian*. You may be thinking: "Whoever wrote this is Biblically illiterate, silly, imbecilic, moronic, stupid, ignorant, uneducated, etc., etc., etc. Let me humbly say to you, dear reader, that while I don't claim to have **_historical_** orthodoxy on this topic, yet I **_do_** claim to have **_true or Biblical orthodoxy_** on it. Let me put it this way: I am pro-Bible all the way! I know what the Bible says and that's what I believe, advocate, and teach in this book.

Friend, if you don't want to read proof that Jesus has already come again, I give you the following options: read this book, but don't take it seriously; OR: read it and take it seriously. My guess is that if you do the first option, you will, in time, do the second option also. Here's a third option: Read the Bible from Genesis to Revelation, meditate on God's word as you read, and pray and ask God to give you the correct understanding of the Bible. If you do this, you won't have to read my book because you will learn that you need to "THINK AGAIN" about "THE SECOND COMING OF JESUS."

The Preferred Audience of This Book

This book is ultimately addressed to any person, Christian or otherwise, who (1) yearns to know the truth; (2) has an open mind; (3) prefers to think for himself; and (4) is not afraid to think "outside of the box."

Truths Are Established Upon the Basis of Two or Three Witnesses!

This book deals with the popular belief among modern Christians that *Jesus is coming again.* My message is that Jesus is _not_ coming again *because He has already come again.* I propose to prove this through the testimonies of THREE BIBLE WITNESSES. Why three? Jesus, in agreement with the Torah [i.e. Law], taught that it takes two or three witnesses to establish a truth or doctrine: ". . . in the mouth of two or three witnesses every word may be established" (Matt. 18:16; see also Deut. 19:15; Heb. 10:28).

(Who Are the Three Witnesses?) The three witnesses are Daniel, Jesus, and the collective apostles. Friends, I hope you will be astonished to hear what these three have been testifying (in _your_ Bible) for centuries without very many Christians ever having understood them! However, there may be a dilemma for you: Will you believe three Holy-Spirit-inspired witnesses, or will you "play it safe" and cling to today's popular but *non-biblical* teaching that Jesus is coming again?

Author

Chapter One

THE WITNESS OF
DANIEL THE PROPHET

INTRODUCTION

Daniel was among thousands of Jews that king Nebuchadnezzar took captive to Babylon in the first deportation, 606 BC. He determined to obey Jehovah. For example, he refused to eat the un-kosher food the king offered him.

God made Daniel a prophet to the Jews in Babylon, and revealed to the Jews through him that Jehovah would continue to favor them for a prophetic period of 490 years.

Daniel prophesied that four beasts would rise up out of the sea:

Daniel spake and said, I saw . . . four great beasts come up from the sea . . . The first *was* like a lion . . . another . . . a second, like to a bear . . . and lo another, like a leopard . . . After this I saw in the night visions, and behold a fourth beast, dreadful and terrible, and strong exceedingly; and it had great iron teeth: it devoured and brake in pieces, and stamped the residue with the feet of it . . . and it had ten horns. I considered the horns, and, behold, there came up among them another little horn, before whom there were three of the first horns plucked up by the roots: and, behold, in this horn *were* eyes like the eyes of man, and a mouth speaking great things.—Dan. 7:2-8; adapted

Each beast represents the same ancient false religion, Babylonian Idolatry, which was carried down to the time of Christ by four powerful, successive Middle East empires. The first empire, "like a lion," was the Babylonian Empire (605-539 BC). The second beast, "like to a bear," was the Medo-Persian Empire (539-331 BC). The third, "like a leopard," was the Grecian Empire (331-168 BC), and the fourth, "great and terrible . . . [that] had ten horns," was **the Roman Empire.** This final empire carried anti-Christ Babylonianism down to the church of Christ, and abominated it! But Jesus' death on the cross overcame it, and delivered all who had been deceived by it.

("MYSTERY, BABYLON THE GREAT . . .") Daniel's vision of these four empires—i.e. kingdoms—is really about an ancient and widespread false religion that Jesus in Revelation called "MYSTERY, BABYLON THE GREAT, THE MOTHER OF HARLOTS AND ABOMINATIONS OF THE EARTH" (Rev. 17:5). This religion had its beginning in the first post-flood city called Babel, whose founder and builder was Nimrod:

And Cush begat Nimrod: he began to be a mighty one in the earth. He was a mighty hunter before the LORD: Wherefore it is said, Even as Nimrod the mighty hunter before the LORD. And the beginning of his kingdom was Babel . . . in the land of Shinar.—Gen. 10:8-10

(When Did Daniel's Prophecy Concerning the Fourth Beast Start?) The Fourth Empire Daniel saw, the Roman Empire, had TEN HORNS on its head (see Dan. 7:7d). Only if we know what or who these horns represent can we determine *when* the Fourth Beast rose from the sea. Let me cut to the chase: THESE HORNS WERE ROME'S FIRST TEN CAESARS, Julius Caesar being the first.

The Ten Horns

These ten "horns," correctly interpreted, were the first ten Caesars of the Roman Empire. The angel told Daniel that they were ten "kings" of that empire—Dan. 7:24a—because Daniel would not have known the meaning of "Caesars." We know now that the angels spoke of:

1.	Julius Caesar	49-44 BC
2.	Augustus	31 BC-AD 14
3.	Tiberius	AD 14-37
4.	Caligula	37-41
5.	Claudius	41-54
6.	Nero	54-68
7.	**Galba**	**68-69 (murdered)**
8.	**Otho**	**69 (suicide)**
9.	**Vitellius**	**69 (murdered)**
10.	Vespasian	69-79*

*Michael Grant, *The Twelve Caesars*

The dates give us a prophetic period of 128 years (49 + 79 = 128). Daniel's prophecy in Chapters 2 and 7, therefore, is concerned with the Roman Empire during these "prophetic" 128 years **only**. Prophecy scholars should stop asking how long the Roman Empire lasted (i.e. in terms of secular history), and start asking how long its *prophetic period* lasted. These Caesars, or "horns," by the way, correspond in time to the "ten toes" on Nebuchadnezzar's "image" in Dan. 2:42.

The Little Horn

In order to fully understand Daniel's witness—*that Jesus' Second Coming took place in midsummer of AD 72*—we must first determine **when** three of the first horns were plucked up by the roots (Dan. 7:8, 20, 24). If the AD 72 date is correct, the Little Horn had to have begun forming in January of AD 69, which would be 3½ years before midsummer of 72. If we check the list of the Ten Caesars above we will see that, indeed, there were three Caesars plucked up in that year: Galba, Otho, and Vitellius. They all three met a violent death and none of them left an heir to take his place on the throne. That is the meaning of "plucked up by the roots" (Dan. 7:8)!

(A Time, Times, and Half a Time") Daniel said that the Little Horn—i.e. the Antichrist—would run his evil course for "a time and times and the dividing of time" (Dan. 7:25). In Revelation we learn that this wording means 3½ years, shown in the two other references to that same *prophetic duration:* (1) "a thousand two hundred *and* threescore days" (Rev. 12:6); and (2) "forty and two months" (Rev.

11:2). All three of these expressions mean 3½ years (i.e. 3½ **prophetic**, not **modern calendar** years).

If you add 3½ years to the Year AD 69, to What Year Do You Come? Here's the point: If the Antichrist's evil course began in **JANUARY** of 69 and continued for 3½ years, to what **year** and to what **season** of that year do we arrive? Isn't it midsummer (perhaps **JUNE**)—the halfway point—of AD 72 (69 + 3.5 = 72.5)? **YES!** Almost any grade school student could calculate this. Thus, according to the **WITNESS OF DANIEL** in *your* Bible, Jesus Christ's Second Coming took place in midsummer of AD 72.

Where in Daniel do we read that Jesus' Second Coming was to occur when this 3½-year course of the Antichrist ended? Find the answer in the following passage:

Then I [i.e. Daniel] would know the truth of the fourth beast [i.e. the Roman Empire], which was diverse from all the others,[1] exceedingly dreadful, whose teeth *were of* iron, and his nails *of* brass; *which* devoured, brake in pieces, and stamped the residue with his feet; And of the ten horns that *were* in his head, and *of* the other that came up, and before whom three fell; even *of* that horn that had eyes, and a mouth that spake very great things, whose look *was* more stout than his fellows. I beheld, and the same horn made war with the saints, and prevailed against them; **UNTIL the ancient of days CAME [i.e. the Second Coming], and judgment was given to the saints of the most High**; and the time came that the saints possessed the kingdom.—Dan. 7:19-22

How Shall the
Kingdom of God
Ever be Seen?

The failure among today's premillennialists to interpret the ten horns as the first ten Roman "kings," or Caesars has caused them to invent a false teaching they call *the revived Roman Empire* (I discuss this topic in the next section).

---

[1] *The others*—i.e. Babylonian, Medo-Persian, and Grecian empires

They had to invent it because they insist that when the kingdom of God comes all men certainly shall be able to see it. Also, like the Jews of Jesus' time they believe that the kingdom is supposed to be on *this earth*. Jesus' teaching contradicts both these misconceptions. He told the Jews: "The kingdom of God cometh not with observation" (Luke 17:20); that is, men won't be able to see it with their physical eyes. Moreover, Jesus assured Pilate: "My kingdom is not of this world" (John 18:36).

This "don't see it" argument reflects a grievous lack of true Biblical *faith* among today's premillennialists. The idea that they won't believe what they don't see is not Biblical. According to the author of Hebrews:

> . . . faith is the substance of things hoped for, the evidence of things **not seen**.—Heb. 11:1

Therefore today's Christians do not please God with their "must see it before I'll believe it" kind of faith:

> . . . without faith *it is* impossible to please . . . God—Heb. 11:6

Note what Paul taught concerning things seen and unseen. Writing to the Christians at Corinth he said:

> (For we walk by faith, **not by sight:**)—II Cor. 5:7

> . . . we look not at the things which are seen, but at the things which are not seen: for the things which are seen *are* temporal; but the things which are not seen are *eternal*—II Cor. 4:18

Jesus taught the Jews not to expect to "see" God's kingdom descend down to earth from Heaven. When they demanded Jesus to tell them:

> . . . when the kingdom of God should come, he answered them and said, THE KINGDOM OF GOD COMETH NOT WITH OBSERVATION; NEITHER SHALL THEY SAY, LO HERE! OR, LO THERE! FOR, BEHOLD, THE KINGDOM OF GOD IS WITHIN YOU."—Luke 17:20-21

The kingdom of God is not ever going to be visible to the physical eye, no more than the invisible God Himself will ever be seen by the fleshly eye. The kingdom of God can only be spiritually *understood*, not seen with the physical eye.

Will There Be A
Revived Roman Empire
So that Daniel's
Prophecies Can Be Fulfilled?

There will never be a revived Roman Empire. Search the Bible from cover to cover and no such doctrine, or grounds for such a doctrine, can be found. The reason this false doctrine was ever invented in the first place stems from today's Christians' lack of understanding of God's word. **First,** they don't understand that the Church was to remain on earth only during Christ's adult-time generation [i.e. from Pentecost to the Danielic Abomination of Desolation, which took place in Asia soon after January 15, AD 69 when Galba was uprooted from the Roman throne.[2]]. Following this Abomination the Great Tribulation commenced and lasted 3½ years until Jesus' Second Coming and the Rapture of the New Testament saints in midsummer of AD 72. When Jesus came one of His Olivet prophecies was fulfilled—i.e. ". . . all things which are written may be fulfilled" (Luke 21:22). Also, Jesus' generation was just four years shy of its end:

> Verily I say unto you, This generation [His own] shall not pass away, till all be fulfilled.—Luke 21:32

---

[2] Galba, Otho, and Vitellius were the three horns that were plucked up by the roots in the year AD 69, during which time "another little horn" formed and persecuted the church. Beginning on this date the Great Tribulation commenced and continued until Jesus' appearing. During the tribulation the church existed but in "the wilderness . . . where she [was] nourished for a time, and times, and half a time" (Rev. 12:14). Thus its work of evangelism had ceased as predicted by Jesus: ". . . the night cometh when no man can work" (John 9:4).

The following passages, correctly understood, teach the same truth:

> Ye [i.e. the twelve disciples] shall not have gone over [i.e. evangelized] the cities of Israel, till the Son of man be come.—Matt. 10:23

> Verily I say unto you, There be some [i.e. of the twelve disciples] standing here, which shall not taste of death, till they see the Son of man coming in his kingdom.—Matt. 16:28

> We [Christians of Christ's generation] shall not all sleep, but we shall all be changed, In a moment, in the twinkling of an eye, at the last trump—I Cor. 15:51b, 52a

> For the Lord himself shall descend from heaven . . . Then we which are alive *and* remain shall be caught up . . . in the clouds, to meet the Lord . . . and so shall we ever be with the Lord.—I Thess. 4:16-17

Conclusion:

The work of the church—i.e. apostolic evangelism—ended in AD 69. Then followed the 3½-year Great Tribulation, which ended in Midsummer of AD 72 with Jesus' Second Coming and the Rapture of the saints. *We must realize that the Roman Empire still existed during these end time events and would never **NEED** reviving!* Hence today's premillennial talk of a revived Roman Empire is only "vanity of vanity" (Eccles. 1:2) and "foolish talking" (Eph. 5:4).

THE SECOND REASON

Second, today's most common Christian eschatology—i.e. premillennialism—is terribly and unwarrantedly flawed inasmuch as Daniel gave not the least hint that there would have to be a revival of the Roman Empire after its **FIRST** and **ONLY** existence.

Nothing Daniel prophesied contains the least hint or suggestion that a "time gap" of any length would be needed between the first time the Roman Empire existed and such end time prophetic fulfillments as the Abomination, the Great Tribulation, the Second Coming, or the establishment of God's eternal kingdom, all of which are hidden in the following passage.

And he[3] shall speak *great* words against the most High [**Abomination**], and shall wear out the saints of the most High . . . until a time and times and the dividing of time [**Great Tribulation and its duration**]. But the judgment shall sit [**Jesus' Second Coming**], and they [Jesus' elect brethren] shall take away his dominion, to consume and to destroy *it* unto the end [**the establishment of the Kingdom of God**]. And the kingdom and dominion, and the greatness of the kingdom under the whole heaven, shall be given to the people of the saints of the most High, whose kingdom *is* an everlasting kingdom, and all dominions shall serve and obey him.—Dan. 7:25-27

Neither in this passage nor in any other passage in Daniel, or for that matter any other passage in the whole Bible, can the hint of a time gap be discerned. Daniel wrote as if all these prophecies would come to pass in an uninterrupted flow of time.

Misconceived Need for a Prophetic Time Gap in Daniel 7

Now we should ask to understand: WHY did premillennialism develop; that is, WHY do most of today's Christian eschatologists and churchmen see a need for a time gap? First, understand that premillennialists **_DO_** know and believe that God's kingdom **_IS SUPPOSED TO BE_** ESTABLISHED **_DURING A TIME WHEN THE ROMAN EMPIRE EXISTS!_** They believe that as well as I. That salient point is too plain for any Bible scholar to miss or deny. What they don't believe is that it happened during the FIRST and ONLY existence of that kingdom. Because they believe only what they can physically see they have concluded that God's kingdom did not appear during the empire's first existence.[4] Thus they look for a revival of the

---

3.   The Little Horn, or Antichrist

4.   In all my writings I show that God's kingdom DEFINITELY DID come about during Christ's ongoing generation, but that it appeared in Paradise, the Third Heaven [see II Cor. 12:1-4], and NOT on this earth. Thus, the premillennialists cannot find the kingdom on **_this_** earth anywhere. In that it exists in Paradise the kingdom is invisible to us on earth. Only when we **enter Paradise for ourselves** will we finally "see" it **_in_** all the inhabitants there. It will then be in us, too!

Roman Empire. It is as simple as that. In short either their unbelief or their lack of understanding (or both, as I suspect) is the reason for the emergence of premillennialism, and its doctrine of a revived Roman Empire. I see unbelief in these Christians because they "invented" a time gap when Scripture nowhere presents a need for it, or gives a hint of it. I see their lack of understanding as resulting from their unbelief.

Jesus' Generation
Corresponded to the
Time of the
First Ten Caesars.

The New Testament either directly or indirectly alludes to all ten of the "horns" on the Fourth Beast [i.e. the Roman Empire]; that is, to the first ten Caesars of that empire. I present the following information, and hopefully "enlightenment," to my unbelieving and confused premillennial friends to help them finally understand and adopt the faith of the first-century Christians, a faith plainly recorded in **their** Bibles. This examination of the New Testament throws light on the ***FACT*** that the Ten Horns [the first ten Roman Caesars] existed during the first time—and ONLY time—the Roman Empire existed. Put in other words, they existed during the lifetime of Jesus and His apostles, AND DURING THE TIME WHEN THE ***TRUE*** CHURCH EXISTED ON EARTH. Let us now "find" the Ten Horns of Daniel's Fourth Beast.

FIRST CAESAR: JULIUS CAESAR
(Reigned 5 years: 49-44 BC)

Julius Caesar [1st Horn], though he had been dead for a generation before Christ was born, nevertheless was the first "horn" in Daniel 7. His name "Caesar" is mentioned 30 times in the New Testament. Also, two cities in Palestine were named after him: (1) Caesarea Philippi, a town north of Galilee; and (2) Caesarea [Maritima], a Palestinian Mediterranean port. Jointly these two cities are mentioned 17 times in the New Testament. Since Caesars' name is seen in the word "Caesarea" we can say that Caesar is mentioned a total of forty-seven times in the New Testament. This biblical evidence alone should suffice any

Christian to believe that Julius Caesar should be counted as the first Horn on the head of the Fourth Beast (Dan. 7:7-8).

SECOND CAESAR: AUGUSTUS
(Reigned 45 years: 31 BC-AD 14)

Augustus [2nd Horn] is mentioned once, and it was in connection with a Roman tax collection in the land of Judea just before the birth of Jesus:

> And it came to pass in those days, that there went out a decree from Caesar Augustus, that all the world [i.e. Roman Empire] should be taxed.—Luke 2:1

Augustus, the first emperor [2nd Caesar], reigned 45 years, the longest reign of any of the first ten Caesars. Jesus was born in the 27th year of his reign and was 18 when he died. The episode of the twelve-year-old Jesus remaining behind in Jerusalem after the Passover feast to discuss the Torah [at the temple] with Jewish doctors took place during the reign of Augustus—ca AD 8, six years before Augustus' death (see Luke 2:41-49).

THIRD CAESAR: TIBERIUS
(Reigned 23 years: AD 14-37)

Tiberius [3rd Horn] is mentioned four times in the Bible, once as the man himself (see below), once as the city of Tiberius on the west shore of the Sea of Galilee (John 6:23), and two times as the alternative name for the Sea of Galilee—i.e. the Sea of Tiberius (see John 6:1 and 21:1). As the Caesar in Rome we find him mentioned in connection with the approximate commencement of the ministries of John the Baptist and Jesus in the Holy Land:

> Now <u>in the fifteenth year of the reign of **Tiberius** Caesar</u>, Pontius Pilate being governor of Judea, and Herod being tetrarch of Galilee, and his brother Philip tetrarch of Ituraea and of the region of Trachonitis, and Lysanias the tetrarch of Abelene, Annas and Caiaphas being the high priests, the word of God came unto John the son of Zacharias in the wilderness.—Luke 3:1

Before Tiberius' reign ended Jesus was baptized and He commenced His public ministry among the Jews (AD 26). He was crucified, buried, and rose again the third day. Pentecost took place, the Church was founded in Jerusalem, Stephen became the first Christian martyr, Saul [i.e. Paul] was converted at Damascus, and "the times of the Gentiles"[5] began (cf. AD 33).

FOURTH CAESAR: CALIGULA
(Reigned 4 years: AD 37-41)

Caligula [4th Horn] is not mentioned in the New Testament. However, it was during his reign that the first "Gentile" was converted (AD 41). Peter, called of God to go to Caesarea [Maritima], preached the gospel to Cornelius [a Roman centurion] and his household. The Holy Spirit fell upon the uncircumcised Cornelius and all others in his house who heard Peter preach.

FIFTH CAESAR: CLAUDIUS
(Reigned 13 years: AD 41-54)

This fourth emperor of Rome [5th Horn] is twice mentioned in Acts of the Apostles:

> And in those days came prophets from Jerusalem unto Antioch. And there stood up one of them named Agabus, and signified by the Spirit that there should be great dearth throughout all the world: which came to pass in the days of Claudius Caesar.—Acts 11:27-28

> After these things Paul departed from Athens, and came to Corinth; and found a certain Jew named Aquila, born in Pontus, lately come from Italy, with his wife Pricilla; (because

---

5   Cf. Luke 21:24; Rom. 11:25. The "Gentiles" to whom Jesus sent Paul were descendants of the lost ten tribes of Israel. After God scattered their fathers among the Gentiles in the 8th century BC, and succeeding generations of them had adopted Gentile manners (including the worship of idols—cf. Deut. 4:28), they became known variously to the Jews as "Gentiles," "barbarians," "Greeks," "Scythians," and "the uncircumcision" [cf. John 7:35; Rom. 1:14; Gal. 2:7-8; Col. 3:11]; yet, they were the genealogical descendants of those fathers.

that Claudius had commanded all Jews to depart from Rome:) and came unto them.—Acts 18:1-2

Other salient Christian events that occurred during Claudius' 13-year reign include:

(1)   Barnabas went to Tarsus to seek Paul.

(2)   The Church members at Antioch began to be called Christians first.

(3)   Herod Agrippa I [grandson of Herod the Great] killed James brother of John and cast Peter into prison, whence an angel of God delivered him.

(4)   Paul's "Gentile" evangelistic missions in Asia and Europe commenced from the first "Gentile" church at Antioch.

(5)   Christian Judaizers opposed Paul and insisted that all "Gentile" converts should be circumcised and follow the Law of Moses.

(6)   The Jerusalem Conference took place to decide whether or not "Gentile" converts should be circumcised. The answer was No!

(7)   Paul took the gospel to Europe (AD 53).

(8)   Lydia a "Gentile" proselyte of Judaism heard Paul preach in Philippi [in Macedonia] and believed on Jesus, becoming the first person to be converted to Christ in Europe. (See *Unger's Bible Dictionary*, pg. 672.)

(9)   Paul and Silas were beaten and cast into prison at Philippi. God sent an earthquake at midnight and the jail doors jarred open. Instead of escaping Paul and Silas stayed within the prison [and persuaded all other prisoners to do the same] so that the city authorities would not kill the jailer. Paul preached Jesus to the jailor and he was converted and baptized, with his entire household (Acts 16:34).

(10) In Athens Paul preached to the Stoic and Epicurean philosophers at the Areopagus, resulting in the conversion of but a few of them (AD 54).

(11) Paul went to Corinth in Achaia and met Aquila and his wife Priscilla, whose occupation was tent making. They were

probably the first to be converted at Corinth. Paul founded the church at Corinth at this time (AD 54).

SIXTH CAESAR: NERO
(Reigned 14 years: AD 54-68)

About six years after Nero became emperor gospel evangelism might well have come to an end. Does the New Testament give any evidence that this could have been the case? Yes. In Colossians for example, written ca. 60-61, Paul said, in so many words, that the Great Commission had already been fulfilled:

> . . . ye heard . . . the truth of the gospel; Which is come unto you, **as *it is* in all the world** . . . the gospel, which ye have heard, *and* **which was preached to every creature which is under heaven;**—Col. 1:5-6, 23

Two other New Testament passages imply the same:

> For we have found this man *a* pestilent *fellow*, and a mover of sedition among all the Jews **throughout the world**, and a ringleader of the sect of the Nazarenes—Acts 24:5

> For the grace of God that bringeth salvation **hath appeared to all men**.—Titus 2:11

Luke's history of the church [i.e. Acts of the Apostles] leads to the conclusion that gospel preaching was over and the Great Commission had been fulfilled. Note that Acts comes to an abrupt end in Acts 28:31. It leaves us hanging as to what became of Paul, and what details preceded his execution by Nero. But this is explainable. Acts was not about Paul. It was about the fulfillment of Jesus' prophecy that before His generation ended "all things which are written" were to be fulfilled (see Luke 21:22, 32).

Paul himself, in effect, said that gospel evangelism was over, and that his life would quickly come to an end. When Paul left Asia he left for the last time, as indicated in this passage:

> And when he [Paul] had thus spoken, he kneeled down, and prayed with them all. And they all wept sore, and fell on Paul's neck, and kissed him, Sorrowing most of all for the words which he spake, that **they should see his face no more**. And they accompanied him unto the ship.—Acts 20:36-38

Paul meant that his mission to the "Gentiles" was about to end with his final task: i.e. to preach Christ to the statesmen and "kings" of his day (cf. Acts 9:15)! Thus, Acts ended with Paul standing before Felix (then governor of Judea) and Ananias (high priest)—Acts 24; Festus (next governor of Judea), and the last of the Herods, King Agrippa II; then on to Rome to testify before Nero and his house:

> Then said Paul, I stand at Caesar's judgment seat, where I ought to be judged . . . Then Festus, when he had conferred with the council, answered, Hast thou appealed unto Caesar? Unto Caesar shalt thou go.—Acts 25:10, 12

This was in accordance to Jesus' previous prophecy to Paul:

> Be of good cheer, Paul: for as thou hast testified of me in Jerusalem, so must thou bear witness also at Rome.—Acts 23:11

Paul's arrest by the Jews in Jerusalem and his subsequent testimony before the rulers of Judea took place during the years AD 60-62. The Acts of the Apostles ends with Paul's year-long journey through a perilous Mediterranean Sea to Rome, where we see him under house arrest from AD 63-65.

Tradition and speculation take over following Acts 28:31 concerning Paul's life after his "first" imprisonment. One tradition says that Nero freed him about AD 65-66 on condition that he no more preach Christ. Paul then, obeying Christ rather than Caesar, went on yet another missionary Journey, probably to Spain (cf. Rom. 15:24, 28). Upon returning to Rome Nero had him arrested and beheaded in AD 67 or 68.

(Paul's Allusion to Nero
In II Thessalonians)

I am persuaded that II Thessalonians chapter two has never been correctly understood and explained, not even close.

Paul, writing ca. AD 54 obtusely alluded to Daniel's **sixth** horn [i.e. Nero], who was about to ascend or had recently ascended to the Roman throne. Fully understanding Daniel's prophecy Paul knew that the sixth "horn"—Roman emperor—would be the last emperor before the appearing of the Antichrist [i.e. Daniel's "another little horn"—Dan. 7:8]. Daniel had written:

> I considered the [ten] horns, and, behold, there came up among them another little horn, before whom there were three of the first horns[6] [i.e. three of the aforementioned ten horns] plucked up by the roots: and, behold, in this horn *were* eyes like the eyes of man, and a mouth speaking great things.—Dan. 7:8

Paul and the Church happened to be alive at the very time when this sixth "horn" [i.e. Nero] was emperor in Rome. Paul knew that before the Antichrist could be revealed and the Great Tribulation take place the church had to first undergo a notable time of apostasy [i.e. many Christians had to forsake the faith and deny Christ before men], and Nero had to die.

The Apostasy Had to
Take Place First.

> Now we beseech you, brethren, by the coming of our Lord Jesus Christ, and *by* our gathering together unto him, that ye be not soon shaken in mind, or be troubled, neither by spirit, nor by word, nor by letter as from us, as that the day of Christ is at hand. Let no man deceive you by any means: for *that day shall not come*, except there come a falling away [i.e. a notable apostasy among Christians] first, and that man of sin be revealed, the son of perdition; Who opposeth and exalteth himself above all that is

---

6   These three horns turned out to be Galba, Otho, and Vitellius (see pages 3, 16-18, & 20).

called God, or that is worshipped; so that he as God sitteth in the temple of God, shewing himself that he is God.—II Thess. 2:1-4

Second, Paul knew that the sixth Danielic "horn" [Nero] had to be "taken out of the way" [i.e. he had to die]. Paul had taught this truth in the church before, and had had to do so in oblique and inoffensive language—apocalyptic language—that Caesar and his spies would not be able to understand:[7]

Nero Had to
Die First.

> Remember ye not, that, when I was yet with you, I told you these things? And now ye know what withholdeth that he [i.e. the Antichrist; Little Horn] might be revealed in his time. For the mystery of iniquity [i.e. the apostasy of many Christians] doth already work [i.e. many Christians had already committed apostasy]: **only he who now letteth [i.e. hindereth] *will let* [i.e. will hinder] until he be taken out of the way.** And then shall that Wicked be revealed, whom the Lord shall consume with the spirit of his mouth, and shall destroy with the brightness of his coming.—II Thess. 2:5-8

The words in this passage—"only he who now letteth *will let* until he be taken out of the way" (v. 7)—refer to Nero, the sixth "horn" or Roman emperor. Paul was saying in hidden language that only when Nero[8] was "taken out of the way" could "that Wicked[9] be revealed."

SEVENTH, EIGHTH, & NINTH CAESARS: GALBA, OTHO, & VITELLIUS
(AD 69: The Great Tribulation Begins)

---

[7] Naturally, if Paul had spoken these things in plain words the authorities would have understood them as grievous libel against Nero, or, as Paul put it elsewhere: ". . . unspeakable words, which it is not lawful for a man to utter" (II Cor. 12:4).

[8] When Nero committed suicide on June 9, AD 68, he was effectively "taken out of the way"!

[9] i.e. the "another little horn" (Dan. 7:8); "man of sin . . . son of perdition" (II Thess. 2:3); "antichrist" (I John 2:18)

In AD 69 these three "horns" or Caesars became the next three Roman emperors in rapid succession. While Galba became emperor sometime in October of AD 68, yet, like Otho and Vitellius after him, he was "plucked up by the roots" in 69. This being "plucked up" is what counts **prophetically**, according to Dan. 7:8. Therefore, we can confidently state that it was in AD 69 that the "another little horn" appeared with Roman backing, authority, and power. It is from this year that the 3½-year "reign" of the Little Horn (Dan. 7:25) began. My reason for saying so is the date of Galba's *plucking up*, which was in the very first month of 69. He was assassinated on January 15th.

His two successors, Otho and Vitellius, were also "plucked up by the roots" in 69. Otho committed suicide on April 16th, and Vitellius was murdered on December 19th. Daniel said that the Little Horn "came up" [Heb. ***ascended***] while these three horns were being plucked up (Dan. 7:8). Since they were plucked up from one end of that year to the other, we conclude that it took that whole year for all seven heads of the Beast to organize and begin their combined anti-Christ persecutions of God's saints.

It is interesting that in Revelation [see Rev. 9:14-18] Jesus said that "four angels" [devils; fallen angels?], loosed from the Euphrates River, planned and commenced a mission to frighten all Christians into committing apostasy. However, because God limited their time to only 3½ years (cf. Matt. 24:22), they wound up "slaying" only "the third part of men" (Rev. 9:15). This means that one out of every three church members in Asia apostatized, and their death was first a spiritual not a physical death.

They died spiritually when they fell away from Christ. Note in Rev. 9:15 that it took these four angels [i.e. devils] a little over a year to cause these third of church members to rise up and organize as the Antichrist. This would have been the year AD 69 while Galba, Otho, Vitellius, and Vespasian ascended to the throne in Rome. When they had all apostatized from Christ they constituted the "beast . . . having seven heads" (cf. Rev. 13:1). That is, they were collectively the Antichrist.

Revelation, correctly exegeted, says that the sixth "head" of the seven-headed "beast"—called "the first beast" in Rev. 13:12—came into Roman-backed power and led a great massacre of Christians in Asia, thus beginning the "war" against Christ and His elect brethren (see Rev. 13:7). By the end of this war in AD 72 the Antichrist had martyred one-fourth of the Elect in the seven churches of Asia:

> . . . And power was given unto them [i.e. "the third of men"—Rev. 9:15] over the fourth part of the earth [i.e. Christ's elect brethren], to kill with the sword, and with hunger, and with death [i.e. pestilence], and with the beasts of the earth.—Rev. 6:8b

THE TENTH CAESAR: VESPASIAN
(AD 69-79: Great Tribulation Ends; Jesus Appears)

It was during Vespasian's reign in Rome [10th Horn] that Jesus' generation came to an end (i.e. AD 76). When he ascended the throne the end time prophetic agenda of God was underway. The apostasy that Paul forecast in II Thess. 2:3 was happening; the Abomination of Desolation that Jesus foretold had begun; and the seven-headed Beast of Revelation was quickly raising its seven ugly heads one after another in Asia. This tenth emperor certainly knew about all this [from his own political perspective, of course, and not from any prophetic or Bible knowledge]. He continued to support and approve what Nero[10] had started: *a campaign to rid the Roman Empire from all vestiges of Christianity.*

Remember, Jesus said that BEFORE His generation ended everything He foretold in His Olivet Prophecy would come to pass:

> Verily I say unto you, this generation [i.e. His own] shall not pass, till all these things be fulfilled.—Matt. 24:34

Jesus knew that His brethren would suffer tribulation from both the Romans and fallen Christians ["antichrists"—I John 2:18] and that their persecutions would be a part of all end time

---

[10] Nero is the emperor who changed Rome's prior neutral policy about the phenomenal growth of Christianity in the empire. Prior to the Great Fire of Rome in 64 AD Nero thought of Christians as a mere branch of Judaism, one of many "legal" and tolerated religions in Rome. When he began to hear rumors that the public was blaming him for the fire he quickly transferred the blame to the Christian community in the city, and began to persecute and martyr them vigorously. This anti-Christian and antichrist stance against Christians continued in the empire up to the time of Constantine in the fourth century AD.

prophetic fulfillment. Everything Jesus foretold in His prophecy did, indeed, come to pass before AD 76. In 69, as we have just seen, the "abomination of desolation" took place (see Matt. 24:15). It happened just before the Beast's sixth "head" ["first beast"—Rev. 13:13] made war on God's saints and when the False Prophet [i.e. the seventh head] threatened all church members in Asia to follow suit if they wanted to stay alive (see Rev. 13:11-12, 14). The False Prophet entered the "temple" [i.e. the Church—cf. I Cor. 3:16] and proclaimed himself "God" in the church:

> Who opposeth and exalteth himself above all that is called God, or that is worshipped; so that he as God sitteth in the temple of God [i.e. the Church], shewing himself that he is God.—II Thess. 2:4

He taught Christians the LIE defined as follows: *if they PUBLICLY DENIED Christ Rome would not persecute or kill them.* But any church member who fell for this lie suffered grave consequences:

> And for this cause [i.e. "they received not the love of the truth"—II Thess. 2:10] **God shall send them strong delusion**, that they should believe a lie: **That they all might be damned** who believed not the truth, but had pleasure in unrighteousness.—II Thess. 2:11-12

> **And said to the mountains and rocks, Fall on us, and hide us** from the face of him that sitteth on the throne, and from the wrath of the Lamb: For the great day of **his wrath is come**; and who shall be able to stand?—Rev. 6:16-17

> The lord of that servant [i.e. apostate church member in Asia] shall come in a day when he looketh not for *him*, and in an hour that he is not aware of, And **shall cut him asunder, and appoint *him* his portion with the hypocrites: there shall be weeping and gnashing of teeth.**—Matt. 24:50-51

> And these shall go away into **everlasting punishment**—Matt. 25:46a

It was during Vespasian's reign that all end time prophecy was finally fulfilled, as Jesus foretold:

> Think not that I am come to destroy the law, or the prophets: I am not come to destroy, but to fulfill. For verily I say unto you, Till heaven and earth pass, one jot or one tittle shall in no wise pass from the law, till all be fulfilled.—Matt. 5:17-18

> For these are the days of vengeance, that all things which are written may be fulfilled . . . Verily I say unto you, This generation shall not pass away, till all be fulfilled.—Luke 21:22, 32

List of End Time Prophetic Events

Below is a list of all things that Jesus said would be fulfilled before His own generation passed away, things that took place during the reigns of Galba, Otho, Vitellius, and Vespasian:

- ✓ The destruction of the Jews' temple (Matt. 24:2);
- ✓ The apostasy or falling away (Matt. 24:5, 11-12; 38, 48-49);
- ✓ The Abomination of Desolation (Matt. 24:15);
- ✓ The Flight of Jewish Christians from Judea (Luke 21:20-21);
- ✓ The End of the church age (Matt. 24:3, 6, 13, 14; cf. I Pet. 4:7)
- ✓ The Great Tribulation (Matt. 24:21);
- ✓ The coming of deceivers and antichrists (Matt. 24:4, 11, 24);
- ✓ The fulfillment of all end time prophecy (Luke 21:22);
- ✓ The heavenly signs (Matt. 24:29);
- ✓ The Second Coming of Jesus (Matt. 24:30, 37, 42, 44, 46, 50);
- ✓ The Rapture of the enduring saints (Matt. 24:13, 31, 40-41);
- ✓ The Judgment and destruction of Antichrist (Matt. 24:51; 25:41, 46b);
- ✓ The Rewarding of the Elect (Matt. 16:27-28; 24:45, 47)

Conclusion

O reader, now you have been shown a biblical and reasonable possibility *and probability* [I believe proof!] that God's entire end time prophetic agenda of events was fulfilled in the first century, during Christ's generation; indeed, BEFORE His generation passed away

(Luke 21:22, 32). That is to say it was fulfilled during the reigns of the first ten Roman Caesars: i.e. the ten horns [i.e. ten "kings"; the first ten Caesars] of Daniel's Fourth Beast! This is the clear testimony of Daniel, our first witness.

Correctly understood Daniel still witnesses to us today from his time of old—2,700 years ago—that _Jesus has already come again_.

NOTES

Chapter Two

THE WITNESS OF
JESUS CHRIST

Jesus taught in clear, unambiguous, easy-to-understand language that His Second Coming would take place during His own generation, which is also to say, the lifetime of His twelve chief disciples. Let us look at the three different ways He either articulated or implied this truth.

The FIRST Way Jesus
Articulated this Truth

FIRST, Jesus said He would come back *before His twelve disciples* [apostles] *had preached in all the cities of Israel's Dispersion.* Speaking to those Twelve (see Matt. 10:2-4) He commanded them to go to "the lost sheep of the house of Israel" (see Matt. 10:6). He added:

YE SHALL NOT HAVE GONE OVER THE CITIES OF ISRAEL, TILL THE SON OF MAN BE COME.—Matt. 10:23b

By this we have proof that Jesus knew that the geographic theater—i.e. the land areas the disciples would go through in fulfilling the Great Commission—was well within the power of His disciples to reach in their own lifetime. By it

we also have proof that the number of people to be saved would be reasonably small [cf. "a little flock" (Luke 12:13)]! Therefore, Jesus did not envision the passage of CENTURIES or MILLENNIA before He would come again!

(The Gospel "Age" Was Brief.) This truth is a clear indication as to how we should interpret the word "age" in Jesus' Great Commission:

> Go ye therefore, and teach all nations, baptizing them in the name of the Father, and of the Son, and of the Holy Ghost: Teaching them to observe all things whatsoever I have commanded you: and, lo, I am with you always, *even* unto the end of the ***world*** [Greek: ***age***]. Amen.—Matt. 28:19-20

In His commission Jesus sent only **the disciples of His own generation** to "go" and preach the gospel to all nations: "Go ***YE***"! Not go any of the innumerable evangelists that have preached on earth *since* Jesus' generation (although they have done and still do much good), but only "Go ***YE***"—i.e. the very twelve disciples who stood before Him as He spoke [i.e. and other *contemporary* evangelists of ***their*** generation, such as Paul; Barnabas; Silas; Timothy; Titus; etc.] (cf. John 17:20; Tit. 1:3, 5).

The word "age," then, is limited in meaning to Jesus' and His disciples' mutual generation.

```
         Jesus' Generation Was
        Enough Time for the
             Fulfillment
        Of the Great Commission!
```

We have but to look in the Book of Revelation—i.e. the book that shows the final meaning of the church and its purpose—to learn how few people on earth God had in mind to believe the gospel and be saved (i.e. have an inheritance in the kingdom of God):

> And I heard the number of them which were sealed: *and there were* sealed an hundred *and* forty *and* four thousand of all the tribes of the children of Israel.—Rev. 7:4

(In the New Testament We Consistently See a Church of Israelite Membership Only!) Note that the church was supposed to have only Israelite members (see also Rev. 7:5-8; cf. Matt. 19:28; Acts 26:7; Rom. 9:4-5; Heb. 2:16-17). Jesus evidently chose His disciples from the twelve tribes of Israel. He said to them: ". . . in the regeneration [gospel or church age] when the Son of man shall sit on the throne of his glory, *ye shall sit upon twelve thrones, judging the twelve tribes of Israel"* (Matt. 19:28).

This truth explains why Paul made some of the signature statements he made to the "Gentile" Galatians, such as: "Wherefore the law was our schoolmaster"; ". . . if ye *be* Christs, then are ye Abraham's seed [i.e. descendants]"; and, ". . . be not entangled AGAIN with the yoke of bondage [i.e. the Law of Moses]"—Gal. 3:24, 29; 5:1.

Also in AD 62 Paul came before King Agrippa II to defend himself against the Jews for being a servant of Christ Jesus (see Acts 26:1-2). He said to the king: "And now I stand and am judged for the hope of the promise made of God unto our fathers: Unto which *promise* **our twelve tribes, instantly serving God day and night,** hope to come, for which hope's sake, king Agrippa, I am accused of the Jews"—Acts 26:6-7.

Paul was here speaking about the church. He was describing its membership as being composed of "our twelve tribes," and he did so when "Gentile" converts had been coming into the faith for decades by the scores of thousands! This can mean only one thing—i.e. those "Gentiles" were really of Israelite descent.

This conclusion is confirmed by Paul's words to the Galatians: ". . . if ye be Christ's, then are ye **Abraham's seed** [descendants of the tribes of Israel] and heirs according to the **promise**" (Gal. 3:29). He did not mean, as many mistakenly teach, that they were only *"spiritual"* Israelites. The statement is emphatic and clear:—i.e. they were **actual, bloodline and genealogical Israelite descendants.**

Note Paul's further description of the church membership: ". . . heirs according to the **promise**" (Gal. 3:29). This clinches it because Paul elsewhere declared by the Spirit that God's promises pertained only to Israel: ". . . Israelites; to whom *pertaineth* the adoption, and the glory, and the covenants, and the giving of the law, and the service *of God*, AND THE **PROMISES**" (Rom. 9:4). God's promises don't pertain to true Gentile peoples, *but only to Israelites!*

(<u>What Are We to Make of All This?</u>) When we consider the things we have just learned from the Bible we can see more clearly why the church age was to be brief. In this vein see what Paul said about how ___short___ the work of gospel evangelism would be:

> For he will finish the work, and cut *it* short in righteousness: because a short work will the Lord make upon the earth.— Rom. 9:28

Consider that, during Christ's generation, God determined to save only 144,000 people to receive eternal life and inherit the kingdom. Consider also that those 144,000 were Israelites only. These things being true, upon what kind of logic should today's churches be teaching that the Great Commission is still in effect these nearly two thousand years later? Are we to believe that it takes God and His church two thousand or more years of dedicated, Holy-Spirit-led and -empowered evangelism to round up a mere 144,000 elect saints?!?

The "Gentile" Church Members in the New Testament

(<u>The True Identity of the "Gentile" Church Members</u>) Some of you, dear readers, are bound to be objecting about now to my statement, above, that the only people God called to church membership were Israelites. Of course you are objecting, and I anticipated it. I fully understand *why* you are objecting. IT IS BECAUSE YOU DON'T KNOW WHO THE "GENTILE" CHURCH MEMBERS OF JESUS' GENERATION WERE. NO ONE HAS EVER **CORRECTLY EXPLAINED** IT TO YOU.

The true identity of the "Gentile" church members in Paul's day has, to my knowledge, rarely if ever been understood by most Bible scholars. The prevailing concept that they were ___true___ Gentiles (people not descended from any of the twelve tribes of Israel) has resulted in an entirely false concept of the **Biblical** or **New Testament** church. The explanation I am about to give you has never heretofore been understood by today's pastors, Sunday-school teachers, or even by degreed college and seminary professors.

"But wasn't Paul," I hear you protesting to me right now, "the apostle to the **_Gentiles?_** How then can you say that all the church members were _Israelites_?!?" Patience, dear reader, I have the answer. Let me, as gently as I can, disabuse you of today's totally false "orthodoxy" on this question. I will start by stating that the "Gentiles" converted under the gospel preaching of Peter, Paul, or any other apostle of Jesus Christ, were all blood-line, genealogical descendants of Abraham through Isaac and Jacob! You have never heard this before, but surprisingly, this truth has been in the Bible for millennia! However, the Bible passages that teach it were unfortunately _wrongly interpreted_ by the early church fathers who tended to be anti-Semitic.

Second, let me advise you that the Jews and Christian scholars in Jesus' day had special ways of referring to these "Gentiles." In hearing Jesus' remark—(Jesus said, "I go to him that sent me. Ye shall seek me, and shall not find _me:_ and where I am, thither ye cannot come" [John 7:33-34])—the Jews wrongly thought He meant that He would soon depart the Holy Land and go preach to "the dispersed among the Gentiles, and teach the Gentiles" (v. 35).

(Gentiles Dispersed Among Gentiles?) Here's my question to you, friends: Why did the Jews say "the DISPERSED" among the Gentiles and then **_call_** the "dispersed" Gentiles _IF THEY KNEW OR THOUGHT Jesus was going to preach to **true** Gentiles?_ Why call them the "dispersed"? Would the Jews have made the least bit of sense to speak of **_true_** Gentile folk being dispersed among other **_true_** Gentile folk? The only sensible way to understand the Jews is if by their first "Gentiles" they meant a _different_ people than their second "Gentiles" ("Gentiles" is used twice in John 7:35)! Wouldn't we, for example, come closer to understanding the Jews' meaning if we associate their word "dispersed" with their second-mentioned "Gentiles," and interpret both as meaning _the centuries-old scattered descendants of Israel's northern tribes?_

Let me explain why it makes perfectly good sense for us to do so. The Jews knew that God had SCATTERED the ten northern tribes of Israel among true-Gentile peoples seven centuries BEFORE their present generation.[11] They knew, also, that during those centuries most

---

[11]   The Assyrians conquered Samaria and scattered the survivors of the ten northern tribes among pagan nations (II Kings 17:5-6). In the days of Moses God had

of the dispersed had ceased worshiping Jehovah and had adopted the same idolatry the native pagan-inhabitants practiced. Also, like their new Gentile neighbors they did not practice circumcision (thus, the Jews and the apostles both called them "the uncircumcision."[12] In short, there were many thousands of bloodline, genealogical Israelite descendants living among true Gentiles in their day who had ***become***, for all practical purposes, "Gentiles"! They were eating Gentile diets, worshiping Gentile gods, and fighting Gentile wars. *They even thought of themselves as Gentiles!*

(The Scattered Ten Northern Tribes of Israel Became "Gentiles"!) In Moses' day God had forewarned Israel that He would scatter them if they forgot Him and began to take up the idolatry of surrounding nations [i.e. true Gentiles]:

> I call heaven and earth to witness against you this day, that ye shall soon utterly perish from off the land whereunto ye go over Jordan to possess it; ye shall not prolong *your* days upon it, but shall utterly be destroyed. And the LORD shall **SCATTER** you among the nations [i.e. true Gentiles], and ye shall be left few in number among the heathen, whither the LORD shall lead you. **AND THERE YE SHALL SERVE GODS, THE WORK OF MEN'S HANDS, WOOD AND STONE, WHICH NEITHER SEE, NOR HEAR, NOR EAT, NOR SMELL.**—Deut. 4:26-28

Dear reader, I'm sure you can understand from this passage why Israelite descendants in Jesus' time were called "Gentiles" by the Jews, and even by Jesus' apostles. It is because they were scattered by the thousands among the Gentiles **and were LIVING like the Gentiles!** It would have been culturally wrong to continue calling them Israelites, or God's people:

> Wherefore remember, that ye *being* in time past [i.e. for seven centuries] Gentiles in the flesh,[13] who are called Uncircumcision

---

forewarned Israel that this would happen if they ever stopped worshiping Jehovah only (see Deut. 4:26-28).

12   See Rom. 2:26-27; 3:30; 4:9-10; Gal. 2:7; Eph. 2:11; Col. 2:13.

13   They had not been CIRCUMCISED "in the flesh" is the meaning here.

by that which is called the Circumcision in the flesh made by hands [i.e. by the Jews]; that at that time ye were without Christ, being aliens [Greek: estranged] from the commonwealth of Israel, and strangers from the covenants of promise, having no hope, and without God in the world: But now in Christ Jesus ye who sometimes were far off [i.e. scattered] are made nigh [i.e. to Jehovah] by the blood of Christ. For he is our peace, who hath made both [the Jewish and scattered "Gentile" Christians] one—Eph. 2:11-13, 14a

The last phrase, "who hath made both one," is a reference to several Old Testament Scriptures prophesying that God would one day reunite the Northern Kingdom [i.e. Israel] and the Southern Kingdom [i.e. Judah]. For example:

In those days the house of Judah shall walk with the house of Israel, and they shall come together [i.e. as one nation]—Jer. 3:18a

. . . Thus saith the Lord GOD; Behold, I will take the stick of Joseph, which *is* in the hand of Ephraim, and the tribes of Israel his fellows, and will put them with him, *even* with the stick of Judah, and make them one stick, and they shall be one [nation] in mine hand.—Ezek. 37:19

Then shall the children of Judah and the children of Israel be gathered together, and appoint themselves one head—Hos. 1:11a

(It Was Logical to Call the Dispersed of Israel "the Uncircumcision"!) Consider now how logical it was for the Jews and the Christian evangelists to call the scattered Israelites "the Uncircumcision." First, note that Paul also called them "Gentiles":

And I . . . communicated unto them [i.e. Judaizers] that gospel which I preach among the **Gentiles**—Gal. 2:2

Paul went on to say that God had called him to be "mighty . . . toward the Gentiles," whom he also called "the uncircumcision": ". . .

they [the Judaizers] saw that the gospel of **the uncircumcision** was committed unto me, as *the* gospel of **the circumcision** [the ubiquitously circumcised Jews] *was* unto Peter; (For he that wrought effectually in Peter to the apostleship of the circumcision, the same was mighty in me toward the Gentiles" (vv. 7-8). We see here that Paul used the terms "Gentiles" and "the uncircumcision" synonymously. This should alert us to the probability that in all his epistles Paul used the word Gentiles to mean the contemporary Israelite descendants of the ten northern tribes.

Dear reader, I trust that you can see the foolishness and redundancy of referring to natural Gentile men—whom the whole world already knew were not circumcised—as "the uncircumcision." The phrase makes sense only if it refers to "Gentiles" who **SHOULD HAVE BEEN but WEREN'T** circumcised; in other words, Israelites God commanded to be circumcised but who had long ago ceased obeying God's commandments (see Gen. 17:10).

```
Jesus Said to
His Disciples:
I will Make You
Fishers of Men
```

Jesus commanded His disciples not to target true Gentile people with the gospel of the kingdom, but rather to take it to "the lost sheep of the house of Israel" (Matt. 10:6; cf. 15:24). Jesus meant primarily the Jews as the "lost sheep" here, but He also spoke of "other sheep . . . which are not of this [Jewish] fold," and added, "them also I must bring, and they shall hear my voice; and there shall be one fold, *and* one shepherd" (John 10:16). By these "other sheep" He no doubt meant the "Gentile" Israelites I have mentioned above.

However, these "other sheep," scattered among the nations as they were, presented a problem to the evangelists—i.e. they would not be able to reach them all with the gospel before Jesus' Second Coming: "Ye shall not have gone over the cities of Israel, till the Son of man be come" (Matt. 10:23). Nevertheless, Jesus commanded the evangelists to:

Go . . . and teach all nations (Greek: Gentiles) . . .—
Matt. 28:19a

Paul's commission to the "Gentiles" brings out the full meaning of Matt. 28:19: ". . . he is a chosen vessel unto me, to bear my name before the Gentiles [i.e. Israelites **acculturated** as Gentiles], and kings, and the children of Israel [i.e. the Jews]"—Acts 9:15

To fulfill Christ's Commission to him Paul would have to traverse much of the Roman Empire, obviously an arduous undertaking that would bring him a great deal of personal and physical suffering: "For I will shew him how great things he must suffer for my name's sake" (Acts 9:16).

Note carefully the wording of Paul's commission: ". . . bear my name **BEFORE** the Gentiles, and kings, and the children of Israel [i.e. the Jews]." Paul was to preach *in their presence* [i.e. "before" them], but not to or for *true* Gentiles. Thus, his preaching was inevitably heard **BY** the true Gentiles and **BY** the kings, and **BY** the Jews, but it was not meant *for* them. It was meant only for the *predestined* "Gentiles" and Jews living in their midst. When Paul preached in the Jewish synagogues, for example, only the *predestined* Jews and "Gentiles" there would believe and be saved.

As Paul preached *before* [i.e. in the presence of] the Gentiles, kings, and Jews, it was the Spirit of God that brought the gospel home in the hearts of only a select few of his hearers, and they were all *Israelites*, none of them true Gentiles.

(The Converted "Gentiles" at Antioch). The Book of Acts **does** speak of "Gentile" converts to the gospel under Paul's preaching. The larger part of Chapter 13 in Acts, for example, is about Paul's ministry at "Antioch in Pisidia" [a part of Asia Minor].

There Paul went into the Jewish synagogue and preached the gospel to a mixed congregation of Jews and "proselytes"—a term always meaning Israelites **acculturated** as "Gentiles"—as implied convincingly in the following passage:

> And when the Jews were gone out of the synagogue, the **Gentiles** besought that these words might be preached to them the next sabbath. Now when the congregation was broken up, many of the Jews and religious **proselytes** followed Paul and Barnabas: who, speaking to them, persuaded them to continue in the grace of God.—Acts 13:42-43

We see in this passage the synonymity between the words "Gentiles" and "proselytes." True Gentiles would never have been admitted into a Jewish synagogue; only circumcised "Gentiles" were admitted—i.e. people known to be descended from Jacob who were studying the Torah under Jewish teachers.

Paul's first sermon in the synagogue proves this point. In that sermon we note Paul's firm doctrine that the gospel was meant only for the descendants of Abraham:

> Of this man's seed [i.e. the seed of David] hath God according to *his* promise raised unto **ISRAEL** a Saviour, Jesus. When John had first preached before his coming the baptism of repentance to all the people of **ISRAEL** . . . Men *and* brethren, **CHILDREN OF THE STOCK OF ABRAHAM**, and whosoever among **YOU** feareth God, to **YOU** is the word of this salvation sent . . . And we declare unto **YOU** glad tidings, how that the promise which was made unto **THE FATHERS**, God hath fulfilled the same unto **US THEIR CHILDREN**—Acts 13:23-24, 26, 32

Peter, also, had earlier made it clear that the gospel was to target only people—Jews and "Gentiles" alike—who were descended from Abraham:

> Him [i.e. Jesus] hath God exalted with his right hand *to be* a Prince and a Saviour, for to give repentance **TO ISRAEL**, and **FORGIVENESS OF SINS**.—Acts 5:31

This means, also, that Cornelius, though an uncircumcised "Gentile" [i.e. a Roman centurion] was also of Israelite descent so that God, notwithstanding his uncircumcision, saved him and his household (cf. Acts 10:44). Note the words Peter first said to Cornelius in his preaching: ". . . Peter opened *his* mouth, and said, Of a truth I perceive that God is no respecter of persons: But in every nation he that feareth him, and worketh righteousness, is accepted with him. The word which *God* sent unto the **CHILDREN OF ISRAEL**, preaching peace by Jesus Christ; (he is Lord of all:)—Acts 10:34-36. It is true, God "is no respecter of persons," but this must be understood in the context of "the children of Israel." In other words, *among Israelites* God is impartial to "whosoever believeth" (cf. Acts 10:43). His not calling true Gentiles does not make Him partial *among Israelites* whom He made His chosen people from ancient times (cf. Deut. 10:15).

Fishers and Hunters

> Behold, I will send for many fishers, saith the LORD, and they shall fish them; and after I will send for many hunters, and they shall hunt them from every mountain, and from every hill, and out of the holes and rocks. For my eyes *are* upon all their ways: they are not hid from my face, neither is their iniquity hid from mine eyes.—Jer. 16:16-17

Fish can be caught by bait or net. Hunters have to go out into the wilderness, over mountains and hills to catch their prey. The above passage from Jeremiah foretold the day [i.e. Jesus Christ's generation] when God would no longer deal with the Jews or any of the children of Israel through the Law of Moses.

Paul made clear that for the Jews the service of the temple and the keeping of the commandments contained in ordinances had come to an end through Christ's death for sin:

> For he [i.e. Jesus Christ] is our peace, who hath made both [Israel and Judah] one, and hath broken down the middle wall of partition *between us* [i.e. deeds of the Law—cf. Rom. 3:20]; Having abolished in his flesh the enmity, *even* the law of commandments *contained* in ordinances; for to make in himself of twain one new man, *so* making peace.—Eph. 2:14-15

Salvation was no longer to be obtained by the Law ordinances: i.e. keeping of the deeds of the law, such as circumcision, tithing, Sabbath and Feast observances, etc. Now it was through grace: ". . . by grace are ye saved through faith; and that not of yourselves: *it is* the gift of God: Not of works [i.e. deeds of the Law], lest any man should boast" (Eph. 2:8-9).

Paul put this truth in the plainest language possible for the Jews still striving for righteousness through the Law:

> . . . Israel, which followed after the law of righteousness, hath
> not attained to the law of righteousness. Wherefore? Because *they
> sought it* not by faith, but as it were by the works of the law. For
> they stumbled at that stumblingstone; As it is written, Behold, I
> lay in Sion a stumblingstone and rock of offence: and whosoever
> believeth on him shall not be ashamed.—Rom. 9:31-33

Through the Holy Spirit Jeremiah foretold the days of grace
through Christ Jesus. It would be a new, a much different day for
Israel. Before grace Israel—the Jews—could be found within her
geographical borders, observing the Law of ordinances Moses wrote
down for them to keep. Up to the time of Christ's death God tolerated
this arrangement—i.e. Law observance, even though Israel never did
attain to the righteousness of the Law. Yet He saved them through
peace- and war-times. No one had to be sent out into the mountains
and hills to "fish" or "hunt" for the Jews, they were right there where
they belonged: in the Holy Land.

However there were millions of Israelites scattered among the
nations who were renegade from their past Israelite heritage, or from
the keeping of the Law. When Christ died He died for THEIR sins as
well as for the sins of the Jews. Yet they were scattered everywhere, as
the prophet said: "every mountain . . . every hill, and . . . the holes and
rocks" of the earth (Jer. 16:16).

The Holy Spirit likened both the Jews and the Israelites as "lost"
(cf. Matt. 10:6), but that among them were those whose hearts were
right before Him. No one could tell by simply looking at them
that their hearts were repentant and that they yearned for God and
righteousness with all their strength, body, and soul. The Law of Moses
could not "find" them or rally them to God. Too many Jews kept the
Law perfunctorily, not from their heart. The scattered Israelites had
totally abandoned the Law centuries before. There was only one way
to "find" them: Holy Spirit ordained and commissioned men had to
"GO" into the nations to "hunt" them out through the preaching of
the gospel:

> . . . **GO** . . . to the lost sheep of the house of Israel—Matt. 10:6

GO ye therefore, and teach all nations, baptizing them in the name of the Father, and of the Son, and of the Holy Ghost: Teaching them to observe all things whatsoever I have commanded you: and, lo, I am with you always, *even* unto the end of the world [Greek: age].—Matt. 28:19-20

. . . it pleased God by the foolishness of preaching to save them that believe.—I Cor. 1:21

. . . a man . . . **GOETH** into the mountains, and **SEEKETH** that which is gone astray—Matt. 18:12

How beautiful upon the mountains are the feet of him that **BRINGETH** good tidings, that **PUBLISHETH**[14] peace; that **BRINGETH** good tidings of good, that **PUBLISHETH** salvation: that saith unto Zion, Thy God reigneth!—Is 52:7

The Apostles Had Help
From the Holy Spirit!

We note, however, that when the Shepherd went into the mountains, He sought a lost SHEEP, not just any wild animal in the wilderness (Matt. 18:12, above). A "sheep" is to be defined as any Israelite whom God had foreordained or predestined unto eternal life. Thus, Jesus said:

. . . the sheep hear his [i.e. the good shepherd's] voice; and he calleth his own sheep by name, and leadeth them out. And when he putteth forth his own sheep, he goeth before them, and the sheep follow him: **for they know his voice. And a stranger will they not follow, but will flee from him: for they know not the voice of strangers** . . . I [Jesus] am the good shepherd, **and know my *sheep*, and am known of mine.**—John 10:3b, 4-5, 14

---

[14]   The apostles not only preached orally, but also preached by **publishing** their Holy Spirit inspired works—i.e. the New Testament! Jesus, for example, commanded John: "Write the things which thou hast seen" Rev. 1:19. When Jesus told the exorcized demoniac to stay at home, we are told that the demoniac "went his way, and **published** [Greek: heralded; preached] throughout the whole city how great things Jesus had done unto him" (Luke 8:39).

Therefore, the Good Shepherd did not seek after his strayed sheep aimlessly, but had help from above. We are told that he **found** it (Matt. 18:13). He had help from God in finding it, as Jeremiah said of God: ". . . mine eyes *are* upon all their ways: they are not hid from my face" (Jer. 16:17).

Also, the apostles of Christ did not **GO** aimlessly into the nations to preach, they had the guidance and leading of the Holy Spirit. Note:

> I am with you . . . unto the end of the world—Matt. 28:20

The apostles were God's "feet" and "legs" [metaphorically], but He was their eyes and unseen Guide. It was God that LED the disciples to the right places—i.e. where and when the lost sheep would be inclined to believe the gospel. We see, for example, that the Holy Spirit forbade Paul to preach in Asia YET (later Paul evangelized in Asia for over two years):

> **NOW** (the time wasn't right) . . . they . . . were forbidden of the Holy Ghost to preach the word in Asia.—Acts 16:6

Paul then would have gone into Bithynia, **". . . but the Spirit suffered them not"** (v. 7). But that night Paul dreamed of a Macedonian who cried out to him, "Come over into Macedonia, and help us" (v. 9b). You see, the Holy Spirit told Paul where not to go, and also where TO go at any given time. I venture to say that not only did the Holy Spirit direct Paul in his way, but also all the other apostles and evangelists during Jesus' generation.

Conclusion

At the Jerusalem Conference (see Acts 15) James, brother of Jesus, understood why God called "Gentiles" to be Christians through Paul's ministry. He knew that they were not **true** Gentiles but only *acculturated* "Gentiles"—i.e. men and women of Israelite descent who themselves and several generations of their forebears had lived among the Gentiles for so long that they in effect and for all practical purposes **were** Gentiles.

Note that James saw God's name in those "Gentiles." He said of them, "Gentiles, upon whom my name is called" (Acts 15:17). There was a reason he saw God's name in them, because He knew that they were of Israelite descent. In Hebrew, which James surely knew and spoke, the word Israel means "he will rule as God" (see *Strong's Concordance*, Greek Dictionary, #3478). The word El means "God," and by inference Jehovah!

(Few Are Chosen) Jesus said, ". . . many are called, but **FEW** *are* chosen"—Matt. 22:14. He called the church a **"LITTLE flock"** (Luke 12:32). He said of the salvation He preached: ". . . strait *is* the gate, and narrow *is* the way, which leadeth unto [eternal] life, AND **FEW** there be that find it" (Matt. 7:14). In Revelation Jesus revealed just how few that number turned out to be at the end of the church age: "And I heard the number of them which were sealed: *and there were* sealed an hundred *and* forty *and* four thousand of all the tribes of the children of Israel" (Rev. 7:4)!

We should not marvel, therefore, or disbelieve, considering all the above discussion of the truths of God's word, that though the elect were scattered throughout many nations, it didn't take long to find them (*the evangelists had the guidance of the Holy Spirit*)! Also, when God had elected [i.e. had finally chosen] 144,000 Israelites from out of the nations, He sent Jesus back for them on earth and caught them all up into Heaven to be with Him!

> . . . I will come again, and receive you unto myself; that where I am, *there* ye may be also.—John 14:3

> For the Lord himself shall descend from heaven, with a shout, with the voice of the archangel, and with the trump of God . . . Then we which are alive *and* remain shall be caught up together with them in the clouds, to meet the Lord in the air: and so shall we ever be with the Lord. Wherefore comfort one another with these words.—I Thess. 4:16-18

It is because of the "few" people God chose for eternal life [i.e. 144,000]; (2) and because His elect would be only *Israelites*; (3) and because of the limited amount of *time* He gave Himself to reach them [i.e. the forty years of Jesus' adult-time generation], that the apostles did not ***need*** to go "over *[all]* the cities of Israel, till the Son of man be come" (Matt. 10:23)!

The SECOND Way Jesus Articulated This Truth

SECOND, Jesus said that *some of the twelve disciples would still be alive in this world when He came again:*

> 27 For the Son of man shall come in the glory of his Father with his angels; and then he shall reward every man according to his works. 28 Verily I say unto you (He said it **only** to His contemporary disciples), THERE BE **SOME** STANDING HERE, WHICH SHALL NOT TASTE OF DEATH, TILL THEY SEE THE SON OF MAN COMING IN HIS KINGDOM—Matt. 16:27-28

It is perplexing and worrisome to me that most Bible expositors DO NOT UNDERSTAND what this passage *obviously* says. Also, I think it is in desperation that they give it a very disingenuous interpretation which, unfortunately, most Christians today have accepted because they are not skilled in Bible exegesis (cf. Heb. 5:13).

(The False Interpretation of Most of Today's Bible Expositors)

First, these "expositors" assert that Jesus fulfilled His words to the disciples **six days later** on the Mount of Transfiguration (see Matt. 17:1ff). This is demonstrably ridiculous! Jesus spoke of **"some"** of His disciples still being alive at His coming (see Matt. 16:28). Why would He say **"some"** when He knew perfectly well that ***ALL*** of them would still be alive just six days later?!?

Second, the expositors are seemingly oblivious to everything Jesus said in v. 27—viz., that He (a) would "come in the glory of his Father with his angels;" and (b) would "reward every man [i.e. disciple] according to his works."

The two verses are of a piece. For example, Jesus' coming "in the glory of his Father" (v. 27) is exactly the same event as His "coming in his kingdom" (v. 28). This alone ties the two verses together. At Jesus' coming He would reward each disciple "according to his works."

There is no hint of the disciples having been rewarded on the Mount of Transfiguration. Also, not one angel appeared with Jesus six days later, to say nothing of "his angels" (plural). Therefore, the Mount of Transfiguration event could not have fulfilled Jesus' words in v. 27. If v. 27 was not fulfilled, then neither was v. 28!

(**"Some"** Compared with **"Most"**) Two or three years later Jesus and His disciples were engaged in their Jewish ministry in Judea. All the disciples were still alive until Judas hanged himself shortly before Jesus' death (see Matt. 27:3-11). This brings up another false interpretation of Jesus' words in Matt. 16:27-28: i.e. that they were fulfilled on Pentecost at the outpouring of the Holy Spirit. These expositors say that the Church was born on that day, and that this fulfilled the coming of Christ in the Father's glory. The Church, they assure us, is the glorious kingdom of God on earth.

This is another deceitful interpretation that under scrutiny falls short of facts and reason. See how it is somewhat viable. First, it might be said that Jesus *did* "come" in the Holy Spirit on Pentecost (cf. John 14:16-18). Second, the Holy Spirit *was* a "gift" (Acts 2:38), and a "gift" may be thought of as a "reward." It is also suggested that "his angels" came on Pentecost, as evinced by the disciples' speaking in tongues (i.e. perhaps they were the "tongues of angels"—I Cor. 13:1).

But all this is mere guessing and speculating, unsupportable by any other Scripture. Was Jesus really talking about the event of Pentecost? There is little or no chance of this being a right interpretation.

My main argument against Jesus' Pentecostal coming is His word **"SOME"** in "**some** standing here . . . shall not taste of death . . . etc." (Matt. 16:28). Actually, only Judas was dead at Pentecost (he "hanged himself"—Matt. 27:5). The other eleven disciples were still alive and well on Pentecost (cf. Acts 1:13).

If Jesus knew—and He surely did—that of the Twelve only Judas would be dead on Pentecost, His word "some" would have made Him a false prophet. He should rather have used the word "most," or perhaps He could have said, "Only eleven of you will still be alive when I come in my kingdom."

Moreover, Jesus' word **"some"** is credible only if we interpret it as denoting a time *NEAR* in the lifetime of His disciples, say, toward the end of their generation (e.g. forty years later—cf. Heb. 3:9, 17). Then it would be believable that "some" of His disciples would still be alive at His coming. Also, it would better fit His prophecy to them that "they shall deliver **you** up to be afflicted, and shall kill **you**" (Matt. 24:9). Thus, we read that James, John's brother, was killed by Herod ca. AD 44, about 14-15 years later in their generation (see Acts 12:2).

(Not Too Much Time) **"Some"** is NOT credible however, in the context of a fulfillment centuries or millennia AFTER their generation, when it is CERTAIN that ALL of them would be dead, which, however, is the way today's un-discerning "expositors" think and teach.

O, dear reader, can you not see and agree with me that the word **"some"** can be true only within a narrow "window of credibility," to be fulfilled not too soon and not too long after Jesus uttered the word? Will you not agree with me that only the disciples' generation could be that "window of credibility"? Let me repeat: **"Some"** of the disciples could no doubt have still been alive before their generation ended. After that *it is certain that ALL the disciples would have been dead*, rendering the word **"some"** as not worthy to have passed from the mouth of the Lord Jesus. See how this interpretation 100% harmonizes with the words Jesus uttered in His Olivet Prophecy: "Verily I say unto you, THIS GENERATION [I.E. HIS AND THE DISCIPLES'] SHALL NOT PASS, TILL ALL THESE THINGS BE FULFILLED" (Matt. 24:34).

Incidentally, it also 100% agrees with an AD 72 Second Coming of Jesus.

The THIRD Way Jesus Articulated this Truth

THIRD, Jesus prophesied that He would come again *before His own generation* would "pass" away:

> When ye shall see **all these things**, know that it [i.e. "the end"—cf. Matt. 24:3, 6, 13-14] is near, *even* at the doors. Verily I say unto you, **THIS** generation shall not pass, till **all these things** be fulfilled.—Matt. 24:33-34

Let us look at Jesus' Olivet Prophecy and see what "all these things" were, one by one. I will show from relative Bible passages and from common historical knowledge that **"all these things"** did indeed take place during Jesus' generation. I will show that they took place during the time of the "fourth kingdom"—the Roman Empire—just as Daniel foretold, and that there has never been any need whatsoever for a revived Roman Empire.

(What Generation Did Jesus Mean?) Jesus meant His **own** generation, as any unbiased reader of the Olivet Prophecy can tell. Note that He said **"THIS"** generation [see Matt. 24:34; Mark 13:30; Luke 21:32], meaning His own contemporary, ongoing generation. That's what the word "this" always means—i.e. something *currently* happening, even as the speaker addresses his audience. Anybody who listened carefully to his English teacher in school will support me in this statement. Had Jesus meant a generation future to His own (such as ours) He would have used the word "that"—i.e. "THAT generation"—in which case we could correctly argue that Jesus did not give His disciples a clear answer to their question: "**When** shall these things be?"—Matt. 24:3.

However, the main reason I know that **"THIS"** generation means Jesus' **_own_** generation is because it is so easy to establish that "all these things" really did take place *during His own generation*. The New Testament historians wrote all about it.

(To Today's Christians New Testament and Ancient History Consist of "Things Not Seen"!) The Bible always calls on a Christian to have faith, to **believe** what Jesus said. They should believe it even though they have not seen it with their own eyes.

> Now FAITH is the substance of things hoped for, the evidence of things **NOT SEEN** . . . without [this kind of] faith *it is* impossible to please *him* [God].—Heb. 11:1, 6

Now I have observed that all high-school students, in reading ancient history, tend to believe it. They may not remember it long enough to make an A on the test, but they do not question it, or try to disprove it. Dear reader, the Bible is also a book of history. Its historians were Matthew, Mark, Luke, John, Peter, Paul, James, and Jude. They all wrote history as it happened. They personally lived it and fully experienced it. Should we not believe them at least as much as school students accept as truthful the things they read in their history books?

I'm going to ask you to do just that, as you read the following material. You have not personally seen its fulfillment, but I want you to trust the divinely-inspired historians.

Jesus foretold history, but He asked His disciples to believe what He said. He told them that the Kingdom of God was nigh, but also informed them that they would never "see" it or "observe" it.[15]

Dear reader, as you read the New Testament from the Book of Acts onward through Revelation, you are reading true history about the fulfillment of a great deal of end time prophecies (cf. Dan. 8:17, 19; 11:35, 40). In Daniel we read that in "the time of the end" these prophecies would be fulfilled, and "unsealed" [i.e. revealed] so that all who desire can understand them: "Go thy way, Daniel: for the words *are* closed up and sealed till the time of the end"—Dan. 12:9. The following sections reveal to us just how these prophecies were fulfilled. Now, let's look at the signs that Jesus gave in His Olivet Discourse, signs that were to be "fulfilled" before Jesus' generation passed away (Matt. 24:34; Luke 21:32).

The Sign of the Destruction Of the Temple

This sign certainly happened in Jesus' own generation—i.e. a historical fact. Titus' Roman army burned the Temple to the ground in AD 70, a year regarded as still in the time of Jesus' generation (cf. Matt. 24:34).

The destruction of the Temple is one sign that even ATHEISTS can believe because all sacred and secular historians **agree** that that Temple was destroyed. The temple mount still exists upon which that Temple stood. There is too much historical evidence for anyone to disbelieve Jesus' words.

This brings up an obvious point: viz., *"All these things"* were actual events that the first-century Christians suffered through. The plentiful historic documentation about the temple's destruction actually <u>*proves*</u> the fulfillment of this sign.

---

[15] Remember, Jesus said, "The kingdom of God cometh not with observation. Neither shall they say, Lo here! Or, lo there! For, behold, the kingdom of God is within you"—Luke 17:20, 21.

The Sign of "All Nations" Hating Christians

"All nations" means the antichrists of Jesus' generation, a huge satanic organization of fallen Christians *from* "all nations" (cf. Matt. 28:19). The writers [and addressees] of New Testament times saw this satanic organization form in their time. Note the following biblical proof of this:

> Not forsaking the assembling of ourselves together, AS THE MANNER OF SOME *IS*—Heb. 10:25

[NOTE: Christians who ceased attending church comprised the "many antichrists" of I John 2:18-19.]

> But it is happened unto them according to the true proverb, The dog *is* turned to his own vomit again; and the sow that was washed to her wallowing in the mire.—II Pet. 2:22

[NOTE: Peter's use of the past tense shows that this proverb had already been fulfilled in many apostate Christians in Jesus' generation. Again, such were antichrists.]

> Little children, it IS the last time: and as ye have heard that antichrist shall come, even now are there many antichrists; whereby we know that it is the last time. They went out from us, but they were not of us; for if they had been of us, they would *no doubt* have continued with us: but, that they might be made manifest that they were not all of us.—I John 2:18-19

[NOTE: John wrote this in the latter half of the first century, while Jesus' generation was still ongoing.]

> I wrote to the church: but Diotrephes, **who loveth to have the preeminence** among them, receiveth us not. Wherefore, if I come, I will remember his deeds which he doeth, prating against us with malicious words: and not content therewith, neither doth he himself receive the brethren, and forbiddeth them that would, and casteth *them* out of the church.—III John 9-10

[NOTE: Diotrephes clearly sat in the temple—i.e. church—as God, acting as God in making arbitrary decisions that were against the will of God. Clearly this was part fulfillment of Paul's warning about the falling away in the church and the revelation of the "man of sin . . . son of perdition" (II Thess. 2:4).]

> For there are certain men crept in unawares [i.e. as self-appointed church authorities], who were before of old ordained to this condemnation, ungodly men, turning the grace of our God into lasciviousness, and denying the only Lord God, and our Lord Jesus Christ . . . Woe unto them! For they have gone in the way of Cain, and ran greedily after the error of Balaam for reward, and perished in the gainsaying of Core. These are spots in your feasts of charity, when they feast with you, feeding themselves without fear: clouds *they are* without water, carried about of winds; trees whose fruit withereth, without fruit, twice dead, plucked up by the roots . . . These are murmurers, complainers, walking after their own lusts; and their mouth speaketh great swelling *words*, having men's persons in admiration because of advantage . . . These be they who separate themselves, sensual, having not the Spirit.—Jude 4, 11-12, 16, 19
>
> [NOTE: Jude's words here clearly show the fulfillment of Dan. 7:25 about the Little Horn, or Antichrist, speaking great words against the most High; wearing out—i.e. persecuting—the saints; and thinking to change times and laws—i.e. church doctrines!]

Not only these passages, but also in the last New Testament book, Jesus, in describing the condition of the seven churches of Asia, proves beyond all doubt that antichrists were already in the church during the latter years of His generation:

> Unto the angel of the church of Ephesus write . . . I have *somewhat* against thee . . . thou hast left thy first love . . . thou art fallen . . .—Rev. 2:1, 4, 5
>
> . . . unto the . . . church in Smyrna . . . *I know* the blasphemy of them which say they are Jews, and are not, but *are* the synagogue of Satan.—Rev. 2:8, 9
>
> . . . to . . . the church in Pergamos write . . . thou hast them that hold the doctrine of Balaam, who taught Balac to cast a stumblingblock before the children of Israel, to eat things sacrificed unto idols, and to commit fornication. So hast thou

also them that hold the doctrine of the Nicolaitans, which things I hate.—Rev. 2:12, 14-15

. . . unto . . . the church in Thyatira write . . . thou sufferest that woman Jezebel . . . to seduce my servants to commit fornication, and to eat things sacrificed unto idols.—Rev. 2:18, 20

. . . unto . . . the church in Sardis write . . . I have not found thy works perfect before God.—Rev. 3:1, 2

. . . to . . . the church in Philadelphia write . . . I will make them of the synagogue of Satan, which say they are Jews, and are not, but do lie . . .—Rev. 3:7a, 9a

And unto . . . the church of the Laodiceans write . . . I know thy works, that thou art neither cold nor hot . . . because thou art lukewarm . . . I will spue thee out of my mouth . . . thou . . . knowest not that thou art wretched, and miserable, and poor, and blind, and naked.—Rev. 3:14, 15, 16, 17

All the above passages prove that the falling away Paul predicted in II Thess. 2:3 was already taking place and was well advanced. They tell us that Jesus' generation was in its last days, as Paul strongly articulated in other words: "The night is far spent, the day [of His coming] is at hand"—Rom. 13:12; and, "the ends of the world [Greek: ages] are come"—I Cor. 10:11. According to Paul this means that "the coming of the Lord Jesus Christ, and . . . our gathering together unto him" (v. 1) was imminent in the latter years of Jesus' generation.

What sincere and thoughtful Christian today reading these passages and seeing from them that the Antichrist had already come [in Jesus' generation] can, notwithstanding, continue to teach that Jesus has **yet** to come in _OUR_ generation or future? Those who so teach are in direct denial of—indeed, _opposition to_—the truth of God's word. Jesus said to all the churches: ". . . behold, I come quickly [Greek: soon; imminently]; and my reward _is_ with me, to give every man according as his work shall be" (Rev. 22:12).

(The Biblical Meaning of "All Nations") We see, then, that Jesus' words "all nations" may signify the antichrist of the last days. In saying to His disciples, "ye shall be hated of **all nations** for my name's sake" Jesus was talking about the Antichrist doing the hating. But how can it be explained that the Antichrist comprised all nations? Here's how. The Antichrist was not just a single man, but also many: "ye have heard that antichrist shall come, even now are there many antichrists" John wrote (I John 2:18). Paul's expressions "man of sin" and "son of perdition" (II Thess. 2:2) are also like "Antichrist." By them Paul meant [depending upon context] a single "man" of sin or more than one, as in an Antichrist *system* or *denomination*. Thus, he also meant either a single Christian or many Christians by his expression "man of God" in the following passage:

> That the **man of God** may be perfect, throughly furnished unto all good works.—II Tim. 3:17

Likewise, the term "all nations" means that the Israelite constituency in both the Church and the Antichrist was the same, in that all antichrists were apostates FROM the church. They were Israelites, but because they were born in different nations, Luke also called them after Gentile names: "Parthians, and Medes, and Elamites, and the dwellers in Mesopotamia, and in Judea, and Cappadocia, in Pontus, and Asia, Phrygia, and Pamphylia, in Egypt, and in the parts of Libya about Cyrene, and strangers of Rome, Jews and proselytes, Cretes and Arabians" (Acts 2:9-11).

The correct interpretation of "all nations," therefore, is understood as Israelites that God called **out** of many Roman Provinces in the time of Jesus' generation. Let's face it, when Jesus commanded His disciples to take the gospel to "the uttermost part of the earth" He had in mind many far off parts of the "earth" found within the borders of the Roman Empire.

Daniel's four kingdoms—Babylonia, Medo-Persia, Greece, and the Roman Empire (see Dan. 2 & 7)—actually define Jesus' "uttermost parts of the earth," inasmuch as His elect brethren were to come into possession of all the peoples who once lived in those regions:

> And the kingdom and dominion, and the greatness of the kingdom under the whole heaven, shall be given to the people of the saints of the most High, whose kingdom *is* an everlasting kingdom, and all dominions shall serve and obey him.—Dan. 7:27

Any astute student of Daniel's prophecy may see that Jesus' kingdom was to be partly made up of the various "dominions" that comprised the four Mediterranean-Bay and Fertile Crescent kingdoms of Daniel's prophetic theater. In other words, by "the uttermost parts of the earth" Jesus meant the same kings and regions of the world of which Daniel spoke. He meant Nebuchadnezzar and the Babylonian peoples; Cyrus and Darius and the Medo-Persian peoples; Alexander the Great and the Greek peoples; and Julius Caesar and the Roman-dominated peoples. It was within these parts of the earth that the Israelite Dispersion resided, to whom Jesus sent His apostles as understood in His words: ". . . other sheep I have [i.e. scattered sheep from the ten tribes of Israel] which are not of this fold [i.e. of the Jews]: them also I must bring, and they shall hear my voice; and there shall be one fold, *and* one shepherd" (John 10:16).

("All Nations" Interpretable as the Rulers Who REPRESENTED "All Nations") Daniel used the term "all nations" also. We see it in chapter 3 of Daniel. The expression is used in the account of the dedication of Nebuchadnezzar's "golden image" that he set up "in the plain of Dura, in the province of Babylon"—Dan. 3:1. Please note that to this dedication Nebuchadnezzar commanded all the **_officials_** and **_rulers_** of his kingdom to come:

> Then Nebuchadnezzar the king sent to gather together the princes, the governors, and the captains, the judges, the treasurers, the counselors, the sheriffs, and all the rulers of the provinces, to come to the dedication of the image which Nebuchadnezzar the king had set up. Then the princes, the governors, and captains, the judges, the treasurers, the counselors, the sheriffs, and all the rulers of the provinces, were gathered together unto the dedication of the image that Nebuchadnezzar the king had set up; and they stood before the image that Nebuchadnezzar had set up.—Dan. 3:2-3

I stress that only these **_officials_** and **_rulers_** attended the dedication. I stress that all the millions of people of all the nations on earth DID NOT ATTEND THE DEDICATION. Repeat: **_All people BY THE MILLIONS were not there in the plain of Dura in the province of Babylon, only their government officials and rulers were there_**.

Now look at the next passage:

> Then the herald cried aloud, To you it is commanded, O
> people, NATIONS, and languages, *That* at what time ye hear
> the sound of the cornet, flute, harp, sackbut, psaltery, dulcimer,
> and all kinds of music, ye fall down and worship the golden
> image that Nebuchadnezzar the king hath set up . . . Therefore
> at that time, when all the people heard the sound of the cornet,
> flute, harp, sackbut, psaltery, and all kinds of music, **ALL**
> the people, the **NATIONS**, and the languages, fell down *and*
> worshipped the golden image that Nebuchadnezzar the king had
> set up.—Dan. 3:4-5

Dear reader, please understand from these passages that the
expression "all nations" is NOT interpreted to mean every last person
from every last nation on the earth, BUT ONLY THEIR OFFICIALS
AND RULERS. When the music sounded only these officials and
rulers bowed down and worshipped the golden image. Of course, there
was one exception. The three officials of the Jews named Shadrach,
Meshach, and Abednego, who represented the nation of the Jews, did
not bow down:

> Then Nebuchadnezzar in *his* rage and fury commanded to
> bring Shadrach, Meshach, and Abednego. Then they brought
> these men before the king.—Dan. 3:13.

We see plainly, therefore, that it is possible, yes common, that in
certain parts of the Bible the expression "all nations" may be interpreted
in a very limited or narrow sense to mean ONLY the *officials* and *rulers*
of "all nations," *not all the millions of people of those nations.*

(Examples of This In the New Testament) Dear reader, let
me strongly suggest to you that *this same limited understanding of
"all nations"* is intended by the Holy Spirit in the following New
Testament passages:

PASSAGE I

When the Son of man shall come in his glory, and all the holy angels with him, then shall he sit upon the throne of his glory. And before him shall be gathered **ALL NATIONS**: and he shall separate them one from another, as a shepherd divideth *his* sheep from the goats. And he shall set the sheep on his right hand, but the goats on the left. Then shall the King say unto them on his right hand, Come, ye blessed of my Father, inherit the kingdom prepared for you from the foundation of the world . . . Then shall he say also unto them on the left hand, Depart from me, ye cursed, into everlasting fire, prepared for the devil and his angels . . . And these shall go away into everlasting punishment: but the righteous into life eternal.—Matt. 25:31-34, 41, 46

PASSAGE II

And I will give *power* unto my two witnesses, and they shall prophesy a thousand two hundred *and* threescore days, clothed in sackcloth . . . And when they shall have finished their testimony, the beast [i.e. the "first beast"—Rev. 13:12] that ascendeth out of the bottomless pit shall make war against them, and shall overcome them, and kill them. And their dead bodies *shall lie* in the street of the great city, which spiritually is called Sodom and Egypt, where also our Lord was crucified. And they of the people and kindreds and tongues and **NATIONS** shall see their dead bodies three days and an half, and shall not suffer their dead bodies to be put in graves.—Rev. 11:3, 7—9

(Let's Understand These Passages!)

In **PASSAGE I** the expression "all nations" clearly cannot mean nations in the sense of their wholeness—i.e. the millions of citizens and subjects of each nation. Nowhere in the New Testament do we find a doctrine that says Jesus or His evangelists were sent out to preach to whole nations, in the sense of the millions of people belonging to each nation. Instead, we find the doctrine that as the apostles preached the gospel in all nations [the Roman provincial territories], *only Israelites* *would be called of the Holy Spirit and only Israelites whom God had predestined of them would believe and be baptized*. We have proof of this in the following passages:

> And when the Gentiles [Greek: NATIONS] heard this [i.e. the gospel], they were glad, and glorified the word of the Lord: and ***as many as were ordained to eternal life believed***. —Acts 13:48

> And we know that all things work together for good to them that love God, **to them who are the CALLED according to *his* purpose. For whom he did foreknow, he also did predestinate to be conformed to the image of his Son**, that he might be the firstborn among many brethren.—Rom. 8:28-29

> Not as though the word of God hath taken none effect. For **they *are* not all Israel, which are of Israel** . . . Esaias also crieth concerning Israel, **Though the number of the children of Israel be as the sand of the sea, a remnant shall be saved**. —Rom. 9:6, 27

> And I heard the number of them which were sealed: ***and there were* sealed an hundred *and* forty *and* four thousand of all the tribes of the children of Israe**l.—Rev. 7:4

PASSAGE II can be correctly interpreted only by scholars who are also thoroughly familiar with Revelation. I hope I am one such scholar, and on that hope I will interpret it for my readers. Let other scholars examine my interpretation and judge for themselves.

First, the "two witnesses" in Revelation should by no means be thought to be only two persons, but many thousands of Christians in Asia that God called on to give up their lives in the witness of the gospel. Also, they were Christians of Christ's generation who had lived in or fled into Asia (cf. Rev. 1:4, 11). God gave these thousands powers that were reminiscent of Moses and Elijah. They had power over the rain, and they could call fire down from heaven (Rev. 11:5-6).

The word "two" in "two witnesses" has reference to **the two different episodes of martyrdom** suffered by Christians in Asia during the 3½ years of the Great Tribulation (cf. Rev. 11:3). Those

3½ years were AD 69-72, years in which Vespasian [Daniel's Tenth Roman Caesar] reigned. We learn of those two martyrdom episodes in the following passage:

> And when he had opened the fourth seal, I heard the voice of the fourth beast say, Come and see. And I looked, and behold a pale horse: and his name that sat on him was Death, and Hell followed with him. And power was given unto them over **the fourth part of the earth, to kill with sword, and with hunger, and with death, and with the beasts of the earth**. And when he had opened the fifth seal, **I saw under the altar the souls of them that were slain for the word of God, and for the testimony which they held**: And they cried with a loud voice, saying, How long, O Lord, holy and true, dost thou not judge and avenge our blood on them that dwell on the earth? And white robes were given unto every one of them; and it was said unto them, that **they [i.e. the first episode of martyrs]** should rest yet for a <u>little season</u>, until their fellow-servants **[i.e. the second episode of martyrs]** also and their brethren, that should be killed as they *were*, should be fulfilled.—Rev. 6:7-11

This passage says that one of every four Christians in Asia [v. 8] died because of giving "testimony" for Christ's name's sake [v. 9]. They did not all die in one martyrdom event, seeing that **"a little season"** intervened between **_two_** different martyrdom events. The first episode took place starting about Jan. 15, AD 69, coinciding with the beginning of the Great Tribulation. The second episode took place at the end of the Great Tribulation about midsummer of AD 72. You can see that the Great Tribulation, which intervened between the two episodes, is called "a little season."

Now, again, in **Passage II**, note that "nations" saw the dead bodies of the witnesses of the Second Martyrdom Episode in AD 72. The reason they saw them is because they had just slain them! These "nations," living during Jesus' generation, did not need TV sets or the Internet You-tube to see them. The killers were on site, and simply looked down on the martyrs' "dead bodies" as they stood near them and walked around them. Those "nations," again, were "rulers" of the nations,[16] not the entire populations of the nations.

In Rev. 1:6 we see that all church members held kingly rank in God's eyes. This is understandable in that shortly they would ascend into Heaven and be rewarded with authority over cities in Paradise (cf. Luke 19:17, 19). David would be the king over all Israel, and the glorified church saints would be lesser kings ruling Israelite cities under him. David himself would be a lesser king than Jesus, who is called "KING OF KINGS, AND LORD OF LORDS" (Rev. 19:16)—cf. Luke 1:32-33.

Even after they apostatized and became antichrists they are still called "kings" in Revelation, as in the following passages:

> And the **kings** of the earth [i.e. the apostate Christians in Asia] . . . hid themselves in the dens and in the rocks of the mountains; And said to the mountains . . . Fall on us, and hide us from the face of him that sitteth on the throne, and from the wrath of the Lamb: For the great day of his wrath is come—Rev. 6:15-17 (selective)

> And there came one of the seven angels which had the seven vials, and talked with me, saying unto me, Come hither; I will shew unto thee the judgment of the great whore that sitteth upon many waters: With whom the **kings** of the earth [Christian apostates in Asia] have committed fornication—Rev. 17:1-2.

Conclusion

Dear reader, I have shown you ample Bible reasoning for interpreting "nations" as persons *from* or *representative of* their various nations of origin. Apostate Christians between Jan., AD 69 and June-July, AD 72—the Great Tribulation period—were these nations (Matt. 25:32 and Rev. 11:9). All church members were *from* their individual nations [i.e. Roman provinces]. Out from the church membership came the apostates, _who were clearly from the same nations_! It was these nations,

---

16   All church members, apostate or faithful, were **rulers** in the sense of being "kings and priests" (see I Pet. 2:9; Rev. 1:6).

therefore, that, at Jesus' Second Coming He judged worthy of being cast into the Lake of Fire.

This knowledge makes us more Biblically literate and wise. By it we may rightly protest modern eschatologists [i.e. premillennialists] who ascribe grandiose [i.e. global or worldwide] meanings to the many passages in the Bible that contain the word "nations." We now know and understand that the word "nations" throughout the New Testament simply means the collective church apostates—i.e. the "many antichrists" of I John 2:18.

The Sign of Enduring to "the End"

The theme of Christians enduring in the faith till Jesus' Second Coming is found everywhere in the New Testament, and understandably so. Only those who endured—kept up their profession of faith in Christ (cf. Heb. 10:23)—would finally be "saved." Those who failed to endure [i.e. those who persisted in their apostasy into the Great Tribulation period] were to be cast into the Lake of Fire and suffer eternal punishment (Matt. 25:46; Rev. 20:14-15).

In His Olivet Prophecy Jesus connected the idea of enduring to the end with the Great Tribulation, a time when there would be false prophets and false Christs [i.e. antichrists] doing their best to coerce Christians, by almost any means of persuasion, into denying Christ before men. Jesus warned that He would also deny such Christians before His Father in Heaven:

> . . . whosoever [among my disciples] shall deny me before men, him will I also deny before my Father which is in heaven.—Matt. 10:33

Note how severe Jesus said the Great Tribulation would be:

> For then shall be great tribulation, such as was not since the beginning of the world [i.e. the Christian church] to this time, no, nor ever shall be. And except those days should be shortened, there should no [Christian] flesh be saved: but for the elect's sake those days shall be shortened.—Matt. 24:21-22

In Revelation, which John wrote around AD 67-68 while imprisoned by Caesar [Nero] on Patmos, we learn that all the seven churches of Asia had some members who had committed apostasy. Jesus told them:

> To him that overcometh [i.e. his apostasy] will I give to eat of the hidden manna [and] . . . power over the nations . . . the same shall be clothed in white raiment; and I will not blot out his name out of the book of life, but . . . will confess his name before my Father, and before his angels . . . I will grant [him] to sit with me in my throne, even as I also overcame, and am set down with my Father in his throne.—Rev. 2:17, 26; 3:5, 21

But to any apostate who did <u>not</u> overcome, Jesus said:

> Depart from me, ye cursed, into everlasting fire, prepared for the devil and his angels.—Matt. 25:41

How many Christians did not endure to the end? Jesus revealed to John that one out of every three Christians in Asia would wind up denying Him and being cast into the Lake of Fire (please read Rev. 8:7-12)! According to Revelation numeric a total of 70,000 Christian apostates there lost their "place" [i.e. inheritance] in God's kingdom:

> And I saw a great white throne, and him that sat on it, from whose face the earth and the heaven fled away; and there was found no place [i.e. inheritance in the kingdom of God] for them.—Rev. 20:11

<u>The Sign of
"the Abomination of Desolation"</u>

The "abomination of desolation" is an apocalyptic expression that has nothing to do with a new Jewish temple such as the so-called "Third Temple" yet to be built [allegedly] on the Temple Mount in Jerusalem [according to premillennial doctrine]. Rather, it pertains to that which became the *true* "temple" that began with Jesus when Jehovah anointed Him with the Holy Spirit at His baptism in the

Jordan River (see Matt. 3:16-17). He then became Jesus Christ, the Anointed One, the Messiah.

The New Testament makes it very clear that during Jesus' public ministry His body was the true Temple: "Destroy this temple," Jesus proclaimed to the Jews, "and in three days I will raise it up . . . he spake of **the temple of his body**" (John 2:19, 21).

In this remark Jesus revealed a profoundly NEW soteriological concept—i.e. the High Calling, not obtainable by the deeds of the Law and the Temple Service—the Levitical or Aaronic priesthood in Jerusalem—but now "By a new and living way," Jesus Christ, a priest after the order of Melchisedec:

> If therefore perfection [i.e. "High Calling," Phil. 3:14] were by the Levitical priesthood, (for under it the people received the law,) what further need *was there* that another priest should rise after the order of Melchisedec, and not be called after the order of Aaron?—Heb. 7:11

> Having therefore, brethren, boldness to enter into the holiest [i.e. God's presence in Heaven] by the blood of Jesus, By a new and living way, which he [Christ] hath consecrated for us, through the veil, that is to say, his **flesh** [i.e. **His born-again body**]—Heb. 10:19-20

> And it is . . . evident: for that after the similitude of Melchisedec there ariseth another priest, Who is made, not after the law of a carnal commandment, but after the power of an endless life. For he testifieth, Thou *art* a priest for ever after the order of Melchisedec.—Heb. 7:15-17

(Christ's Elect Saints Were Jesus' "Body" During His Ongoing Generation, and Therefore the True Temple of God.) The New Testament teaches that the called and elect saints of God were the "body" of Christ on earth, Jesus being the "head":

> And [God] hath put all *things* under his feet, and gave him *to be* the **HEAD** over all *things* pertaining to the church, Which is his **BODY**, the fullness of him that filleth all in all.—Eph 1:22-23

Christ, as it were, was the only Member of His "body" before Pentecost, and that explains why He pointed to His own body by itself as "the temple" (John 2:19). Later, however, when God poured out His Spirit also upon Christ's disciples, THEY became God's True Temple on earth (Jesus was then in Paradise above). Beginning from Pentecost, Christ's body was the church, and He their Head. Thus, of the church Paul wrote:

> Know ye not that ye are the temple of God,[17] and *that* the Spirit of God dwelleth in you? If any man defile the temple of God, him shall God destroy; for the temple of God is holy, which *temple* ye are.—I Cor. 3:16-17

(The Jews' Idea of Daniel's Abomination of Desolation) The Jews had their own idea of how to define Daniel's "abomination of desolation." It would be any unlawful or idolatrous person or thing that entered (or even came too near to) God's Temple in Jerusalem. For example, in 169 BC the Seleucid king Antiochus IV (Epiphany) entered the Holy Place of the ["second"] Temple and removed everything he found therein. He removed to his own country the "golden altar [i.e. of incense], the lampstand . . . and all its utensils. He took also the table for the bread of the Presence, the cups for drink offerings, the bowls, the golden censers, the curtain, the crowns, and the gold plating off the Temple façade" (I Macc. 1:20-22). That was certainly an "abomination of desolation" to the Jews.

In the days of Jesus, however [after He became "Christ" at his baptism] He revealed to the Jews that their Herodian Temple was already defiled:

> And Jesus went into the temple of God, and cast out all them that sold and bought in the temple, and overthrew the tables of the moneychangers, and the seats of them that sold doves, And said unto them [i.e. the chief priests], It is written, My house shall be called the house of prayer; but ye have made it a den of thieves.—Matt. 21:12-13

---

[17] See also I Cor. 6:19; II Cor. 6:16; Eph 2:21; II Thess. 2:4; I Pet. 2:5.

> Behold, your house [i.e. the Herodian Temple] is left unto you desolate.—Matt. 23:38

This is all to say that the Herodian Temple could not become abominated any more than it already was. Daniel's "abomination of desolation," in other words, when it happened, would have nothing to do with the defiling of the Temple at Jerusalem, *but everything to do with the TRUE Temple, the Church of God!*

(The Falling Away—I.e. the Apostasy Paul Predicted) Note that Jesus said to His disciples: "When ye [i.e. His disciples, not the Jews] shall see the abomination of desolation, spoken of by Daniel the prophet, stand in the holy place, (whoso readeth, let him understand:) Then let them [i.e. Christians] which be in Judea [i.e. in the church; in the true Temple] flee into the mountains" (Matt. 24:15-16).

In speaking these words to His disciples (not to the Jews) it is evident that a new and different understanding of Daniel's abomination of desolation [than that of the Jews] was intended. Furthermore, it is evident that a new and altogether different Temple was intended by those words. That's why we see the words "whoso readeth, let him understand"! The common or Jewish understanding of the abomination of desolation would no longer do; now the abomination of desolation had to do with the new, true Temple of God—i.e. the Church of God—being somehow abominated.

("Whoso Readeth, Let Him Understand") It is clear that Paul and the Thessalonian Christians [after Paul wrote them and explained it to them] UNDERSTOOD Daniel's abomination of desolation. Note his words:

> Let no man deceive you by any means: for *that day shall not come* [i.e. the Great Tribulation—cf. II Thess. 2:2], except there come a falling away first [i.e. in the church], and that man of sin be revealed, the son of perdition; Who opposeth and exalteth himself above all that is called God, or that is worshipped; so that **he as God sitteth in the TEMPLE of God, shewing himself that he is God.**—II Thess. 2:3-4

In the above passage the new understanding of Daniel's abomination of desolation is hidden [but was discernable to the wise—Rev. 13:18; 17:9a]! The **TEMPLE** intended was not the Herodian temple, but the **NEW** and **TRUE** "temple" that came into existence at Jesus' baptism (and on Pentecost the Church of God became a part of that same temple). Paul said that the time was imminent when "the son of perdition" [Antichrist] would enter the "temple" [i.e. the Church] and seek to steal away its pure doctrines and holy way—as Daniel put it, ". . . think to change times and laws" (Dan. 7:25)—and substitute doctrines of devils, such as "the doctrine of Balaam" and "the doctrine of the Nicolaitans"—Rev. 2:14, 15.

Revelation Proves that the
Abomination of Desolation Was Already in
Its First Stages In the Church
Toward the End of Jesus' Adult-time
Generation!!

Dear reader, I cannot impress upon you enough (for it is hardly discerned among today's Christians) that it was apostate **Christians**—baptized church members during Jesus' generation—who, toward the end of Jesus' generation, committed the abominable sin that led to their desolation [i.e. having their names blotted out of the Book of Life and being cast into the Lake of Fire—cf. Rev. 3:5; 20:12, 15].

False teachers **ALREADY IN** the church (because they were bona fide members of the church) began to teach doctrines that were anti-Christ. More and more Christians accepted these doctrines until the church "institution" began to totter and fall. By the time John wrote Revelation [AD 67-68] the abomination of desolation [i.e. the Apostasy] was in advanced stages in the seven churches of Asia. Jesus wrote [i.e. He dictated] letters to each church, pointing out its strengths on the one hand and its abominations on the other (see Rev. 2-3). He said they still had time to repent, but they would have to hurry and do it, or else put it off past *a line of demarcation* and wind up being "frozen" in their apostasy—i.e. "without remedy":[18] **"I GAVE HER SPACE TO REPENT OF HER FORNICATION; AND SHE REPENTED NOT"** (Rev. 2:21). Here's how Jesus described the antichrists when that point of no return came:

---

[18]   Cf. II Chr. 36:16; Prov. 6:15; 29:1.

Babylon the great [i.e. the church institution] is fallen, is fallen, and is become the habitation of devils, and a cage of every unclean and hateful bird. For the nations [fallen Christians] have drunk of the wine of the wrath of her fornication [i.e. have imbibed her Satanic, anti-Christ doctrines], and the kings of the earth [apostate Christians in Asia] have committed fornication with her [i.e. have listened to the "great whore"—Rev. 17:1-2]

He that is unjust [i.e. apostate], let him be unjust still: and he that is filthy [spiritually deceived], let him be filthy still —Rev. 22:11a

Jesus also commanded that when that point came all faithful Christians were to "jump ship":

Come out of her, my people, that ye be not partakers of her sins, and that ye receive not of her plagues. For her sins have reached unto heaven, and God hath remembered her iniquities.—Rev. 18:4-5

Conclusion

Thus, O reader, you have just read Jesus' testimony that it was in His day and during His ongoing generation that the Danielic Abomination of Desolation took place. Both the abomination of desolation and His Second Coming were certainly two things that He said—in His Olivet Prophecy—would take place before His generation passed away.

The Sign of False Prophets
And Apostasy in the Church

In His Olivet Prophecy Jesus said to His disciples:

Take heed that no man deceive you, for many shall come in my name, saying, I am Christ; and shall deceive many . . . And many false prophets shall rise, and shall deceive many. And because iniquity shall abound, the love of many shall wax cold . . . For there shall arise false Christs, and false prophets, and shall shew great signs and wonders; insomuch that, if *it were* possible, they shall deceive the very elect.—Matt. 24:4-5, 11-12, 24

(Here's an Important Statement, Question, and Answer.) STATEMENT: Jesus foretold this sign before the church age started on the day of Pentecost.

QUESTION: Are there any New Testament books written at the end of the church age that tell us whether or not this prophecy was being fulfilled?

ANSWER: Yes! They are Hebrews, Jude, Peter's second epistle, John's first and third epistles, and Revelation. These books were all written between AD 61 and 68, shortly before Jesus' Second Coming.

FALSE PROPHETS: FULFILLED!

Little children, it is the last time . . . even now are there many antichrists . . . let no man deceive you.—I John 2:18; 3:7

. . . Diotrephes, who loveth to have the preeminence among them, receiveth us not . . . prating against us with malicious words: and not content therewith, neither doth he himself receive the brethren, and forbiddeth them that would, and casteth *them* out of the church.—III John 9-10

For there are certain men crept in unawares, who were before of old ordained to this condemnation, ungodly men, turning the grace of our God into lasciviousness, and denying the only Lord God, and our Lord Jesus Christ.—Jude 4

Nicolaitans . . .—Rev. 1:5, 15

. . . them that hold the doctrine of Balaam, who taught Balac to cast a stumblingblock before the children of Israel, to eat things sacrificed unto idols, and to commit fornication. —Rev. 1:14

. . . thou sufferest that woman Jezebel, which calleth herself a prophetess, to teach and to seduce my servants to commit fornication, and to eat things sacrificed unto idols.—Rev. 2:20

. . . them of the synagogue of Satan, which say they are Jews, and are not, but do lie;—Rev. 3:9

CHRISTIAN APOSTATES: FULFILLED!

. . . forsaking the assembling of ourselves together, as the manner of some [i.e. church members] *is*—Heb. 10:25

Of how much sorer punishment, suppose ye, shall he [i.e. a Christian] be thought worthy, who hath trodden under foot the Son of God, and hath counted the blood of the covenant, wherewith he was sanctified, an unholy thing, and hath done despite unto the Spirit of grace?—Heb. 10:29

. . . cursed children [i.e. apostate church members]: Which have forsaken the right way, and are gone astray, following the way of Balaam . . . For it had been better for them not to have known the way of righteousness, than, after they have known *it*, to turn from the holy commandment delivered unto them. But it is happened unto them according to the true proverb, The dog *is* turned to his own vomit again; and the sow that was washed to her wallowing in the mire.—II Pet. 2:14-15, 21-22

. . . thou hast left thy first love . . . thou are fallen . . . except thou repent.—Rev. 2:4-5

. . . them that commit adultery with her . . . except they repent.—Rev. 2:22

. . . thy works, that thou hast a name that thou livest, and art dead.—Rev. 3:1

I know thy works, that thou art neither cold nor hot: I would thou wert cold or hot. So then because thou art lukewarm, and neither cold nor hot, I will spue thee out of my mouth. —Rev. 3:15-16

What Was the Chief Message of the False Prophets?

This section would not be complete unless I commented on the "lie" that the false prophets told in Jesus' generation, and TO WHOM THEY TOLD IT. First, it was Paul that foretold this "lie":

> And for this cause God shall send **THEM** strong delusion, that **THEY** should believe a **LIE.**—II Thess. 2:11

Reason tells us that the pronouns "them" and "they" in this passage refer to Christians. The lie could not reasonably be aimed at worldly or unbelieving people. Why lie to people who had long time been deceived by Satan, already hopeless captives of that wicked serpent? One more lie would not make them any more hopeless.

Paul implied that the lie was aimed at Christians—i.e. people once delivered from God's wrath, but who could apostatize and fall back into Satan's camp and God's condemnation:

> **That they all might be damned** who believed not the truth, but had pleasure in unrighteousness.—II Thess. 2:12

In other words, anyone falling for this lie would have to be a person **not** at the time under God's wrath—i.e. a Christian. Non-Christians, according to Jesus, were "condemned <u>already</u>" (John 3:18).

Satan first started the lie, telling it to Christians in Asia on the verge of being persecuted by Rome. Coming under persecution was a scary thought, even for Christians. Earlier, thinking that the Great Tribulation was upon them, the disciples at Thessalonica became "shaken in mind," and "troubled" (cf. II Thess. 2:2). Satan knew Christians dreaded the coming persecutions predicted by Jesus (see e.g. Matt. 24:9). Jesus also knew it, and forewarned His followers NOT to fear man:

> . . . fear not them which kill the body, but are not able to kill the soul: but rather fear him which is able to destroy both soul and body in hell . . . whosoever shall deny me before men, him will I also deny before my Father which is in heaven.—Matt. 10:28, 33

Jesus knew that that fear would cause many of His disciples to publicly "deny" Him. He would give them "space"[19] [time] to repent from their fear, but if they failed to "overcome" it during that "space" He would cast them into the Lake of Fire in the Great White Throne judgment (Rev. 20:14-15).

(What Was the "Lie"?) Satan lied first to the Christians under fear and stress in Asia. When they fell from the faith they became antichrists, and in turn the antichrists [Antichrist] told the same lie to their erstwhile Christian brethren to coax *them* to also deny Christ and join them. Sinners like company.

Now that we know the effect the lie had on Christians, we have a very strong idea of what the lie actually was. Was it not the "Peace and safety" message Paul mentioned? See the following:

> . . . when they [antichrists] shall say, **Peace and safety;** then sudden destruction cometh upon them, as travail upon a woman with child; and they shall not escape.—I Thess. 5:3

In other words the Lie was that "peace and safety" would come upon Christians who denied Christ before men. Satan told this lie first. Directing it into the hearts of fearful Christians, he intimated that if they would deny Christ before the Roman magistrates [in Asia] the magistrates would exempt them from persecution; hence, they would be at peace. Hence, they would be safe!

(The "Depths" of Satan) But the Lie went deeper into Satanic deception. Satan suggested that when the winds of persecution ceased they could simply ask for forgiveness and return to Christian life as before. "After all," Satan lied, "there was no sin that God would not forgive." But remember, Jesus said that there WAS a sin that God would not forgive:

> . . . I [Jesus] say unto you [i.e. you disciples], All manner of sin and blasphemy shall be forgiven unto men: but the blasphemy *against* the *Holy* Ghost [i.e. against the Father] shall not be forgiven unto men. And whosoever speaketh a word against the Son of man, it shall be forgiven him: but whosoever

---

[19]   See Rev. 2:21.

speaketh against the Holy Ghost [i.e. against God], it shall not be forgiven him, neither in this world [Greek: age], neither in the *world [age]* to come.—Matt. 12:31-32

Persistently and consistently denying Christ before men [i.e. throughout a "space" or trial period] was the unpardonable sin. To do so the Christian was defiling and searing his own innermost conscience and heart of hearts, which the Holy Spirit of Truth had enlightened [cf. John 14:17; 16:13] and filled with God's love and the hope of eternal life.

(More About the Unpardonable Sin) Lest any Christian reading this become fearful or doubtful as to whether or not he has committed the unpardonable sin, let me say a few more words. **FIRST** only Christians of the time of Jesus Christ ACTUALLY had the baptism of the Holy Spirit, and so could blaspheme the Holy Spirit. One could not truly blaspheme the Holy Spirit unless he had been "enlightened" by or "tasted" the Holy Spirit (Heb. 6:4). Paul, for example, blasphemed God [i.e. the Holy Spirit] *before his conversion,* and was forgiven because he had never HAD the Holy Spirit at the time; therefore, he did not KNOW GOD. He did not PERSONALLY have the Holy Spirit. To Timothy he wrote:

> I think Christ Jesus our Lord, who hath enabled me, for that he counted me faithful, putting me into the ministry; **Who was before a blasphemer,** and a persecutor, and injurious: but I obtained mercy, **because I did *it* ignorantly in unbelief**.—I Tim. 1:12-13

Paul blasphemed God as an unbeliever, as one who had never truly known God. Christians who DID know God and blasphemed Him out of fear of man were the ones capable of committing the unpardonable sin, and ONLY they.

Many Christians today, of course, have a conviction that they have been baptized with the Holy Spirit, which I believe is self-deception. God's Spirit certainly helps people today, but baptism with the Holy Spirit belonged only to the Christians that partook in the High Calling Salvation rank during Jesus' generation. This is evident all through the New Testament.

SECOND, even Christians of the time of Jesus' generation—those "many antichrists" who ACTUALLY had the baptism of the Holy Spirit and yet blasphemed Him—were EVENTUALLY forgiven! Jesus said that such blasphemers would not be forgiven during His generation ["this world" or age] nor in the *world* to come (Matt. 12:32). But what was that age or world to come? The "AGE" or "WORLD" to come was Paradise where they would live out their millennial life span in flesh and blood bodies. Paradise was not only an "age" for them, but truly another "world" for them. The Greek word for "age" [aion; eon] can also be correctly translated "world." Proof that God did not forgive them of the unpardonable sin in Paradise, so long as they were in flesh-and-blood bodies, is shown in that they during that time did not receive their ultimate, glorified bodies,[20] nor did they in the flesh enter into the very Presence of Jehovah in the Highest Heaven. After being in Paradise till the end of their life span in the flesh, GOD CERTAINLY FORGAVE THEM **AT THAT TIME**, and welcomed them into His Presence as His children in the Kingdom of God! O dear reader, thank God for His eternal love and unfailing mercy, "For the LORD *is* good; his mercy *is* everlasting; and his truth *endureth* to all generations" (Psalm 100:5; cf. 89:2).

Summary

The false prophets [antichrists] that appeared in the church toward the end of Jesus' generation fell for a Satanic "LIE" and were "damned" for it (II Thess. 2:11-12). They then passed that lie on to other members of the church—most of whom resisted it and successfully endured in the faith to the end (cf. Matt. 24:13).

The lie was that a Christian could deny Christ publicly and still get forgiveness later, return to the Christian life, and make it into Heaven at Jesus' Second Coming. Many church members fell for this lie and committed the unpardonable sin. Jesus came back "in a day when [they looked] not for him, and in an hour that [they were] not aware of" (Matt. 24:50). By denying Christ publicly they had, in effect, blasphemed the Holy Spirit.

---

[20]   i.e. their "immortal" and "incorruptible" bodies (cf. I Cor. 15:52-54)

The Christians that did NOT fall for this lie were those who recognized the lie as that which Paul foretold (II Thess. 2:11), and the liars as the "false prophets" and "false Christs" that Jesus foretold (see Matt. 24:11, 24). They put off the "fear" of man and many "loved not their lives unto the death" (Matt. 10:28; Rev. 21:11).

The Sign of the Gospel
Preached in All the World

Jesus said that when the gospel had been preached "in all the world [Greek: *Roman Empire*] . . . then shall the end come" (Matt. 24:14).

(Be Sure to Interpret "World" Correctly Here.) In order to correctly interpret "world" in Matt. 24:14 one must keep the following thoughts in mind:

- Jesus gave the Great Commission (as seen for example in Matt. 10:5ff; 28:19-20; and Acts 1:8) to His contemporary disciples **_only_**. The responsibility for its fulfillment was not to pass down to evangelists of future generations.
- In the disciples' minds the "world" correctly meant the *Mediterranean world* wherein could be found predestinated descendants of the twelve tribes of Israel (cf. Matt. 19:28; Acts 26:7; Rom. 8:29-30; Eph. 1:5; Rev. 7:4-8).
- The disciples heard Jesus say that He would be with THEM [includes other evangelists of their generation: e.g. Barnabas, Silas, Timothy, Titus, etc.] "unto the end of the world [Greek: age]." They correctly interpreted "age" to mean their own generation, **_and before it passed away_** (cf. Matt. 24:34).
- The disciples did not think or believe that fulfilling the Great Commission would take centuries or millennia. In fact, Paul declared it already fulfilled in Col. 1:5-6, 23.
- The Great Commission pertained only to the high-ranking Salvation Paul called "high calling of God in Christ Jesus" (Phil. 3:14), and which the Hebrews author called the "heavenly calling" (Heb. 3:1).
- Those so called and chosen were to be kings and priests over the lately resurrected people of the four Danielic [i.e.

Mediterranean and Fertile Crescent] kingdoms (cf. Dan. 2 &
7) in the kingdom of God, ruling over nations and cities in
Paradise (Luke 19:17, 19; I Pet. 2:5, 9; Rev. 1:6).

(Be Sure to Interpret "the End" Correctly.) By "the end" [see Matt.
24:14] Jesus did not mean the end of man's secular history on earth,
but He DID mean the end of the *sacred history of the TRUE Church*
on earth. This is seen in Jesus' command to His elect brethren to "flee"
when they saw Daniel's "abomination of desolation":

> When ye . . . see the abomination of desolation, spoken
> of by Daniel . . . Then let them which be in Judea flee into
> the mountains . . . For then shall be great tribulation, such as
> was not since the beginning of the world [Gk. cosmos; i.e. the
> beginning of the Church age] to this time, no, nor ever shall
> be.—Matt. 24:15-17, 21

The Church that Jesus said would "end" was the one He was to
found and "build" (Matt. 16:18). It was also the one He said would
"flee" before His generation came to an end. But the Church we see
on the earth today was founded and built by men, beginning with the
church fathers late in the first century and early in the second century
AD. This was a whole generation removed from Jesus' generation.
These two churches are not to be confused with each other.

("The End" Was 3½ Years Before Jesus' Second Coming.) Moreover,
we are not to confuse "the end" with the Second Coming of Jesus Christ.
Jesus' coming did not take place until 3½ years AFTER "the end" [i.e.
the start of the "abomination of desolation"]![21] The Great Tribulation
[that lasted 3½ years] took place between "the end" and Jesus' coming.
During those years Jesus' elect brethren (Jesus called them "the woman")
were fled into the "wilderness . . . where she is nourished for a time, and
times, and half a time, from the face of the serpent" (Rev. 12:14).

---

[21] Jesus was talking about "the end" of the viable [i.e. functional] church—before
the antichrist members abominated it. Jesus' Second Coming did not end the
church age, it ended the Great Tribulation that followed the church age. This is
an important distinction.

("The Gates of Hell" Did not "Prevail Against" Christ's Church!)
Just because Christ's Church ended in AD 69 [i.e. the year the Great
Tribulation began] we are not to conclude that Satan and the "gates of
hell . . . prevailed against" it, as promised by Jesus in the following passage:

> And I say also unto thee, that thou art Peter, and upon this
> rock I will build my church; and the gates of hell [Greek: Hades]
> shall not prevail against it.—Matt. 16:18

See the following reasons the Gates of Hell did not prevail over
Christ's Church:

- o The church age ended before Jesus' generation passed away,
  just as Jesus foretold.
- o Not one of Jesus' martyrs perished, not even a single hair of
  their head (Luke 21:18).
- o When Satan attacked the "woman" in the "wilderness" God
  protected her (see Rev. 12:7-16).
- o Though Satan [i.e. Antichrist] devoured the woman's
  "man child"—i.e. the 31,500 First-Episode martyrs (cf.
  Rev. 6:8)—"her child was caught up unto God, and *to* the
  throne"—Rev. 12:5.
- o In AD 72 Christ appeared with His angels and raptured the "woman"
  and "the remnant of her seed" into Heaven. See Rev. 11:11-12;
  12:1, 6, 14, and 17; I Thess. 4:16-17; and Matt. 24:30-31.
- o In Heaven Jesus' brethren ate and drank together at "the
  marriage supper of the Lamb (Rev. 19:9).
- o God rewarded Jesus' raptured brethren with suzerainty over
  cities of Israel in Paradise (Luke 19:17, 19).
- o ". . . the devil . . . was cast into the lake of fire and brimstone . . . and
  shall be tormented day and night for ever and ever"—Rev. 20:10

The Sign of the
Great Tribulation

Jesus said, "For then shall be great tribulation, such as was not
since the beginning of the WORLD [Gk. *cosmos*; i.e. the Church

of Christ] to this time, no, nor ever shall be. And except those days should be shortened, there should no flesh [i.e. of Christ's elect brethren] be saved; but for the elect's sake those days shall be shortened."—Matt. 24:21-22

(What "World"?) The Greek word "world" in this passage [i.e. cosmos] is greatly misunderstood by most commentators. Let us look carefully at the definition Dr. James Strong gives "cosmos" in his Greek Dictionary: "orderly arrangement or decoration; the world in a wide **_or NARROW sense_**, including its inhabitants" (#2889); emphasis added.

I am suggesting to you, dear reader, that in Matt. 24:21 the Greek word *cosmos* must be understood <u>in its **narrow** sense</u> to signify a much smaller "world" than the entire global planet. I am persuaded that it means the church of God, a new and tiny cosmos during Jesus' generation that had an "arrangement" or "decoration" that was pleasing to God but liable to persecution by the larger world [Roman Empire].

If we give it this meaning then we can understand Jesus' true meaning that the <u>church</u> [He wasn't talking about the Jews[22]] would never suffer a greater tribulation. It would not suffer a greater because immediately after they suffered the "great tribulation" Jesus came and raptured the church off the face of the earth:

> Immediately after the tribulation of those days [i.e. AD 69-72] . . . shall appear the sign of the Son of man in heaven . . . And he shall send his angels with a great sound of a trumpet, and they shall gather together [i.e. rapture; catch up] his elect from the four winds, from one end of heaven to the other.—Matt. 24:29a, 30a, 31

O reader, do you now understand? How could the Church ever suffer a greater tribulation when in AD 72 Christ appeared and caught all His elect brethren up into heaven? If they were in heaven, weren't they out of Satan's reach? In Revelation we see them after they were caught up. They were with God and at peace, never to be persecuted again:

---

[22]   While it is true that the Jews during WWII suffered a much greater tribulation [i.e. the Holocaust], yet this does not negate Christ's words. He was not talking about the Jews, but about Christians, His elect brethren.

These [i.e. "a great multitude," Rev. 7:9] **ARE** they which came out of great tribulation, and have washed their robes, and made them white in the blood of the Lamb. Therefore **ARE** they before the throne of God, and serve him day and night in his temple: and he that sitteth on the throne [Christ] shall dwell among them. They shall hunger no more, neither thirst any more; neither shall the sun light on them, nor any heat. For the Lamb which is in the midst of the throne shall feed them, and shall lead them unto living fountains of waters; and God shall wipe away all tears from their eyes.—Rev. 7:14b, 15-17

(What Caused the Apostasy and What Caused the Great Tribulation that Followed?) In the year AD 64 almost all of Rome was destroyed in a great fire. At first the Romans blamed Nero for setting it in order to make room to build his golden palace. But Nero diverted attention away from himself by blaming the Christians in Rome. From that day on Roman policy toward Christians became hostile and deadly.

History speaks of the Neronian Persecution, in which Nero cruelly attempted to exterminate all Christians, not just from Rome but everywhere they were found.

Most Christians at that time had fled into Asia because of (a) open war against the Jews in the Holy Land [i.e. the First Jewish Revolt: AD 66-70], and (b) outbreaks of Christian persecutions from Rome through Greece. Asia, being on the other side of the Aegean Sea, had become the last best sanctuary for Christians. Nero commanded that ten additional magistrates[23] be sent into Asia to launch a policy of Christian extermination there also. Seeing this development, Asian Christians began to commit apostasy [i.e. in anticipation of persecution and martyrdom], fulfilling the prophesies by Jesus, Peter, and Paul that many brethren would fall away in the last days (see e.g. Matt. 10:28-33; 24:9-13; II Thess. 2:3; I Tim. 4:1; II Tim. 4:3-4; II Pet. 2:1-2).

When John wrote Revelation this apostasy was well underway, as seen clearly in Jesus' mini-epistles in chapters 2 and 3. In Jesus' epistle to the Christians at Smyrna He warned of a soon-to-occur ten-day "tribulation" just in Smyrna:

---

[23]   These ten magistrates are signified in Revelation as the "ten horns" (see e.g. Rev. 1:1; 12:3; 13:1; 17:12).

Behold, the devil shall cast *some* of you into prison, that ye may be tried; and ye shall have tribulation ten days: be thou faithful unto death—Rev. 2:10.

Why just ten days there? I believe it was because God gave them "a way of escape":

> . . . God is faithful, who will not suffer you to be tempted [Greek: tried; tested] above that ye are able; but will with the temptation also make a way to escape, that ye may be able to bear it.—I Cor. 10:13

They escaped to a wilderness area evidently not too far from the seven churches of Asia (cf. Rev. 12:6, 14). But wouldn't they have soon died in a wilderness environment where there supposedly was insufficient shelter, water, food, medicine, and clothing? Well, yes, but who says that there were no such amenities in this particular wilderness? Apparently **"mammon"*** [i.e. **very rich men***] owned property and houses there. God had placed **them*** there long before the Christian refugees needed **them.*** [Note: These and all following emboldened words with an asterisk have synonymity of subject matter and basic meaning.]

> And the woman[24] fled into the wilderness, where she hath a place prepared of God, that **THEY*** [i.e. the **Mammon***][25] should feed her there a thousand two hundred and threescore days—Rev. 12:6

Thus we see what caused the Apostasy [i.e. the Neronian Persecution] and the Great Tribulation [i.e. the Ten Horns, or the ten ad hoc magistrates ordered into Asia by Nero], and how God protected most of the elect brethren following their escape into the wilderness.

---

[24]   In Revelation the "woman" was Christ's espoused [betrothed], His soon-to-be bride—cf. II Cor. 11:2; Eph. 5:25, 32; Rev.12:1; 21:2, 9.

[25]   Jesus prophesied to His disciples that one day there would be **"mammon"*** to help them in a time of great need (Luke 16:9).

The Identity of the Sheep*
In Jesus' Sheep and Goat Parable

NOTE: Remember, all words with the asterisk (*) indicate synonymity of subject matter and meaning.

(The Initial Persecution at Smyrna Saved Most Christians in Asia.) The persecution at Smyrna lasted only ten days, but that was long enough to sound the alarm to all the other churches in Asia, and give their members a chance to flee into the wilderness. It also gave the **Mammon*** a chance to think about what was happening to the Christians and make hard decisions. **They*** determined to help the Christians, chiefly because God moved them to, but also because Christians were their best workers and friends.

The **Mammon,*** by the way, were **non-church-member Israelite elect.*** **They*** were no doubt the chief entrepreneurs and business men of Asia. **They*** had long-time been the chief **employers*** of Christians in Asia. As God used Joseph to make Pharaoh rich [i.e. during the seven years of plenty] so He used the Christians to make their **employers*** *extremely* successful in their companies and stores throughout Asia, especially in the ports on the east-Aegean coast. To accomplish their business successfully **they*** had to hire all kinds of workers, and many of them. Along with pagan employees **they*** also hired many Christian workers: e.g. longshoremen, warehousemen, manufacturers, and product transporters. In the cities [e.g. Smyrna, Ephesus, Pergamos, Philadelphia, etc.] **they*** hired Christian artificers, shopkeepers, bookkeepers, and salesmen.

They loved hiring Christians as their workers because they were honest, industrious, and punctual. By contrast their pagan employees were often pilferers, foot-draggers, drunken, foul-mouthed, inept workers who were frequently absent, unmotivated, and undependable.

When the Great Tribulation spread from Smyrna to the other cities suddenly all Christians fled into the wilderness and their **Mammon*** employers wound up not having dependable workers. Thinking that the persecution would soon end and everything go back to normal, the **Mammon*** offered to temporarily take their Christian workers into their wilderness homes, hide them from the authorities, and generally just take care of them, thinking that they could all soon return to their jobs and resume their work as usual.

However, Christ was about to appear and catch Christians up into heaven—*including their **mammon hosts**.** This infers that the **Mammon*** were "lost **sheep*** of the house of Israel" (Matt. 10:6; cf. John 10:16), as well as the "**sheep**"* in Jesus' Sheep/Goat Parable. When Jesus came and caught the **Mammon*** up into Heaven [along with their Christian workers] He spoke the following unexpected words to **them**:*

> Then shall the King say unto **them*** on his right hand [i.e. the **sheep*** or **Mammon***], Come, ye blessed of my Father, inherit the kingdom prepared for you from the foundation of the world [Greek: cosmos, or the church]: For I was an hungered, and ye gave me meat: I was thirsty, and ye gave me drink: I was a stranger and ye took me in: Naked, and ye clothed me: I was sick, and ye visited me: I was in prison, and ye came unto me. Then shall the **righteous*** [i.e. the **Mammon***] answer him, saying, Lord, when saw we thee[26] an hungered, and fed *thee?* or thirsty, and gave *thee* drink? When saw we thee a stranger, and took *thee* in? or naked, and clothed *thee?* Or when saw we thee sick, or in prison, and came unto thee? And the King shall answer and say unto them, Verily I say unto you, Inasmuch as ye have done *it* unto one of the least of these my <u>brethren</u> [i.e. the church elect], ye have done *it* unto me.—Matt. 25:34-40

---

[26]   This question asked by the "**sheep**"* proves that the **Mammon*** [i.e. the "**sheep**"*] were never church members, but mere **compassionate Israelites*** who gave Christ's brethren aid and comfort during their persecutions in the Great Tribulation. Had **they*** once been church members **they*** would surely have understood the principle that in helping Christians **they*** were also helping Christ Jesus the Lord of the Christians. That **they*** didn't understand this explains their surprise at being inducted into God's eternal kingdom along with the Christians **they*** helped (Matt. 25:37-39).

The Parable of the Hired Workers Regarding the Eleventh Hour Hires*

Jesus' testimony that His Second Coming would occur before His generation passed away is seen also in another of His parables.—i.e. "The Parable of the Workers" (see Matt. 20:1-16)—summarized as follows.

One day a "householder" went to the market place on five different occasions [at three-hour intervals] and hired workers to work in his vineyard. He hired workers at 6 a.m., 9 a.m., noon, 3 p.m., and 6 p.m. The first hires, or the "early in the morning" hires[27]—wound up working for the householder longer than the four subsequent hires—agreed to be paid a "penny," or a whole day's wage. The four following hires, however, worked for him for a reduced number of hours respectively:

➤ the 9 a.m. hires for 10-12 hours;
➤ the 12 (noon) hires for 7-9 hours;
➤ the 3 p.m. hires for 4-6 hours.

But the 6 p.m. hires—called the **"eleventh hour" hires***[28]—wound up working for only "one hour" [note that their work time was drastically "shortened" from a usual three-hour segment to only one hour [cf. Matt. 24:22]! But at pay time the paymaster commanded the workers to line up in reverse order—i.e. the **"eleventh hour" hires*** first in line and the "early morning" hires last. Unexpected by the first hires the paymaster paid the **last hires*** a penny as well as to themselves. They murmured that that was unfair, because they had worked in the field during the "heat of the day,"[29] but the **last hires*** had worked in the cooler time of day and for only one hour (Matt. 20:12). Then the householder said to one of them:

> Friend, I do thee no wrong: didst not thou agree with me for a penny? Take *that* thine *is*, and go thy way: I will give unto **this last***, even as unto thee. Is it not lawful for me to do what I will with mine own? Is thine eye evil, because I am good?—Matt. 20:13-15

---

27 See Matt. 20:1.
28 See Matt. 20:9.
29 See Matt. 20:12.

(The Explanation)

Dear reader, this parable is about Jesus' Second Coming and the "pay" [i.e. reward] He would then give to all His elect brethren according to their works (Matt. 16:27). It raises the question of why **people*** who worked for Him only "one hour" [i.e. the **"eleventh hour" hires***] should receive the same pay as others who worked for Him for perhaps thirteen plus hours [i.e. the first or "early . . . morning" hires].

In explaining the parable Jesus focused on only the first and **last hires.*** He wanted to make the point that all His elect brethren, whether those who had served Him for five decades, or others who had served Him for only three and a half years [i.e. during the Great Tribulation], would both receive eternal life and an inheritance in the eternal Kingdom of God!

Both the first and **final hires*** were to have served the Lord in the most difficult of times. Acts might strongly suggest to us, for example, that the very first Christians [cf. the first hires]—e.g. the twelve apostles of Jesus Christ and the church in Jerusalem that suffered severe persecution at the hands of the chief priests and Saul the Pharisee—deserved a better reward than the **last hires**.* This is understandable when you realize who the **last hires*** were.

The Identity of the Last Hires*

Some might contend that I should interpret the **last hires*** to be ***Christians*** that labored in God's vineyard during the Great Tribulation. Perhaps their argument would be that though they worked only one hour, yet their persecutions for Christ's name's sake was much more severe than that of Christians who served the Lord *before* the Great Tribulation (cf. Matt. 24:21). That sounds very plausible, but they were not the hires Jesus had in mind. The following passage tells us that there were people—**non-church-member Israelite elect***—who stepped up to the plate during the Great Tribulation in Asia and gave aid and comfort to Christ's elect church "brethren" (Matt. 25:40):

> **He*** [any rich and compassionate Israelite "Gentile"] that
> receiveth a prophet in the name of a prophet shall receive a

prophet's reward; and **he*** that receiveth a righteous man shall receive a righteous man's reward. And **whosoever*** shall give to drink unto one of these little ones a cup of cold *water* only in the name of a disciple, verily I say unto you, **he*** shall in no wise lose his reward.—Matt. 10:40-42

By interpretation this passage says that some **unidentified Israelites helped*** Christians being persecuted in some day of distress would receive the SAME eternal reward as those **they*** helped.

The passage is no doubt a prophecy of Jesus concerning the time of the Great Tribulation when His elect brethren in Asia would suffer terrible persecution and martyrdom, unequaled by any church persecution before or after it (cf. Matt. 24:21). But notice who Jesus stresses in the passage—i.e. not the Christians being aided and comforted but the mysterious, unidentified people who helped them! In the Sheep and Goat Parable these people are identified as the **"sheep"*** who, by giving aid and comfort to Jesus' "brethren" [see Matt. 25:40] also gave aid and comfort to Jesus. And it is clear that the "sheep" did not expect such a great reward.

We may now understand, also, that the **Mammon*** who would "receive" Christ's brethren "into everlasting habitations" (Luke 16:9) were the **Last Hires.*** In His "Parable of the Unjust Steward" Jesus pointed out that the reason the **Mammon*** would receive His "brethren" would be *because Christians had already helped them first* [i.e. to prosper in their businesses in Asia]. That is, it was mainly because of the Christians who worked for them that they had become **Mammon*** [filthy rich] in the first place!

For three and one-half years [during the Great Tribulation period] these **Mammon,*** therefore, would put their lives and money on the line to save as many Christians from the Ten Horns as possible, which turned out to be three-fourths of the Christian population in Asia at that time.

O dear reader, can you not see that the **"sheep"*** in Jesus' "Sheep and Goat" parable and the **"Mammon"*** in His "Parable of the Unjust Steward" are the same with the **"eleventh hour" hires*** in the "Parable of the Workers" (Matt. 20:1-16)? They were also *"**the rest of the dead**"** in Rev. 20:5! [30]

---

[30] This clear harmony of several Scriptures from different parts of the Bible is why there is such a thing as <u>Biblical Theology</u>.

If this is so, we can understand why the persecuted saints of the First Hires would be upset when they learned that the **Last Hires*** [i.e. the **Mammon***] had received eternal life and an inheritance in the kingdom without ever having been a member of the Church of God, and without ever having suffered [from what they could see], or been born again, or baptized with water by a qualified minister of the Church. They also knew that the **Mammon*** had had an easy life in comparison to themselves—the "early . . . morning" or first-hour hires (Matt. 20:1). They were rich, owned businesses, had city and country [cf. "wilderness"] properties and houses, and they had many servants [Christian workers]. Also, they remembered—and were now puzzled by—Jesus' words, "How hardly shall they that have riches enter into the kingdom of God" (Mark 10:23)! They also recalled, no doubt, that *they themselves*, as church members in Jerusalem, gave up all that they had, took up their crosses, and followed the impoverished Christ to a potential martyrdom.

<u>God's Protocol in
Saving the 4,000 Mammon* Was Quite Different
from that of Saving Church Members
During Jesus' Generation.</u>

But remember, dear reader, that when the Great Tribulation began the Church age simultaneously ended. Therefore, to save the **Mammon*** [i.e. the 4,000 **"rest of the dead"***] during the ensuing Great Tribulation [3½-year period: ca Jan. 15, AD 69 to midsummer of 72] God waived the special High Calling Salvation Rank requirements such as Repentance, Water Baptism, Public Confession of Faith, the New Birth, and Baptism with the Holy Spirit.

Rather, He saved **_them_*** [i.e. gave them eternal life and an inheritance in the kingdom] by the protocol Jesus required of the rich young ruler—i.e. "Sell all that thou hast, and distribute unto the poor . . . and come, follow me"—Luke 18:22. This is exactly what was required of the 4,000 **Mammon*** who, in the Asian wilderness "fed" and "nourished" 105,000 Church refugees [i.e. the woman in the wilderness] throughout the 3½-year Great Tribulation period.

By the time the Tribulation came to a close all the wealth the **Mammon*** had gained during the church age was gone! How so? Answer: ***They*** * *used up all their money and resources taking care of Christ's elect brethren*. And don't forget, those 105,000 elect brethren were called "the woman" in Revelation:

> And when the dragon saw that he was cast unto the earth [i.e. in Asia], he persecuted the woman which brought forth the man *child*. And to the woman were given two wings of a great eagle [i.e. the **Mammon**,* whose money (i.e. coinage) showed the Roman eagle], that she might fly [i.e. flee] into the wilderness, into her place, where she is nourished for a time, and times, and half a time, from the face of the serpent.—Rev. 12:13-14

In effect, therefore, the **Mammon*** *DID* fulfill a godly and Heaven-approved protocol for inheriting the kingdom and having everlasting life. Though they had not previously been saved church members, yet now in the Great Tribulation of Christ's brethren **they*** spent all their wealth on *receiving* Jesus' elect brethren into their homes and lives. **They*** spent all that **they*** had on them, distributing food, water, clothing, shelter, medicine, etc., to each "poor" saint of God as he had need (cf. Acts 2:45). In this way **they*** fed and nourished 105,000 people, supplying **_all_** their human needs for a total of "a thousand two hundred *and* threescore days" (Rev. 12:6)! What an unheard of sacrifice by people that did not even know God was about to accept them into His everlasting kingdom (Matt. 25:34-30)!

After the Tribulation ended, Jesus came. He gathered these 4,000 **mammon*** unto Himself [i.e. raptured them] together with His 140,000 High-Calling brethren. Then He explained to **them,*** "Inasmuch as ye have done *it* unto one of the least of these my brethren, ye have done *it* unto me. And **these . . . righteous*** shall go away . . . into life eternal" (Matt. 25:40, 46)

Chapter Three

THE WITNESS OF
THE APOSTLES

Dear reader, in this chapter I lay out for your perusal in meticulous detail the *collective* witness of six different apostles that says that Jesus' Second Coming was about to take place in their day and time, and that, in fact, it **_did_** take place in their time.

The six apostles are Paul, John, the Hebrews author, James, Peter, and Jude. I could as easily have said that the third witness was the Holy Spirit, for it was He that inspired each apostle to teach this truth.

(Are you a Divine Visitor from the Past?)

Dear reader, in order for you to comprehend these six apostolic witnesses you must forget yourself. Not a single one of these apostles was writing to YOU or to ME. *The apostles' audience was strictly and forever the Christians who lived contemporaneously with themselves.* In short, except for academic purposes, you and I have no direct or immediate interest in either the High-Calling Salvation that they preached, or the eternal rewards God gave them. If you do not agree with this, and are staunchly determined **_NEVER_** to agree with it no matter what, then you are wasting your time finishing this book or reading the New Testament itself.

The only way you might have an immediate part in the "apostles' doctrine" (Acts 2:42) is if you can somehow demonstrate that you LIVED in the first century, knew the apostles first hand, and were a

Christian *at that time*. You must also be about a two-thousand-year-old "time traveler" sent from God to us 21ˢᵗ century Christians!

If you are indeed come to us from two thousand years ago (I beg you indulgence), then I will know that I do not have to convince **YOU** that the doctrine stated above (first paragraph) is true. You will already know it is. In fact, you must have been sent to this generation on an errand from God to help put the record and doctrines of the New Testament straight for today's woefully mistaken and Biblically illiterate Christians, and to advance their religious education.

The Witness of Paul: Quotes from Paul's Epistles

The following quotes from Paul were all inspired by the Holy Spirit and written to and meant strictly and ONLY for first-century Christians. Both Paul and the Holy Spirit had in mind ONLY Christians of Christ's generation. Neither Paul nor the Holy Spirit had US in mind, not even remotely, not at all, zilch! They were NOT sending their message to Christians who would be living two millennia later. If Paul could speak to you from Heaven, and you asked him if what I am saying here is correct, he would answer in the positive, and urge you to apply II Tim. 3:16 to yourself.

ROMANS

- For I reckon that the sufferings of this present time are not worthy *to be compared* with the glory which shall be [Greek: **ABOUT to be**] revealed in **US**.—Rom. 8:18
- For he will finish the work [i.e. of the Great Commission], and cut *it* short in righteousness: because **A SHORT WORK** will the Lord make upon the earth.—Rom. 9:28
- And that, knowing the time, that *it is* high time to awake out of sleep: for **NOW** *is* **OUR** salvation nearer than when **WE** believed. The night is far spent, the day is **AT HAND**—Rom. 13:11, 12a
- And the God of peace shall bruise Satan under **YOUR** feet **SHORTLY**—Rom. 16:20
- . . . the preaching of Jesus Christ [i.e. concerning the kingdom of God] . . . which was kept secret since the world began . . . **NOW**

is made manifest . . . **TO ALL NATIONS** for the obedience of faith—Rom. 16:25-26

I CORINTHIANS

- . . . **YE** come behind in no gift; **waiting for the coming of OUR** Lord Jesus Christ: Who shall also confirm **YOU** unto the end . . . blameless in the day of **OUR** Lord Jesus Christ.—1:7-8
- . . . this I say, brethren, **THE TIME IS SHORT**—I Cor. 7:29a
- Now all these things happened unto them [Israelites in the Sinai Wilderness], for ensamples: and they are written for **OUR** [i.e. Corinthians'] admonition, **UPON WHOM THE ENDS OF THE WORLD [Greek: AGES] ARE COME**—I Cor. 10:11
- For as often as **YE** [not "we"] eat this bread, and drink this cup, **YE** [not "we"] do shew the Lord's death **TILL HE COME.**—I Cor. 11:26
- Behold, I shew **YOU** [not "us"] a mystery; **WE** shall not all sleep [die]—I Cor. 15:51
- Maranatha [Greek: O (our) Lord come]—I Cor. 16:22

II CORINTHIANS

- For **WE** know that if **OUR** earthly house [born-again body] were dissolved, **WE** have a building [immortal body] of God, an house not made with hands, eternal in the heavens.—II Cor. 5:1
- For he says, **"AT THE ACCEPTABLE TIME** I listened to you, and on **THE DAY OF SALVATION** I helped **YOU"** [not *us*] Behold, **NOW** [when Paul lived] is **"THE ACCEPTABLE TIME"**; behold, **NOW** is **"THE DAY OF SALVATION"**—II Cor. 6:2, NASB

GALATIANS

- Who gave himself for **OUR** sins, that he might deliver **US** from [Greek: take us out of[31]] this *present* evil world [Greek: *age*; i.e. the time of Jesus' generation], according to the will of God and **OUR** Father—Gal. 1:4

---

[31] i.e. rapture us!—from the Greek εχελητται [exaletai], meaning, "to *tear out . . .* pluck out . . . rescue" (see *Strong's Concordance*, Greek Dictionary, #1807).

- Stand fast therefore in the liberty wherewith Christ hath made **US** free, and be not entangled **AGAIN**[32] with the yoke of bondage [i.e. the Law of Moses].—Gal. 5:1

EPHESIANS

- Having made known unto **US** the mystery of his will, according to his good pleasure which he hath purposed in himself: that in the dispensation of the **FULNESS** of times[33] he might gather together in one all things [i.e. "all" Israel's 12 tribes] in Christ, both which are in heaven [i.e. 3rd heaven, Paradise], and which are on earth; *even* in him:—Eph. 1:9-10
- . . . not only in this world, but also in that which is to come [Greek: about to come[34]]—Eph. 1:21
- Wherefore take unto **YOU** the whole armour of God, that **YE** may be able to withstand in the evil day [the Great Tribulation], and having done all, to stand.—Eph. 6:13

PHILIPPIANS

- Being confident of this very thing, that he which hath begun a good work in **YOU** will perform *it* UNTIL THE DAY OF JESUS CHRIST:—Phil. 1:6
- . . . that **YE** may be sincere and without offence TILL THE DAY OF CHRIST;—Phil. 1:10

---

32 **"AGAIN"** shows the Galatians were **Israelites**. Why? Only Israelite Christians who had once been under the Law could fall from it [as in Hos. 1:6-9-10], then come under it **"AGAIN"**! This supports my thesis that in the Great Commission Jesus sent the Evangelists ONLY to such nations or "Gentiles" that had once been under the Law (Matt. 28:19).

33 "THE FULNESS OF TIMES"—Jesus equated His own generation as "THE FULNESS OF TIMES" with His words "I am come to . . . fulfil" (Matt: 5:17), and "The time is fulfilled, and the kingdom of God is at hand" (Mark 1:15).

34 Greek: μελλοντι [mellonte], means "about (to be) . . . at the point of being . . . or on the verge of being (see *Strong's Concordance,* the Greek Dictionary, #3195). Knowing this is crucial to the correct meaning of this passage. Christ was on the verge of rapturing His elect brethren into a world about to open up to them—i.e. the Holy Land *in Paradise*. This Greek word gives the lie to the common interpretation put forth by today's expositors that Christ's coming has yet to happen these two thousand years after Paul's day.

- For unto **YOU** [not unto *us*] it is given in the behalf of Christ, not only to believe on him, but also to suffer for his sake [i.e. in the Great Tribulation];—Phil. 1:29
- I [Paul] press toward the mark for the prize of the high calling[35] of God in Christ Jesus.—Phil. 3:14
- For **OUR** conversation [Greek: citizenship] is in heaven; from whence also **WE** look for the Saviour, the Lord Jesus Christ: Who shall change **OUR** vile body, that it may be fashioned like unto his glorious body, according to the working whereby he is able even to subdue all things unto himself.—Phil. 3:20-21
- The Lord is at hand.—Phil. 4:5b

COLOSSIANS

- . . . the truth of the gospel: Which is come unto **YOU** as *it is* in all the world . . . the hope of the gospel, which **YE** have heard, *and* which was preached to every creature which is under heaven; whereof I Paul am made a minister—Col. 1:5b, 6, 23b
- . . . that **WE** may present **EVERY MAN** [predestinated in Christ's generation to inherit the kingdom of God] perfect in Christ Jesus.—Col. 1:28
- When Christ, *who is* **OUR** life, shall appear, then shall **YE** also appear with him in glory.—Col. 3:4
- Knowing that of the Lord **YE** shall receive the reward of the inheritance: for **YE** serve the Lord Christ.—Col. 3:24

I THESSALONIANS

- . . . **YE** turned to God from idols to serve the living and true God; And to wait for his Son from heaven, whom he raised from the dead, *even* Jesus, which delivered **US** from the wrath to come. —I Thess. 1:9b, 10
- That **YE** would walk worthy of God, who hath called **YOU** unto his kingdom and glory.—I Thess. 2:12

---

[35] High-Calling Salvation rank; cf. "the heavenly calling" (Heb. 3:1). God was calling Paul and all other Christians of his day to soon enter a HIGH or a HEAVENLY dwelling [cf. II Pet. 1:11], i.e. His own eternal abode. This is the salvation Jesus offered His followers, seen in His words "the gospel of the kingdom [i.e. of God or, of heaven]" (see e.g. Matt. 4:23; 6:33; 9:35; 12:28; 13:11; et. sequentia; e.g. Matt. 24:14 and Mark 1:14).

- For what is **OUR** hope, or joy, or crown of rejoicing? *Are* not even **YE** in the presence of our Lord Jesus Christ at his coming? —I Thess. 2:19
- To the end he may stablish **YOUR** hearts unblameable in holiness before God, even **OUR** Father, at the coming of **OUR** Lord Jesus Christ with all his saints.—I Thess. 3:13
- But I would not have **YOU** ignorant, brethren, concerning **THEM** which are asleep, that **YE** sorrow not, even as others which have no hope. For if **WE** believe that Jesus died and rose again, even so **THEM** also which sleep in Jesus will God bring with him. For this we say unto **YOU** by the word of the Lord, that **WE** which are alive *and* remain unto the coming of the Lord shall not prevent **THEM** which are asleep. For the Lord himself shall descend from heaven with a shout, with the voice of the archangel, and with the trump of God: and the dead in Christ shall rise first: Then **WE** which are alive *and* remain shall be caught up together with **THEM** in the clouds, to meet the Lord in the air: and so shall **WE** ever be with the Lord. Wherefore comfort one another with these words. —I Thess. 4:14-18
- But **YE**, brethren, are not in darkness, that that day should overtake **YOU** as a thief . . . Therefore let **US** not sleep, as *do* others; but let **US** watch and be sober . . . For God hath not appointed **US** to wrath, but to obtain salvation by **OUR** Lord Jesus Christ.—I Thess. 5:4, 6, 9
- . . . I *pray God* **YOUR** whole spirit and soul and body be preserved blameless unto the coming of **OUR** Lord Jesus Christ. Faithful *is* he that calleth **YOU** who also will do *it*.—I Thess. 5:23-24

II THESSALONIANS

- And to **YOU** who are troubled rest with **US** when the Lord Jesus shall be revealed from heaven with his mighty angels . . . when he shall come to be glorified in his saints— II Thess. 1:7, 10a
- Now we beseech **YOU**, brethren, by the coming of **OUR** Lord Jesus Christ, and by **OUR** gathering unto him—II Thess. 2:1
- Whereunto he called **YOU** by **OUR** gospel, to the obtaining of the glory of **OUR** Lord Jesus Christ.—II Thess. 2:14
- And the Lord direct **YOUR** hearts into the love of God, and into the patient waiting for Christ.—II Thess. 3:5

I TIMOTHY

- Now the Spirit speaketh expressly, that in the latter time[36] **SOME** shall depart from the faith,[37] giving heed to seducing spirits, and doctrines of devils—I Tim. 4:1
- . . . godliness is profitable unto all things [i.e. Christians of Jesus' generation], having promise of the life that now is, and of that which is to come [Greek: της μελλουσης, the one **ABOUT** to come].—I Tim. 4:8
- Fight the good fight of faith, lay hold on eternal life . . . I give **THEE** [i.e. Timothy] charge in the sight of God . . . and *before* Christ Jesus . . . That **THOU** [Timothy] keep *this* commandment without spot . . . until the appearing of **OUR** Lord Jesus Christ—I Tim. 6:12a, 13-14
- Laying up in store for **THEMSELVES** [the "rich in this world"; mammon—v. 17; cf. Luke 16:9] a good foundation against the time to come [Greek: μελλον, **ABOUT** to come], that **THEY** [the rich; mammon] may lay hold on eternal life.—I Tim. 6:19

II TIMOTHY

- Who hath saved **US**, and called *US* WITH AN **HOLY CALLING**[38] . . . according to . . . grace, which was given **US** in Christ Jesus before

---

[36] Paul and the other apostles testified that they were already, in their own generation, living in the last days (see e.g. Heb. 1:2; 9:26; I John 2:18; I Pet. 1:20).

[37] This passage connects the last days with "the falling away" Paul foretold (see II Thess. 2:3). The New Testament gives ample evidence that the apostasy period was well underway even as Paul wrote to Timothy. This is yet another important thesis of this book. In this book I often address the question: How is it that serious readers of the Bible [New Testament especially] have not seen this connection? See e.g. I Tim. 1:19-20; II Tim. 1:15; 2:17-18; 3:8; 4:10; Heb. 10:25, 39a; II Pet. 2:10, 15, 21-22; I John 2:18-19; III John 9-10; Jude 4; Rev. 2:4, 9, 14-15, 20; 3:1-2, 9, 15-17.

[38] **HOLY CALLING**—i.e. salvation unto eternal life and an inheritance in the kingdom of Heaven. This "**HOLY CALLING**" salvation is commensurate with the "high calling" [Phil. 3:14] and the "heavenly calling" [Heb. 3:1] salvation. The **HOLY CALLING** salvation rank was given *only* to the 140,000 church elect and later granted to the additional 4,000 Tribulation-Elect Israelites [cf. "rest of the dead"—Rev. 20:5; also called "Mammon"—Luke 16:9; the "eleventh hour" hires—Matt. 20:6, 9; the "receivers"—Matt. 10:40-41; and the "sheep"—Matt. 25:33a]. These together comprised the 144,000 Israelites or the totality of Christ's Elect brethren during His generation. Salvation to Israel by the deeds of the Law

the world began, But is **NOW** [39] made manifest by the appearing of our Saviour Jesus Christ [i.e. Jesus appeared as the "Christ," or the "Messiah," at His baptism in AD 26], who hath abolished death, and hath brought life and immortality to light through the gospel—II Tim. 1:9-10

• . . . Instructing those that oppose **THEMSELVES**;[40] if God peradventure will give **THEM** repentance[41] to the acknowledging of the truth; and *that* **THEY** may **recover THEMSELVES**[42] out of the snare of the devil.—II Tim. 2:25-26

• This know also, that in the last days[43] perilous times shall come.[44] II Tim. 3:1

---

preceded it (cf. I John 17a; Gal. 3:23-25). Salvation by the deeds of the Law never offered Israel eternal life or an inheritance in the kingdom of God, but only a long life in Canaan, good crops, a peaceful earthly life, and protection from enemies. Moreover, the **HOLY CALLING** ceased after (a) the fulfillment of the Danielic "abomination of desolation" (Matt. 24:15), and (b) the Great Commission, which Paul indicated was fulfilled as early as AD 60-61 [see Col. 1:5-6, 23].

[39] i.e. Christ's adult-time generation (i.e. AD 26-69)

[40] Those "that oppose themselves"—i.e. These had to be born-again church members ca. AD 65-69 with conflicting fears: **(1)** the fear that the Roman magistrates in Asia [i.e. the Ten Horns] would martyr them for their faith in Christ—Rev. 2:10; cf. Matt. 10:28; and **(2)** the fear that God who, for their apostasy, **would blot out their names from the Book of Life**, resulting in their being cast into the Lake of Fire—Rev. 3:5; 20:12, 15.

[41] Apostate Christians did not know that God would cut them off from Christ if they did not repent before a deadline date known [at the time] only to God. This deadline date turned out to be around January 15, AD 69 when the Danielic "abomination of desolation" was set up in the seven churches of Asia. Scripture pertaining to this deadline date are: II Thess. 2:11; Heb. 2:1-4; 3:7-11; 6:1-6; 12:16-17; Rev. 2:21; 22:10-11.

[42] "**recover** themselves"—i.e. successfully return to their public profession of faith in Christ before the deadline date, and thus "recover" their eternal life and their inheritance in the kingdom of God

[43] This passage tells us that both Paul and Timothy understood that the closing years of Christ's generation constituted the last days. Since Paul wrote II Tim. ca. AD 65, the last days were already ongoing. This was common knowledge at the time, as seen in the following passages (Rom. 13:11-12; I Cor. 7:31b; 10:11; 11:26; 15:51; Eph. 1:21 (read in Greek); Phil. 4:5; I Thess. 1:10; Heb. 1:2; 10:37; James 5:7-9; I Pet. 1:20; 4:7, 17; II Pet. 3:12; I John 2:18; Rev. 1:1, 3; 22:7, 12, 20).

[44] "Perilous times"—In the Roman Empire perilous time began, as far as Christians were concerned (and Christians are the central and continual subject of the New Testament) in AD 64 due to the burning of Rome. Nero accused the Christians

- • . . . men shall be lovers of their own selves, covetous, boasters, proud, blasphemers, disobedient to parents, unthankful, unholy, incontinent, fierce, despisers of those that are good, Traitors, heady, highminded, lovers of pleasures more than lovers of God;[45]—II Tim. 3:2-4
- • Having a form of godliness[46]—II Tim. 3:5a
- • . . . but denying the power thereof:[47]—II Tim. 3:5b
- • . . . from such turn away.[48]

---

of doing it and immediately began killing them in Rome. But surviving Christians fled Rome and went into Asia. In the Book of Revelation we have strong indication that Nero had a long arm that reached into Asia to continue his persecution of Christians there (cf. Rev. 2:10; 6:8-11; 11:7-8; 12:11; 13:7, 15; 17:14a). I don't know of any power other than the Roman Empire that could have caused the massive massacring of Christians in Asia from about January 15, AD 69 through midsummer of AD 72 (Rome had thousands of accomplices in Asia that helped in the killing of Christians—i.e. "the beast having seven heads and ten horns"—cf. Rev. 13:1ff).

[45] This passage is about **the apostasy in the church** during the "last days" [i.e. of Jesus' generation], _it is not about the unsaved world_. It wouldn't make any sense if it were about people outside the church because they were always of this description . . . nothing new there! But for Christians it WAS new—i.e. a sudden, unexpected dive into the "depths" of the devil [Rev. 2:24]. The Church started out holy, and remained holy and faithful unto God until the last days when Nero blamed the Christians for burning Rome. Then, fearing reprisal and persecution many church members in Asia purposely began publicly vilifying the name of Christ by practicing the debauched manners described in this passage. Their hope was that the Romans would see them as pagans and exempt them from persecution. The following passage supports this interpretation: "They [i.e. Christian apostates] went out from us [started acting like sinners] . . . that they might be made manifest that they were not all of us [enduring Christians]" (I John 2:19; cf. Matt. 24:9).

[46] "Form"—from the Greek μορφωσιν [morphosin]: "form" or a shape [i.e. of a male human body]. Paul is saying that the apostate Christians, having been born again, were still in the shape of man [i.e. God is also in the form of man—Gen. 2:27]. O reader, know that the apostates were all born-again persons with entirely "new" physical bodies in the image of God and man, which shape by itself signifies "godliness" [cf. II Cor. 5:17].

[47] That is, they lost their faith that God would preserve them body, soul, and spirit in the event of their martyrdom (I Thess. 5:23; cf. Matt. 10:28; Luke 21:18). It was largely this loss of faith that caused them to commit apostasy.

[48] All Christians in the face of an imminent Great Tribulation were "troubled" in their spirits (II Thess. 2:1-2). Paul's idea here is that if any Christian trying

TITUS

- . . . **WE** should live soberly, righteously, and godly, in this **PRESENT** [i.e. the first century] world; looking for that blessed hope, and the glorious appearing of the Great God and **OUR** Saviour Jesus Christ; Who gave himself for **US**, that he might redeem **US** from all iniquity, and purify unto himself a peculiar people, zealous of good works.—Tit. 2:12b, 13-14

PHILEMON

- For perhaps he [i.e. the bondservant Onesimus] therefore departed for a season, that thou [Philemon his master] shouldest **receive**[49] him for ever; Not now as a servant, but above a servant, a brother beloved . . . unto thee . . . in the Lord.—Philem. 15-16 (compare Luke 16:9)

The Witness of John:
Quotes from I, II, and III John,
and the Book of Revelation

I JOHN

- ➢ Little children, it **IS** the last time: and as ye have heard that antichrist shall come, even **NOW** are there many antichrists; whereby **WE** know that it **IS** the last time.—I John 2:18

---

hard to remain faithful to Christ continued to mix with these apostates in the church *he ran a great risk of committing apostasy himself.* So "turn away" from them, Paul exhorted.

[49] **"receive"**—These expressions—**"receive** . . . forever" and **"receive** you into everlasting habitations"—have a meaning peculiar and unique to the Christian persons being alluded to in Philemon 15 and Luke 16:9 [i.e. those living in Jesus' generation] because **THEY** were among the scores of thousands soon to be "received" into the kingdom in the Rapture event at Jesus' AD 72 Second Coming (John 14:3; I Thess. 4:17; cf. Matt. 24:31; II Pet. 1:11).

> ➤ **THEY** [i.e. Christians in Christ's generation who fell away from the faith[50]] went out [51] from **US**: for if **THEY** had been of **US**, **THEY** would *no doubt* have continued with **US**; but *THEY went out*, that **THEY** might be made manifest[52] that **THEY** were not all of **US**. —I John 2:19

> ➤ Who is a liar but **HE** that denieth that Jesus is the Christ? He **IS**[53] antichrist—I John 2:22a

> ➤ Let that therefore abide in **YOU**, which **YE** have heard from the beginning.[54] If that which **YE** have heard from the beginning shall remain in **YOU**, **YE** also shall continue in the Son, and in the Father.—I John 2:24

> ➤ These *things* I have written unto you concerning **THEM** that seduce **YOU** [i.e. the "antichrists" of I John 2:18; see above].—I John 2:26

> ➤ And now, little children, abide in him; that, when he shall appear, **WE** may have confidence, and not be ashamed before him at his coming.—I John 2:28

---

50 Christian apostasy is predicted frequently in the New Testament as part of the "last days" scenario: see e.g. Matt. 13:20-21; 24:12; Gal. 5:4; II Thess. 2:3; II Tim. 4:2-4; Heb. 6:6; 10:25, 38; II Pet. 2:1-2.

51 "went out"—see Jude 19: "These are they who **separate themselves** [i.e. from Christian fellowship], sensual, having not the Spirit."

52 "Manifest"—Church apostates wanted desperately to be *manifested*—publicly and widely understood—as no longer being believers in Christ Jesus. Why? Because the Great Tribulation period—i.e. AD 69-72—was about to start and they knew the chances were great that they would be persecuted and martyred for Christ's name's sake (see e.g. Matt. 10:22; 19:29; 24:9; John 15:21; Acts 9:16). Their intention was to publicly deny Christ before the Roman magistrates so as to become exempt from persecution. Little did they know that the Romans would kill them anyway (see Rev. 17:12-16); therefore, their scheme proved futile and fatal. It turned out to be the "delusion" and the "lie" Paul predicted that would bring God's judgment on them (see II Thess. 2:11-12).

53 The apostate Christian "**IS** antichrist"—Note the present tense of this excerpt. It tells us that Paul's "falling away" prophecy [II Thess. 2:3] was underway in the church at the time John wrote this epistle.

54 This imperative sentence shows that in the end it was the responsibility of the believer to remain faithful to Christ: "Let that [i.e. faithfulness to Christ] therefore abide in you." Christians in v. 9 that "went out" of the church [and thereby denied Christ publicly] had ceased obeying this command. It cannot be said, therefore, that they were never Christians in the first place. Peter's description of Christian apostates in II Pet. 2:20-22 applies to them in every sense. Also, the Hebrews author gave an accurate description of them (Heb. 10:26-29).

➤ Beloved, **NOW** are **WE** the sons of God, and it doth not yet appear what **WE** shall be: but **WE** know that, when he shall appear, **WE** shall be like him; for **WE** shall see him as he is.—I John 3:2

➤ Beloved, believe not every spirit, but try the spirits whether they are of God: because many false prophets **ARE** gone out into the world.—I John 4:1

➤ . . . every spirit that confesseth not that Jesus Christ is come in the flesh is not of God: and this is that *spirit* of antichrist, whereof **YE** have heard that it should come; and even **NOW ALREADY** is it in the world.—I John 4:3

➤ Herein is **OUR** love made perfect, that **WE** may have boldness in the day of judgment—I John 4:17

➤ If any man [who was a Christian during Jesus' generation] see **HIS** brother [another Christian] sin a sin *which is* not unto death,[55] **HE** shall ask, and **HE** shall give **HIM** life for **THEM** that sin not unto death. There **IS**[56] a sin unto death: I do not say that **HE** shall pray for it.—I John 5:16

II JOHN

➤ I rejoiced greatly that I found **of**[57] **THY** children walking in truth —II John 4:a

---

[55] "Sin *which is* not unto death"—Examples of sins not unto death would be those repented of before the deadline date of ca. January 15, AD 69. John said that all sins had to be confessed to God, and God would forgive them (I John 1:9). I suspect, however, that John had in mind here primarily the sin of apostasy, also to be repented of before the deadline date. Other inspired writers of the New Testament were also very concerned about apostates/antichrists repenting *before* it was too late. Cf. II Thess. 2:11; Heb. 6:3-6; 12:17; Rev. 22:11a.

[56] The word "is" in this brief passage is important to take note of. It means that the "sin unto death" was possible only for Christians that lived when John wrote this epistle [i.e. during Christ's generation]. The reason it was possible at that time only is because it was only during Christ's generation that God gave His Holy Spirit to believers (John 7:39; Acts 1:4-5; 2:1-4; I Pet. 1:12b). What the "sin unto death" amounted to, therefore, was that blasphemy against the Holy Spirit that Jesus warned against: ". . . the blasphemy *against* the *Holy* Ghost shall not be forgiven unto men [i.e. unto Christians of Jesus' generation]" (Matt. 12:31b).

[57] Only some **"OF** thy children" were walking in the truth. This wording is significant in that it indicates that many others **of** her children must NOT have been continuing in the truth. In other words, John wrote II John during the time

➤ For many deceivers are entered into the world, who confess not that Jesus Christ is come in the flesh. This is a deceiver and an antichrist. Look to yourselves, that **WE** lose not those things which **WE** have wrought—II John 7:8a

III JOHN

➤ For I rejoiced greatly, when the brethren came and testified of the truth that is in **THEE**, even as **THOU** walkest in the truth, I have no greater joy than to hear that my children walk in truth.—III John 3-4

➤ Diotrephes,[58] who loveth to have the preeminence among **THEM**, receiveth **US** not. Wherefore, if I come, I will remember his deeds which **HE** doeth, prating against **US** with malicious words: and not content therewith, neither doth **HE HIMSELF** receive the brethren, and forbiddeth **THEM** that would, and casteth *THEM* out of the church.—III John 9b, 10

REVELATION

➤ The Revelation of Jesus Christ, which God gave unto him, to shew unto his servants things which must **SHORTLY** come to pass; and he sent and signified *it* by his angel unto his servant John—Rev. 1:1

➤ Blessed *is* **HE** that readeth, and **THEY** that hear the words of this prophecy, and keep **those things which are written therein:** for the time is **AT HAND**.—Rev. 1:3

---

of apostasy in the church (cf. Paul's "falling away" II Thess. 2:3). The fact that there were still "some" walking in the truth, therefore, was enough to make John "rejoice greatly"!

58 Diotrephes was clearly one of the many deceivers/antichrists that was encouraging apostasy in the church during the "last days" of Jesus' generation. Note how he had taken control of a local church! This is partly what Daniel meant when he prophesied that the Little Horn [i.e. Antichrist] would seek to "change times and laws" (Dan. 7:25). Jesus also prophesied this apostasy, calling it Daniel's "abomination of desolation" (Matt. 24:15). Finally, it is exactly what Paul meant when he foretold "the son of perdition; Who opposeth and exalteth himself above all that is called God, or that is worshipped; so that he as God sitteth in the temple of God [i.e. in the church of God—cf. I Cor. 3:16], shewing himself that he is God . . . whom the Lord shall consume with the spirit of his mouth, and shall destroy with the brightness of his coming" (II Thess. 2:3c, 4, 8b)!

- ➤ I [John] was in the Spirit on **THE LORD'S DAY**[59]—Rev. 1:10a
- ➤ What thou seest, write in a book [i.e. the Book of Revelation], and send *it* unto the seven churches which are in Asia;[60] unto Ephesus, and unto Smyrna, and unto Pergamos, and unto Thyatira, and unto Sardis, and unto Philadelphia, and unto Laodicea.—Rev. 1:10b, 11
- ➤ Fear not; I [Jesus] am . . . the last[61]—Rev. 1:17b
- ➤ Because thou [members of the church at Philadelphia] hast kept the word of my patience, I also will keep thee from [Greek: through] the hour of temptation,[62] which shall come [Greek: is about to come] upon all the world [i.e. the church world in Asia], to try them [i.e. Christians] that dwell upon the earth [Asia].—Rev. 3:10
- ➤ Behold, I come quickly [Greek: soon; shortly]: hold that [i.e. faith] fast which thou hast, that no man take thy crown[63]—Rev. 3:11
- ➤ And white robes were given unto every one of them; and it was said unto them that they should rest yet for a little season, until their fellow-servants also and their brethren, that should be killed as they *were*, should be fulfilled.[64]—Rev. 6:11

---

59 Cf. "the day of the Lord" (see also: I Cor. 1:8 & 11 Thess. 2:2, NASB). The "day of the Lord" was not *Sunday*, but the "day" of the Great Tribulation and Jesus' Second Coming that would immediately follow (cf. Matt. 24:29-30). Nowhere is this phrase used in the Bible to indicate a day of the week, Sunday or otherwise. John's first-century audience knew his meaning—i.e. that the Spirit of God took John up and showed him all the visions of what was "shortly" to happen in Asia. Other such occasions for John can be seen in Rev. 4:2; 17:3; 21:10; and 22:17.

60 Here we see strong indication [I would venture to say proof] that the Great Tribulation was a horror that would happen in Asia in the first century. It would target the seven churches of Asia, both those committing apostasy and those remaining faithful to Christ.

61 Jesus' words "Fear not" indicate that the churches were about to enter the fearful end-time event called "the Lord's day" (v. 10; cf. II Thess. 2:2), or the Great Tribulation (see Rev. 7:14; cf. Matt. 24:21). Also, His words "I am . . . the last" indicate that the church had come to its last days on earth.

62 "The hour of temptation"—i.e. the Great Tribulation. Jesus promised that if Christians would "Watch . . . and pray always" God would deliver them safely through or out of the Great Tribulation. Such, evidently, was the case of the Philadelphian Christians (see Luke 21:36).

63 Cf. ". . . a crown of righteousness, which the Lord, the righteous judge, shall give me at that day: and not to me only, but unto all them also that love his appearing" (II Tim. 4:8).

64 This passage teaches that there were to be two *episodes* of Christian martyrdom in Asia during the Great Tribulation (the 1st Episode in January of AD 69 and

> And she [i.e. the "woman clothed with the sun"[65]—see Rev. 12:1] brought forth a man child, who was [Greek: was about] to rule all nations with a rod of iron: and her child was **CAUGHT UP**[66] unto God, and *to* his throne.—Rev. 12:5

> Here is wisdom. Let him that hath understanding count the number of the beast: for it is the number of a man; and his number *is* six hundred threescore *and* six.[67]—Rev. 13:18

> . . . and no man could learn that song but the hundred *and* forty *and* four thousand, which were redeemed from the earth . . . *being* the firstfruits[68] unto God and to the Lamb.—Rev. 14:3

---

the 2nd Episode in midsummer of AD 72). Here Revelation speaks of the 1st Episode because it took place at the start of the Great Tribulation *(the four horsemen speak of the beginning of the Great Tribulation: see Rev. 6:1-8)*. We know the 2nd Episode happened in midsummer of AD 72 because the Two Witnesses were martyred just at the time of the last trumpet, the time of Jesus' Second Coming and the Rapture (see Rev. 11:12).

[65] This "woman" was with child (Rev. 21:2), the child being the thousands of martyrs of the 1st Episode and the woman [their "mother"] being the child's Christian-brethren survivors who escaped into the Asian wilderness (Rev. 12:6). The "serpent/dragon" [i.e. Satan] tried to kill the "woman" too but God miraculously saved her (Rev. 12:13-16) until the end of the Great Tribulation [i.e. midsummer of AD 72]. Then Satan killed the martyrs of the 2nd Episode, called "the remnant of the woman's seed" (Rev. 12:17). This "remnant" is also called the "Two Witnesses" in Rev. 12:3.

[66] "caught up to God"—i.e. into Heaven. The child [i.e. the 1st Episode martyrs] remained "under the altar" [i.e. Paradise, Rev. 6:9] until the Rapture, on which occasion they came "with" Jesus to Asia (cf. I Thess. 4:14), then "caught up" into Heaven to God.

[67] This passage gives strong support to the doctrine that Revelation was fulfilled toward the end of Christ's generation; that is, during the reigns of Nero, Galba, Otho, Vitellius, and Vespasian (ca. AD 54-72). Those were the years when the practice of the Hebrew gematria [called isopsephia by the Greeks]—i.e. the assigning of numerical values to letters of the alphabet—reached its zenith in the distiches of Leonidas of Alexandria, a poet contemporary also with Seneca and the apostle Paul. See *Clarke's Commentary*, vol. VI, p. 1025. See Appendix A: "Regarding '666,'" p. 237.

[68] The "firstfruits" were Christians of the First Century only; that is, of the time of Christ's adult-time generation: i.e. AD 29-69. In short, the firstfruits were Christ plus the 144,000 elect brethren who endured to the end—Matt. 24:13, 24. Cf. Rom. 8:23; 16:5; I Cor. 15:20, 23; 16:15; James 1:18; Rev. 7:3-8 and 14:4. Here we are told that they numbered only 144,000 and **no more!** These also constituted the Bride of Christ as seen in Rev. 21:2. Here's the point: We

➤ And I saw another sign in heaven, great and marvelous, seven angels having **the seven last plagues**[69]; for in them is filled up the wrath of God . . . And I heard a great voice out of the temple [about] the wrath of God upon the earth.—Rev. 15:1; 16:1

➤ Behold, I come quickly; blessed *is* he that keepeth the sayings of the prophecy of this book . . . And, Behold, I come quickly; and my reward *is* with me, to give every man according as his work shall be . . . He which testifieth these things saith, Surely I come quickly. Amen. Even so, come, Lord Jesus.—Rev. 22:7, 12, 20

➤ I Jesus have sent mine angel to testify unto you these things in the churches.[70] I am the root and the offspring of David, *and* the bright and morning star.—Rev. 22:16

The Witness of
the Hebrews Author

❖ God, who at sundry times and in diverse manners spake in time past unto the fathers by the prophets, Hath IN THESE LAST DAYS spoken unto **US** by *his* Son, whom he hath appointed heir of all things, by whom also he made the worlds [Greek: *ages*]—Heb. 1:1-2

❖ Are not they [i.e. the "holy angels'—cf. Luke 9:26; Heb. 1:7; Rev. 14:10] all ministering spirits, sent forth to minister for **THEM** [i.e.

"Christians" who have existed on earth since Christ have no Biblical warrant for including ourselves as Firstfruits of Christ additional to the 144,000 "firstfruits" mentioned in Rev. 14:4. A mere 144,000 Elect also supports the thesis of this book that the church age was not to continue on earth past Christ's adult-time generation. Forty years, one should think, was sufficient time for God to call and choose a mere 144,000 faithful believers in Christ.

[69] According to Rev. 1:1-3 and 22:7, 12, & 20 "the seven last plagues" were fulfilled in the first century, or AD 72. This means they took place 1,940 years ago—from the publication of this edition [2012 – 72 = 1,940]!

[70] I.e. the "seven churches of Asia"—Rev. 1:4, 11. This passage confirms that everything prophesied in Revelation was to happen "shortly" [i.e. after John wrote Revelation]. It stands to reason, therefore, that since Jesus returned in AD 72 to rapture the living NT saints, that also the antichrists died in that same year by order of the Ten Horns [see Rev. 17:12-13, 16]. Moreover, the seven churches of Asia suddenly ceased existing at that time.

Jesus' elect "brethren"—cf. Heb. 2:10-12] who shall be [**Greek:** who are **ABOUT** to be] heirs of salvation?[71]—Heb. 1:14

❖ For unto the angels hath he not put in subjection the world [Greek: the inhabited earth: ***Paradise***] to come [Greek: **ABOUT** to come[72]], whereof we speak.—Heb. 2:5

❖ And have tasted the good word of God, and the powers of the world [Greek: age] to come [Greek: **ABOUT** to come]—Heb. 6:5

❖ But Christ being come an high priest of good things to come[73] [Greek: **ABOUT** to come], by a greater and more perfect tabernacle, not made with hands, that is to say, not of this building;[74] —Heb. 9:11

❖ For the law having a shadow of good things to come [Greek: **ABOUT** to come], *and* not the very image of the things, can never with those sacrifices which they offered year by year continually make the comers thereunto perfect [i.e. immortal].—Heb. 10:1

---

71   The author is speaking here of the **highest** salvation rank, belonging only to the elect brethren of Christ during His generation. In Hebrews this salvation rank is called "so great salvation" (Heb. 2:3) and "heavenly calling" salvation (Heb. 3:1). Elsewhere in the New Testament it is called "high calling" salvation (Phil. 3:14), and "holy calling" salvation (II Tim. 1:9). Note that when the Hebrews author penned his treatise [AD 63], Jesus was ***ABOUT*** to come again (He came just nine years later in AD 72) and saved His elect brethren—i.e. raptured them up into Heaven (cf. I Thess. 4:17) having instantly "changed" them to immortal and incorruptible bodies (I Cor. 15:50-53). See also Heb. 10:37!

72   Premillennialists cannot, according to their eschatology, rightly deal with the expression here, "the world [**ABOUT**] to come." Their teaching that that world has not YET come, these nearly two thousand years later, is a patent denial of scriptural truth plainly stated [in Heb. 2:5]. They wind up ridiculously teaching that the word "about" means thousands of years later. Their error stems from their poor faith, or frequently believing only what they see (cf. John 4:48; 9:39-41; Heb. 11:1-3; II Cor. 4:18; 5:7). Thus, they also disbelieve Christ's teaching that the church would be gone from earth before His own generation passed away. See Matt. 24:30-31, 34, and I Thess. 4:16-17.

73   These "good things" would include anything and everything pertaining to "heavenly calling" salvation, such as glorified bodies, eternal life, inheritance in the kingdom of God, and rulership in Paradise.

74   I.e. the collective born-again bodies of the church membership during Jesus' generation, which Paul called "the temple of God" (I Cor. 3:16). The Christians of that time looked for a "greater" and "more perfect" body to be given them at Jesus' coming, one that would be **immortal, incorruptible,** and **eternal** (I Cor. 15:51-53).

❖ Not forsaking the assembling of **OURSELVES** together, as the manner of **SOME** *is*, but exhorting **ONE ANOTHER**: and so much the more, as **YE** see the day approaching.—Heb. 10:25

❖ For if **WE** sin wilfully[75] after that **WE** have received the knowledge of the truth, there remaineth no more sacrifice for sins, But a certain fearful looking for of judgment and fiery indignation, which shall devour [Greek: which is **ABOUT** to devour] the adversaries. —Heb. 10:26-27

❖ For yet a little while [Greek: a **VERY** little while] and he that shall come will come, and will **NOT TARRY**.—Heb. 10:37

❖ By faith Abraham, when he was called to go out into a place which he should after receive for an inheritance, obeyed; **and he went out, not knowing whither he went**.[76]—Heb. 11:8

❖ By faith Isaac blessed Jacob and Esau concerning things to come [Greek: **ABOUT** to come[77]].—Heb. 11:20

---

[75] The author is referring to Christian apostasy here [cf. II Thess. 2:3], which was a sin that could be committed **_only_** during Christ's generation. It was committed out of fear as a willful, calculated act in order to avoid persecution and possible martyrdom at the hands of the Romans.

[76] People often get upset or disturbed when I so boldly tell them that Jesus has already come again. Though I point out many Bible passages that prove this, they can hardly accept it. They have been conditioned to believe that salvation is unthinkable without the Second Coming of Jesus accompanying and confirming it. But where is their faith? Abraham had no such expectations of a Second Coming, nor did he have any knowledge of Jesus Christ. All he knew was obedience to the Word of Jehovah; therefore God imputed righteousness to him (Gen. 15:6). Today we Christians are also expected to believe and do whatever God's word teaches, and it definitely teaches that the 2nd Coming of Jesus occurred in AD 72. We cannot please God if we cannot find a way to adjust to this truth or to any other truth taught in the Bible ["without faith *it is* impossible to please *him*"—Heb. 11:6]. Note, also, what our passage says about Abraham: "he went out, **not knowing** whither he went"! Dear Christian reader, you may not yet know where you are going, either, in your Christian journey; but if in the meantime you will simply believe God's Word you **will** know in due time, as Abraham did. Just believe God; have faith in His Word. This is good and profitable counsel for today's Christians.

[77] Isaac told Jacob and Esau what was going to happen to them at some distant time in the prophetic future (see Gen. 27:27-29, 39-40), and **this** passage—Heb. 11:20—told the first readers of Hebrews in AD 63 [and us, in AD 2012] that Isaac's prophecies were only THEN—in the "last days" (see Heb. 1:2)—"**ABOUT**" TO COME TO PASS. And, incidentally, in Paradise Jehovah

❖ For here [i.e. on earth] **WE** have no continuing city [Jerusalem—cf. Gal. 4:25], but **WE** seek one[78] to come [Greek: **ABOUT** to come].—Heb. 13:14

The Witness of James

NOTE: The author of the Book of James was the half-brother of Jesus [or cousin-german] called "James *son* of Alphaeus" (Matt. 10:3). Considering that he wrote so emphatically that Jesus' Second Coming drew "nigh" and that He "stood before the door" [James 5:8-9], he was likely a part of the fulfillment of Jesus' promise to His disciples that, "There be **SOME** standing here, which shall not taste of death, till they see the Son of man coming in his kingdom" (Matt. 16:28).

o James, a servant of God and of the Lord Jesus Christ, to the TWELVE TRIBES[79] which ARE scattered abroad, greeting.—James 1:1

o Be patient therefore, brethren, UNTO THE COMING OF THE LORD.—James 5:7a

o Be YE also patient; stablish YOUR hearts: FOR THE COMING OF THE LORD DRAWETH NIGH.—James 5:8

o . . . behold, the judge [i.e. Jesus Christ] STANDETH BEFORE THE DOOR.—James 5:9b

---

was on the verge of finishing off the massive armies of Edom and Gog and Magog on "the mountains of Israel" (Ezek. 38: 8, 21; 39:2, 4, 17; cf. Psalm 83:6)! These still unlearned warrior peoples had been **in Paradise** since the Universal Resurrection on Nisan 14, AD 29 [see John 5:28-29], but had resisted God's command for them to repent (see Acts 17:30). When they rebelliously attacked the tribes of Israel who then were living peacefully in "unwalled villages" God miraculously destroyed them. See Ezek. 37-38.

78 i.e. a Jerusalem **"ABOUT"** to come [i.e. in AD 72]: see Gal. 4:26; Rev. 3:12; 21:2

79 The "twelve tribes" to whom James addressed his epistle cannot refer to any body of persons except the church of Christ in Jesus' generation. By his reference to the "twelve tribes" James meant the scattered church membership (including the Jewish Christian refugees recently fled from Judea—cf. Luke 21:20-21). That the church was made up _only_ of descendants from **all twelve tribes of Israel** is well attested to in the pages of the New Testament (see e.g. Matt. 10:6; 15:24; 19:28; Acts 26:7; Rom. 9:4-5; Gal. 3:16, 29; 6:16; Rev. 7:4-8).

The Witness of Peter

I PETER

⇒ Peter, an apostle of Jesus Christ, to the **strangers**[80] scattered throughout Pontus, Galatia, Cappadocia, Asia, and Bithynia—I Pet. 1:1;

⇒ **WHO** are kept by the power of God through faith unto salvation READY[81] TO BE REVEALED IN THE LAST TIME—I Pet. 1:5;

⇒ That the trial of **YOUR** faith [i.e. the "trial" would be the imminent Great tribulation] . . . might be found unto . . . THE APPEARING OF JESUS CHRIST[82]—I Pet. 1:7;

⇒ Receiving the END of **YOUR** faith, *even* the salvation of **YOUR** souls—I Pet. 1:9;

⇒ Of which salvation [i.e. "high calling" salvation] the prophets [*Old Testament* prophets, such as Isaiah, Jeremiah, Ezekiel, Daniel, etc.] have inquired and searched diligently, who prophesied of the grace *that should come* unto **YOU**[83]—I Pet. 1:10;

⇒ Searching what . . . ***time*** the Spirit . . . did signify . . . Unto whom [i.e. unto those same Old Testament prophets] it was revealed, that not unto themselves, but unto **US** they did minister the things, which are **NOW** [i.e. in the days of the New Testament apostles] reported unto **YOU** by them [i.e. Jesus' apostles] that have preached the gospel unto **YOU** with the Holy Ghost sent down from heaven[84]—I Pet. 1:11-12;

---

[80] The "strangers" in this passage were Christians. Peter called them "strangers" because, having fled from Jerusalem according to the commandment of Jesus (see Matt. 24:16 & Luke 21:21), they soon found themselves scattered in these Roman provinces of Asia Minor.

[81] The strangers were "READY" for Jesus' Second Coming at the time they received Peter's epistle, and the reason is because they were living in the "LAST TIME" and they ***knew*** it! (See I Pet. 1:18-20).

[82] This passage shows that the 3½-year Great Tribulation period was imminent when Peter wrote this epistle, and that it would end with the *immediate* Second Coming of Jesus! Cf. Matt. 24:29-30.

[83] This passage clearly says that the "salvation" foretold by the Old Testament prophets was to have its fulfillment ONLY and SOLELY in the Christians that lived **in Christ's generation.**

[84] "With the Holy Ghost sent down from heaven"—This phrase is vital to the understanding of this passage. The only time the Holy Spirit came down from heaven was during Christ's generation. It came down first to Jesus when He was

⇒ Wherefore . . . hope to THE END[85] for the grace that is to be brought unto **YOU** at the revelation [i.e. Second Coming] of Jesus Christ.—I Pet. 1:13;

⇒ . . . redeemed with . . . the precious blood of Christ . . . Who verily was . . . manifest in **THESE LAST TIMES** for **YOU**—I Pet. 1:18, 19, 20;

⇒ And this is the word which by the gospel **IS** preached unto **YOU**. —I Pet. 1:25;

⇒ . . . **YE** *are* a chosen generation[86] . . . a peculiar people; that **YE** should shew forth the praises of him who hath called **YOU** out of darkness into his marvelous light.—I Pet. 2:9;

⇒ Which in time past *were* not a people of God [see Hos. 1:9]: which had not obtained mercy [see Hos. 1:6], but **NOW** [cf. II Cor. 6:2] have obtained mercy . . . For **YE** were as sheep going astray; but are **NOW** [i.e. in Jesus' generation] returned unto the Shepherd and Bishop of **YOUR** souls [i.e. through the gospel, not through the Law].—I Pet. 2:10, 25;[87]

⇒ Christ . . . being put to death in the flesh, but quickened[88] by the Spirit: By which also he went and preached unto the spirits in prison;[89] Which

---

baptized [see Matt. 3:16], and second upon the church, starting on Pentecost [see Acts 2:1-2]. There is no indication anywhere in Scripture that it would come down again for any future person or generation. Thus, we see Jesus promising to be "with" His disciples "unto the end of the age":—". . . lo, I *[through the agency of the Holy Spirit]* am with **YOU** alway, *even* unto the end of the world [Greek: age; generation]. Amen."—Matt. 28:20b

[85] "THE END"—i.e. the end of Jesus' generation and of the church age. This passage says, in effect, that Peter's **first-century addressees** [not us 21st century readers] would still be alive on this earth at the Second Coming of Jesus Christ [i.e. in AD 72]!

[86] "a chosen generation"—O reader, if you will receive it this first-century generation to whom Peter addressed his epistle is the exact same generation Jesus said would not "pass away" until all end-time prophecies had been fulfilled (see Luke 21:22, 32).

[87] This passage is remarkable for revealing that Peter's two epistles were written not just to Jewish Christians, but also to the "Gentile" Christians of whom Paul wrote: "Hath God cast away his people? God forbid. For I also am an Israelite, of the seed of Abraham"; and, ". . . be not entangled **AGAIN** with the yoke of bondage [i.e. the Law]"—Gal. 5:1.

[88] "Quickened"—i.e. made alive again in a Christophany, or a temporary incarnation. Matthew called it a "resurrection" in Matt. 27:53.

[89] "Spirits in prison"—These were the departed spirits of the wicked antediluvians who were being kept or guarded by their personal angels. Their collective angels

sometime were disobedient, when once the longsuffering of God waited in the days of Noah while the ark was a-preparing ["Whereby the world that then was, being overflowed with water, perished;"—II Pet. 3:6].—I Pet. 3:18, 19, 20;[90]

⇒ For for this cause was the gospel preached also to them that are dead [i.e. that _were_ dead] that they might be judged according to men in the flesh[91]—I Pet. 4:6. See FN#s 200 & 208 in Chapter Five of this book; compare also "**ARE** in the graves"—John 5:28 and FN#207 in Chapter 5;

⇒ The END OF ALL THINGS IS AT HAND [i.e. at hand in AD 64 when Peter wrote his second epistle[92]]: be **YE** therefore sober, and watch . . ."—I Pet. 4:7

⇒ For the time _is come_ that judgment [i.e. the Great Tribulation] must begin at the HOUSE OF GOD [i.e. the Elect]: and if _it_ first _begin_ at **US**, what shall the end _be_ of them [i.e. antichrists; Christian apostates] that obey not the gospel of God?—I Pet. 4:17

⇒ . . . I [Peter] . . . am . . . an elder, and a witness of the sufferings of Christ, and also a partaker of the glory [i.e. the kingdom of God] that shall be [Greek: **IS ABOUT TO BE**[93]] revealed.—I Pet. 5:1

---

were, in effect, their "prison." Jesus called these spirits "captives," and said that one of His missions was to set them free (see Luke 4:18-19). Peter and the Hebrews author described their liberation as being reincarnated for the purpose of being judged, with that judgment culminating in righteous living through the Holy Spirit: I Pet. 4:6, RSV; cf. Heb. 9:27; 12:11.

[90] These passages say that after dying on the cross [on Nisan 14, AD 29] Christ went into Paradise (cf. Luke 23:43) and preached to the antediluvians that had perished in the Flood of Noah.

[91] "In the flesh"—i.e. reincarnated. God cannot judge men except they are in fleshly bodies. He had to reincarnate "all that are in the graves" before He could judge them. Scripture says that it is after men die that God judges them (see Heb. 9:27). This was true even of the wicked dead of olden times whose resurrection was delayed for millennia. As soon as God reincarnated them He judged them (cf. Matt. 12:41-42).

[92] "In AD 64"—The end of the church generation came in AD 69 and Jesus' Second Coming occurred in AD 72. THAT'S what I can accept as "at hand"!

[93] Over and over again we see this Greek word μελλω (see _Strong's Concordance_, Greek Dictionary, _#3195) overlooked and ignored_ in the KJV and other English versions of the Bible _as if it has no significance whatsoever._ I can only conclude that the translators did not want to deal with it. Perhaps they loathed translating it because if they did they would have to teach it and defend it as obviously meaning that Jesus had to have come back during His generation!

⇒ . . . when the chief Shepherd shall appear, **YE** shall receive a crown of glory[94] that fadeth not away.—I Pet. 5:4

⇒ Humble **YOURSELVES** therefore under the mighty hand of God, that he may exalt[95] **YOU** in due time [i.e. "shortly," cf. Rev. 1:1] —I Pet. 5:6

⇒ . . . the God of all grace, who hath called **US** unto his eternal **glory** by Christ Jesus, after that **YE** have suffered a while [i.e. in the imminent Great Tribulation—cf. I Pet. 4:12], make **YOU perfect** [i.e. glorify you], stablish, strengthen, settle **YOU**.—I Pet. 5:10[96]

II PETER

⇒ According to his divine power hath given unto **US** all things that *pertain* unto [eternal] life and godliness, through the knowledge of him that hath called **US** to glory and virtue: Whereby are given unto **US** exceeding great and precious promises: that by these **YE** might be partakers of the divine nature [i.e. be perfected; glorified; made immortal and incorruptible—cf. I Cor. 15:51-53], having escaped the corruption that is in the world through lust. II Pet. 1:3-4

⇒ Wherefore . . . brethren, give diligence to make **YOUR** calling and election sure: for if **YE** do these things, **YE** shall never fall: For so an entrance shall be ministered unto **YOU** abundantly into the everlasting kingdom of **OUR** Lord and Saviour Jesus Christ. —II Pet. 1:10-11

⇒ **WE** have also a more sure word of prophecy [i.e. the Old Testament **and** the New Testament Scriptures]; whereunto **YOU** do well that **YE** take heed, as unto a light that shineth in a dark place, UNTIL

---

94   "Crown of glory"—These are regal words. Scripture teaches that only Israelites called and elected during the time of Jesus' generation—i.e. before it ended (Luke 21:22, 32)—stood to see Christ's return and have eternal life and an inheritance in the kingdom of God.

95   "Exalt"—This is another regal term that can pertain only to 1st century Christians. See Matt. 23:11-12; Acts 2:33-34; Psalm 89:19-20; 97:9.

96   See in this passage two more terms—"glory" and "perfect"—that in Jesus' generation pertained only to (1) the elect during Jesus' generation and (2) the Old Testament saints. The latter also had to wait until Jesus' Second Coming in AD 72 to be perfected (see Heb. 11:40).

THE DAY DAWN, AND THE DAY STAR ARISE IN **YOUR** HEARTS[97]—II Pet. 1:19

⇒ But there were false prophets also among the people [of ancient Israel], even as there [soon] shall be false teachers ["antichrists"—I John 2:18] among **YOU**, who privily shall bring in damnable heresies, even denying the Lord that bought **THEM**, and bring upon **THEMSELVES** swift[98] destruction.—II Pet. 2:1

⇒ And through covetousness shall **THEY** [the antichrists; Christian apostates] with feigned words make merchandise of **YOU** [i.e. you enduring Christians—cf. Matt. 24:13]: whose judgment **NOW** of a long time lingereth not, and their damnation slumbereth not.—II Pet. 2:3

⇒ . . . the heavens and the earth,[99] which are **NOW** [i.e. "now" meaning Peter's generation, not ours today!], by the same word are kept in store, reserved unto fire against the day of judgment and perdition of ungodly men . . . the day of the Lord will come as a thief in the night; in the which the heavens shall pass away with a great noise,[100] and the elements[101] shall melt with fervent heat,

---

[97] Here is yet another passage that says, in effect, that Peter and the **SPECIFIC** Christians he **ORIGINALLY** addressed knew that they would still be "alive *and* remain" on earth on the day of Christ's Second Coming, to be "caught up . . . in the clouds, to meet the Lord in the air" (I Thess. 4:17).

[98] "swift"—i.e. **soon, shortly, near at hand, impending.** That is, the antichrist's destruction was to take place **shortly** *after Peter's epistles arrived in the hands of his* **FIRST** *reading audience.* In this passage "Swift"—Greek: [ταχινην]—is from the same root as "shortly" [ταχει] in Rev. 1:1 and "quickly" [ταχυ] in Rev. 22:7, 12, and 20.

[99] In Peter's 3rd-chapter apocalyptic language he speaks of the "heavens" and "earth" as being "reserved unto fire against the day of judgment and perdition [i.e. destruction] of ungodly men." These ungodly men were the "antichrists" (I John 2:18); the "false teachers among you" (II Pet. 2:10. Jesus spoke of them as "false Christs" and "false prophets" (Matt. 24:24). Paul spoke of them as "man of sin," and "son of perdition" (II Thess. 2:3). The point is, these varied phrases are all synonymous—i.e. equivalents with Peter's "heavens" and "earth."

[100] "noise"—i.e. the collective screams and loud cries of thousands of antichrists burning **"alive"** at the stake simultaneously [cf. Rev. 19:20], and augmented by the roar of a vast "lake" of fire with flames leaping heavenward and consuming flesh and large amounts of wood (wooden stakes and various other flammable "fuels"). I should also add the tremendous noise produced by the mayhem and ruckus of the spectators.

[101] The human body is composed of 28 "elements" and "trace elements" (trace elements italicized): oxygen, carbon, hydrogen, nitrogen, calcium, phosphorus,

the earth also and the works[102] that are therein shall be burned up. —II Pet. 3:7, 10

⇒ *Seeing* then *that* all these things [i.e. these antichrists: the elements of their bodies] shall be dissolved, what manner *of persons* ought **YE** to be in *all* holy conversation and godliness, LOOKING FOR **AND HASTING UNTO** THE COMING OF THE DAY OF GOD, wherein the heavens [i.e. antichrists; Christian apostates] being on fire shall be dissolved, and the elements [in the antichrists' bodies] shall melt with fervent heat?[103] Nevertheless **WE**, according to his promise, LOOK FOR NEW HEAVENS AND A NEW EARTH, WHEREIN DWELLETH RIGHTEOUSNESS. Wherefore, beloved, seeing that **YE** look for such things, be diligent that **YE** may be found of him in peace, without spot, and blameless.—II Pet. 3:11-14

⇒ **YE** therefore, beloved, seeing **YE** know *these things* before, beware lest **YE** also, being led away with the error of the wicked, fall from **YOUR** own stedfastness. But grow in grace, and *in* the knowledge of our Lord and Saviour Jesus Christ. To him *be* glory both now and for ever. Amen.—II Pet. 3:17-18

The Witness of Jude

Note: Jude [also: Judas] is another of Jesus' half-brothers [or cousins-german]. He is named in Matt. 13:55. This would make him a full brother of James, the author of the New Testament Book of James. It appears that both these men most likely were still alive here on earth when Jesus came back again in AD 72. The reason I say this is because

---

potassium, sulfur, sodium, magnesium, copper, zinc, selenium, molybdenum, fluorine, chlorine, iodine, Manganese, cobalt, iron, *lithium, strontium, aluminum, silicon, lead, vanadium, arsenic,* & *bromine* (http://chemistry.about. com/cs/howthingswork/f/blbodyelements.htm). It was these elements that God burned up in the persons of the antichrists at the hands of the Ten Horns: "And the ten horns which thou sawest upon the beast, these shall hate the whore, and shall make her desolate and naked, and shall eat her flesh, and **burn her with fire**" (Rev. 17:16).

102 By "works" is probably meant the formation of the beast having seven heads—i.e. the Antichrist system—and the persecutions and martyrdoms this system committed against Jesus' elect brethren.

103 In this passage we have a perfect description of what happens to human flesh when burned at the stake: it is "dissolved," and the elements comprising it "melt with fervent heat"! *Important:* see also Zech. 14:12.

they both complained of Christian teachers who taught that grace permitted Christians to commit apostasy and still be in the "faith."

- Beloved, when I gave all diligence to write unto **YOU** of the **common** salvation,[104] it was needful for me to write unto **YOU** and exhort **YOU** that **YE** should earnestly contend for **the faith which was once delivered unto the saints.**[105]—Jude 3
- For there are certain men [i.e. false teachers/prophets—Matt. 24:4, 11-12; cf. II Pet. 2:1] crept in unawares, who were before of old ordained to this condemnation,[106] ungodly men, turning the grace of our God into lasciviousness,[107] and denying the only Lord God, and our Lord Jesus Christ.—Jude 4

---

[104] **"The common salvation"** here is most likely not the same salvation that Paul called "high calling," or the Hebrews author called "so great salvation," and "heavenly calling" (see Phil. 3:14; Heb. 2:3; 3:1). Rather, it may be the *universal salvation* Paul occasionally stressed (e.g. I Tim. 4:10; Rom. 5:18). Thus, Jude seemingly changed his topic to High Calling salvation, seeing all around the signs Jesus foretold would take place (Luke 21:31-32).

[105] Jude's words, **"faith which was once delivered unto the saints"** *do* refer to "high calling" salvation, also called "so great salvation," and "heavenly calling" salvation (see Heb. 3:1). Paul once referred to it as a *special* salvation: "**specially** [belonging to] those that believe" (I Tim. 4:10). Thus, Jude knew that THIS salvation was way more crucial to his readers, all of whom God had called through apostolic evangelism during Jesus' still-ongoing generation (cf. Matt. 24:34). We Christians today cannot claim that Jude's epistle pertains directly to us, therefore, since only universal salvation relates to us. Ours is that "common" salvation Jude at first was about to teach his followers. Jude, like Paul, knew that it was important for Christians to know about this lesser salvation rank. However, at the last moment Jude switched to the High-Calling rank as his topic, which tells us that conditions had suddenly worsened for Christians! Thus, they needed exhortation on *their special rank* of salvation (which could be forfeited through apostasy), not on salvation common to all men (which could not be forfeited for any reason).

[106] "This condemnation"—Note the word "this." It always means something close at hand, either in location or in time. The whole tenor and content of Jude's epistle signifies that God's wrath was "at hand," and about to fall upon the antichrists in the church. Remember, we are talking the first century here. Jude's dire warnings do not directly apply to us Christians living almost two thousand years later.

[107] ". . . grace . . . into lasciviousness [Greek: licentiousness; immorality]." The antichrists had believed a "lie" that allegedly *allowed* them to have "pleasure in unrighteousness" and still be saved by grace [see II Thess. 2:11-12]. In

- These be they that separate themselves, [108] sensual, having not the Spirit.—Jude 9
- Now unto him that is able to keep **YOU** from falling, and to present **YOU** faultless before the presence of his glory[109]

Decision Time

Dear reader, you have now seen from this book and your own Bible that there are three powerful and unassailable *witnesses* to the truth that Jesus came again before His own generation ended.

Here is what each witness said concerning this truth:

(1) DANIEL: His 2nd coming would take place in AD 72;
(2) JESUS CHRIST: His 2nd coming would take place before His own generation passed away;
(3) THE COLLECTIVE APOSTLES: His 2nd coming was imminent in their own generation.

(Your Response) O reader, this may be the only time in your life that someone will ever give you a "three-witness formula" that biblically proves Jesus' *first century* Second Coming. Here's a quick review showing this formula:

. . . at the mouth of two witnesses, or at the mouth of three witnesses, shall the matter be established.—Deut. 19:15b

---

Revelation we see this heresy being played out in the seven churches of Asia [see e.g. Rev. 2:2, 9; 3:9]. Apostates in those churches were advocating idolatry and fornication [e.g. Rev. 2:14, 20], and teaching that God would excuse these sins because, after all, if Jesus died for all sin, God would forgive all sin, etc., etc., etc. This was the same false doctrine that sinners of olden times used to excuse their sin; for example, Israelites in the wilderness (v. 5); angels that sinned (v. 6); and the Sodomites (v. 7).

[108] See e.g. Acts 20:30; Heb. 10:25; II Pet. 2:15a; and I John 2:19.

[109] "Present **YOU** before the presence of his glory"—Here Jude says, in effect, that Jesus' Second Coming would happen during the life time of the *original* addressees of his epistle! This turned out to be true. Jude wrote this epistle ca. AD 65, and Jesus came again in AD 72, just seven years later!

But if he will not hear *thee*, *then* take with thee one or two more, that in the mouth of two or three witnesses every word may be established.—Matt. 18:16

It is also written in your law, that the testimony of two men is true.—John 8:17

This is the third *time* I am coming to you. In the mouth of two or three witnesses shall every word be established.—II Cor. 13:1

Against an elder receive not an accusation, but before two or three witnesses.—I Tim. 5:19

He that despised Moses' law died without mercy under two or three witnesses.—Heb. 10:28

You see, dear reader, that even **LIFE AND DEATH MATTERS** were frequently judged and decided on the basis of just two or three witnesses. I am now asking **YOU** to make a decision on the important issue of whether or not Jesus has already come again, and to do it on the basis of the three witnesses I have given you in this book.

If you make a "yes" decision—i.e. Jesus has already come again—you have God's total, 100% approval. You may stand firm on your decision based upon the truth of the Bible even if the Christian world ostracizes you for it.

(You May Delay Your Decision.)

Note that there is much more to be read and studied in the remainder of this book. If you feel unsure about this question, please read on. These pages contain powerful, Biblical arguments and interpretations to give you confidence in making a "yes" decision on this question; ***Biblical*** arguments, I repeat, not mine. I simply give you in them a great deal more evidence from YOUR Bible. Yes, I *explain* and *interpret* other doctrines for you also, but I *encourage you to see if you can determine a better or a different interpretation to the Bible passages and arguments I provide for your consideration.*

If you can in all purity and honesty successfully refute my interpretations, you may make a "no" decision and feel correct and good about it and yourself.

Finally, no matter if you decide "no." You can say that you have at least read this book, made an honest effort to understand it, and come to your own decision without previous prejudices or biases. If you do this, that is an admirable thing and you are to be commended. Please use the form below to record your decision.

PERSONAL RECORD

I, having read and studied this book, and having prayed sincerely for God to help me in my understanding, make the following decisions on the explanations and interpretations the author gives in this book about:

1. Daniel's witness:	Correct____	Incorrect____
2. Jesus' witness:	Correct____	Incorrect____
3. Apostles' witness:	Correct____	Incorrect____

⇒ I *did* read this entire book: Yes___ No___
⇒ I believe Jesus' Second Coming took place in AD 72 as explained by the author:
    Yes___ No___

Signed by:_____

Date:_____

Chapter Four

SUPPORTING BIBLICAL DOCTRINES

I add this chapter as a means of helping you, dear reader, to more firmly grasp why I say that Jesus has already come again and that therefore His coming is no longer to be awaited or expected. I have written this chapter in a Q and A form.

The questioner is you, dear reader, but I ask the questions *for* you, questions that I believe you *would* ask if you and I were in private conversation. I deeply respect your questions, and try to answer them as thoroughly and clearly as I can.

Daniel's 70 Weeks Prophecy

QUESTION #1: Doesn't Daniel's prophesied 490 years[110] allow for a time gap of unknown duration—already about two millennia!—between its 483rd and 484th years [i.e. between its 69th and 70th weeks]?

ANSWER: No. First, Daniel spoke of the 70 Weeks [i.e. the 490 years] as flowing straight through [*uninterruptedly*] from beginning to end. There is no man or devil in all creation that has the authority to put a time gap between any of those years. Second, if God meant us to understand a time gap He surely would have made it plain (not throw us a curve). Arguing for the gap is like arguing for a deceptive

---

110   See Dan. 9:24-27.

and tricky God (such as atheists and agnostics are wont to do). If God's word cannot be trusted as written how can anyone build or establish truth upon it?

QUESTION #2: What *were* the beginning and ending years of Daniel's 70 Weeks prophecy?

ANSWER: The first year was **457 BC**, the year Artaxerxes decreed for the Jews to return home and rebuild their city and temple [see Dan. 9:25; cf. Ezra 7:13]. The last year was AD 33, calculated by subtracting **457 BC** from the total 490 years.

Year 483, by the way, is very important. It translates to AD 26 in which, according to Daniel, the Messiah would appear. Jesus Christ, indeed, did appear to the Jews in that very year! If that part of God's word has been proven trustworthy, why not also trust Him that the 490 years flowed *uninterruptedly* from beginning to end? Daniel certainly said nothing about a time gap.

QUESTION #3: If God was going to bless the Jews throughout the entire 490 years, uninterruptedly, in what way did He bless them AFTER year 483; that is, ***during the so-called "70th Week" [last seven years]?***

ANSWER: Year 483, of course, was the date of Jesus' baptism, and the beginning of His ministry to the Jews as their Messiah. The act of His baptism "confirmed" God's intention to go the full 490 years with the Jews, and do it uninterruptedly from year **457 BC** (Dan. 9:27; cf. Matt. 5:17-18). Thus, Daniel's 70th Week commenced immediately after year 483, and the 70th Week of years were the final seven of the total of the 490 "determined" ***Jewish*** years (John 1:11 and 4:22b).

Look again at the actual years comprising the 70th Week—i.e. AD 26-33. Remember, Daniel said that the Messiah would be "cut off" [i.e. crucified] "in the midst of the week."[111] (Jesus died on Nisan 14, AD 29, so marking "the midst" of that Week.) Thus, the first half of the Week was from Jesus' baptism to His crucifixion. The second half was from Jesus' crucifixion to Paul's conversion (at Damascus) in AD 33. The 490 *Jewish* years then ended. Most Jews did not even realize any of this. I say this not to put the Jews of those days down, for remember, their blindness to the gospel of the kingdom of God was

---

[111] See Dan. 9:27.

God's doing. Jesus said that God had purposely blinded the Jews until a later time, when "all Israel"—that same generation of Jews—would be saved (Matt. 13:10-11; Rom. 11:7, 26). Thus, they continued on in blindness until AD 70, when Titus destroyed Jerusalem and the temple and slaughtered about a million of them in Palestine from north to south.

The Seventieth Week

God mightily blessed the Jews in the 70th Week. He sent both John the Baptist and Jesus Christ the only-begotten Son of God to preach the coming wrath of God upon the Jews if they did not repent (cf. Matt. 3:7). This repentance had nothing to do with the kingdom of God, but everything to do with whether or not God would save the Jews' _nation and religious polity_. Had they repented God would have protected them from the Romans, and they would not have been destroyed.

But it is evident throughout the New Testament that they did NOT repent. Nevertheless, for the first half of the 70th Week Jesus ". . . went about doing good [to the Jews], and healing all that were oppressed of the devil; for God was with him" (Acts 10:38). Why did He do that knowing of their sure imminent destruction [i.e. before Jesus' generation would end]?

First, it is because He was obligated to fulfill the prophecy of Daniel 9:27: to continue blessing the Jews during the final seven of their "determined" 490 years. Again, those final seven years constituted Daniel's 70th Week.

Second, and ironically, it was God's way of saving the Jews. Remember, His Son was going to die for _**them**_ "in the midst" of that week. It was their unbelief and ignorance about Him that made them reject Jesus and turn Him over to Pilate for crucifixion. Paul said: "But we speak the wisdom of God in a mystery, _even_ the hidden _wisdom_, which God ordained before the world [Gk. _ages_] unto our [i.e. the Christians'] glory: Which none of the princes of this world [i.e. the Jewish rulers] knew: FOR HAD THEY KNOWN _IT_, THEY WOULD NOT HAVE CRUCIFIED THE LORD OF GLORY" (I Cor. 2:7-8). Had Christ not died for sin the Jews, nor anyone else, could ever have been saved! It is plain, therefore, that the blindness of the Jews was necessary if God was to save "all men" (I Tim. 4:10).

Third, He was **_going_** to save "all Israel" [i.e. the Jews of Jesus' generation]; that is, reincarnate and bring them into Paradise during the years of their destruction by the Romans, which took place in the years AD 66-70.

In short, it was in the 70ᵗʰ Week that God laid the foundation [i.e. "Jesus Christ," I Cor. 3:11] for the Jews' RESTORATION, but He would not actually save them until later in His generation. He would save them *nationally* and *en masse* by supernatural means [resurrection] unseen by the world. The Romans thought that the Jews were cursed by the gods, and cursed even by their own God. However, God was restoring them as fast as the Romans slew them!

Peter told the Jews that Heaven would "receive" Jesus [i.e. keep Him out of their sight] until the time of their restoration: "Whom the heaven must receive until the times of restitution of <u>all things</u> [i.e. of "all Israel"—Rom. 11:26a], and THEN He would "bless" them and "turn away every one [of them] from his iniquities" (Acts 3:21, 26). It would be only then that the Jews would mourn over their rejection of Christ (see Zech. 12:10). It was also then that they laid eyes on Jesus once more, as Jesus told them: "<u>Ye shall not see me henceforth, till ye shall say, Blessed *is* he that cometh in the name of the Lord</u>"—Matt. 23:39. Paul later said this same thing only in slightly different words: "And all Israel [i.e. Palestinian Jewry] shall be saved [i.e. RESTORED[112]]: as it is written, There shall come out of Sion [i.e. out of Jerusalem in Paradise] the Deliverer, and shall turn away ungodliness from Jacob" (Rom. 11:26).

QUESTION #4: Why would God make the Jews wait till the end of Jesus' generation before actually punishing and then restoring them in this manner?

ANSWER: There is a twofold answer.

---

[112] Saved, but not in the High Calling rank. That is, God did not give them an inheritance in the kingdom, nor the eternal life that came with that inheritance (He restored them only to a *millennial* life span). He did not change them from mortal to immortal beings. He DID give them the new birth; that is, He "changed" them from flesh to flesh—i.e. from Adamic to non-Adamic flesh (see Job 14:14; 19:25-27).

First, God's justice and vengeance obliged Him to nationally punish the Jews for rejecting His Son and handing Him over to Pilate for crucifixion. Even though they did it because God had blinded them, yet they were guilty as human beings, whether they knew God's will or not. Even the blind Jews knew that they had ulterior motives for rejecting Christ. For this God held them guilty and deserving of punishment. There is a principle throughout the Bible that we cannot ignore, which is seen in the following passages:

> To me [i.e. to Jehovah] *belongeth* vengeance, and recompence . . . I will render vengeance to mine enemies, and will reward them that hate me . . . I will make mine arrows drunk with blood, and my sword shall devour flesh—Deut. 32:35a, 41b, 42a

> Vengeance *belongeth* to me, I will recompense, saith the Lord. And again, The Lord shall judge (punish) his people.— Heb. 10:30

In short, God is just and punishes the wicked. However, there had to come a worsening of the political climate and relationship between Jerusalem and Rome. Later, in AD 66 war broke out between the Jews and the Romans, and Titus brought in his Roman troops and destroyed the entire Jewish polity. The blood of about a million Jews was shed by the Roman sword from the Galilee in the north to Jerusalem in the south.

But look now at the second reason God waited until the last years of Jesus' generation before punishing and saving the Jews.

The Times of the Gentiles

Paul said that God would not save "Israel"—restore Palestinian Jewry to Garden of Eden conditions—**"until the fullness of the Gentiles be come in"** (Rom. 11:25b). Paul told this to the Christians at Rome because he did not want them to be *ignorant*: "For I would not, brethren, that ye should be **ignorant** of this mystery, lest ye should be wise in your own conceits; that blindness in part is happened to Israel" (v. 25a).

When we talk of "the times of the Gentiles" we are actually talking about the Christian church for the longest period of the time of Jesus' generation [while the church continued on earth]. The picture is this: (1) God had saved most of the Jews He ordained during the 70th Week [AD 29-33]; and (2) then it was time to save the "Gentiles." Saving the "Gentiles" would require a lot more time than just seven years. Why? Three reasons.

First, the disciples would have to "**GO** . . . and teach all nations," a commandment that, in order to fulfill, would involve their traveling thousands of miles back and forth from Antioch in Syria to Asia Minor and Europe. Jesus prophesied that before His Great Commission was fulfilled the church would have lasted "unto the end of the world [Gk. age]"; that is, unto the "last days" of His generation. See Matt. 28:19a, 20b. Sometimes the travel time alone, just to go from point A to point B, would consume much of the apostles' time. For example, Paul's last journey [from Caesarea Maritima in Palestine to Rome, Italy] took him over a year, and that was after he had already spent two years in prison defending himself before kings and magistrates from his arrest in Jerusalem in AD 60 to his departure to Rome in AD 62.

Second, when the apostles' travels brought them into a city they often had to remain, preach, and teach there until all that God had ordained came into the Faith and were established in it. Paul, for example, remained in Ephesus for two years and three months until "all they [i.e. the predestined] which dwelt in Asia heard the word of the Lord Jesus, both Jews and Greeks" (Acts 19:8, 10). See how long that took? And that was just in Ephesus. There were other cities where Paul had to dwell and preach until the predestined could be reached and secured in the Faith. Paul's missionary journeys [as recorded in Acts] took him 22 or 23 years to accomplish (from AD 45 to ca. 67-68).

Third, for every Jew God ordained to believe during their 70th Week there were three Gentiles so ordained that had to be reached. To be specific, the Jewish elect constituted only one-fourth of the final, total church elect. The Jews comprised three tribes (Levi, Benjamin, and Judah), but the Gentiles comprised the remaining nine tribes.[113]

---

[113] It is a mistake to call converts from the nine tribes "Jews." No, they were mostly *acculturated* "Gentiles" descended from Abraham, Isaac, and Jacob.

It is revealed in Revelation that there would finally be 36,000 elect Jews, as compared to 108,000 Gentiles. Most of the Jewish converts after Pentecost came to Christ in Jerusalem and Judea, but the Gentile converts were scattered from Syria all the way to places like Ephesus, Asia, Macedonia and Achaia, Greece, and Rome, Italy. See Rev. 7:4-8.

QUESTION #5: How long did "the times of the Gentiles" last?

ANSWER: About twenty-four years [AD 45-69]! Daniel's 70 Weeks Prophecy [explained above] and several New Testament Scriptures, taken together, indicate this. We have just learned from Daniel that the times of the Jews ended in AD 33, the same year in which their "determined" 490 years were fulfilled. Then God stopped favoring them. It was also the same year that Jesus called Paul to evangelize the "Gentiles."

(The First Year of "the Times of the Gentiles")

However, the "times of the Gentiles" did not begin *in earnest* in AD 33, but about 12 years later [AD 45] when the Holy Spirit called Paul to go out on his first missionary journey [see Acts 13:1ff]. Thus, the "times of the Gentiles" went into high gear when Paul, the apostle to the Gentiles, began **preaching** to the "Gentiles" (most of the first "Gentiles" he converted were likely *proselytes* associated with the Jewish synagogues).

(The Last Year of "the Times of the Gentiles") The "Gentile" times would have had to end *before* the Romans destroyed Jerusalem, because Jesus said:

> Jerusalem shall be trodden down of the Gentiles UNTIL the times of the Gentiles be fulfilled.—Luke 21:24

In other words, when the "Gentile" times ended, the Romans would stop trodding down Jerusalem. This is in accordance with both Daniel and Jewish history. Daniel's "another little horn" [i.e. the Antichrist] would arise in AD 69 and "set up" the Abomination of Desolation in the "temple" [i.e. the *church*—cf. II Thess. 2:4; cf. I Cor. 3:16] and change <u>times</u> and <u>laws</u>" (Dan. 7:25).

Regarding "times," the antichrists would change [i.e. debunk] the apostles' interpretation of Daniel's "times" prophecies [e.g. the AD 69 rise of the Antichrist, and the imminent return of Jesus and the last judgment (see Dan. 7:25-27)]. Regarding "laws," they would conveniently re-explain the gospel so as to allow apostasy as a heaven-approved means of exempting oneself from Roman persecution [i.e. the "lie" predicted by Paul in II Thess. 2:11]. Thus, the "times of the Gentiles," ended in AD 69.

With these events, starting ca. Jan. 15, AD 69, both the true gospel and the true church (see Matt. 16:18) suddenly ceased on earth (cf. Matt. 24:3, 6, 13-16).

The Identity of the "Gentiles"

QUESTION #6: Would you please give a fuller explanation of who the <u>Gentiles</u> in the New Testament were?

ANSWER: Great question. Yes, I will do that for you, but warning: this answer will take up the remainder of this chapter. I will divide the answer, with interpretations of certain key passages from the New Testament, into four parts. I begin by discussing two basic passages from Luke 2 and Acts 15.

PART 1

(Jews and "Gentiles" Joined
Together as in Former Times)

13 And after they held their peace, James answered, saying, Men *and* brethren, hearken unto me:

14 <u>**SIMEON**</u> (not Simon Peter) hath declared how God at the **FIRST** did visit the Gentiles, to take out of them a people [i.e. Christians] for his name.—Acts 15

<u>A Discussion Focusing on Simeon</u>:

The "Simeon" of Acts 15:14 is not Peter because Peter was not the "**FIRST**" New Testament saint or prophet to speak of Gentile conversions. It was the Simeon of Luke 2:25ff that had that honor. Second, Peter's given name Simon is never spelled S-i-m-e-o-n in the Greek New Testament. Let's look first at the two different Greek spellings of Simeon and Simon.

(<u>Simon Vs. Simeon in Greek</u>) Commentators on Acts 15:14, to a man, say that the Greek word **Συμεών** ["Simeon"] refers to Peter because it is the <u>Hebrew</u> spelling for the Greek Simon. Thus, they conclude, it means Peter. This is a very poor reason for their interpretation.

Their reasoning is unsound Biblically because everywhere else in the New Testament the Greek word **Σιμων** ["Simon"] is used to refer to Peter. Altogether in the New Testament the Greek spelling **Σιμων** [Simon] is used 44 times for Peter's given name.

By contrast the word **Συμεών** [Simeon] is used in the New Testament only 5 times:

1) Luke 2:25 (a devout man that blessed Jesus);
2) Luke 2:34 (the same devout man that blessed Jesus);
3) Luke 3:30 (Father of Levi; an ancestor of Jesus);
4) Acts 13:1 (a prophet of Antioch); and
5) Acts 15:14 (*erroneously* said to be Peter, but actually refers to the devout man in #s 1 and 2)

Notice that for each of these five times Luke was the writer (Luke wrote both the Gospel of Luke and Acts of the Apostles). If Luke meant Peter by the spelling S-i-m-e-o-n (in Acts 15:14) it would have been a surprising and unexpected (to say nothing of a *mysterious*) spelling change for him in the Bible. Furthermore, the Holy Spirit who inspired Acts 15:14 would have known better to use the anomaly **Συμεών** to signify Peter—i.e. God's Spirit would avoid any such confusion ("For God is not *the author* of confusion—I Cor. 14:33).

(<u>Was Simeon in Acts 15:14 the First to Speak of Gentile Salvation?</u>) Certainly. Let us now look at what *this same* **SIMEON**—in Luke's Gospel—said on the day that Jesus was circumcised.

(Luke 2:25-34)

25 And, behold, there was a man in Jerusalem, whose name *was* **Simeon**; and the same man *was* just and devout, **WAITING FOR THE CONSOLATION OF ISRAEL:** and the Holy Ghost was upon him.

26 And it was revealed unto him by the Holy Ghost, that he should not see death, before he had seen the Lord's Christ.

27 And he came by the Spirit into the temple: and when the parents brought in the child Jesus, to do for him after the custom of the law,

28 Then took he him up in his arms, and blessed God, and said,

29 Lord, now lettest thou thy servant depart in peace, according to thy word:

30 For mine eyes have seen **THY SALVATION**,

31 Which thou hast prepared before the face of **ALL PEOPLE**;

32 A light to lighten **THE GENTILES**, and the glory of **THY PEOPLE ISRAEL**.

33 And Joseph and his mother marveled at those things which were spoken of him.

34 And **Simeon** blessed them, and said unto Mary his mother, Behold, this *child* is set for **THE FALL AND RISING AGAIN OF MANY IN ISRAEL;** and for a sign which shall be spoken against;

35 (Yea, a sword shall pierce through thy own soul also,) that the thoughts of many hearts may be revealed.—Luke 2:25-34

(The Interpretation)

Note the stressed parts of this passage. Here is my brief interpretation of each:

(Luke 2: 25)

WAITING FOR THE CONSOLATION OF ISRAEL.—Here Israel means both Jews and "Gentiles," with "Gentiles" interpreted as descendants of the northern tribes of Israel. The idea of **CONSOLATION** here means the rejoining of "Judah" and "Israel" as one nation, just as they were in the days from Jacob through Solomon, as per the following passages:

> In those days [i.e. Jesus' generation], and in that time, saith the LORD, the children of Israel shall come, they and the children of Judah together . . . *saying*, Come, and let us join ourselves to the LORD in a perpetual covenant *that* shall not be forgotten.—Jer. 50:4a, 5b

> And I [Jehovah] will make them one nation in the land upon the mountains of Israel; and one king shall be king to them

all: and they shall be no more two nations, neither shall they be divided into two kingdoms any more at all:—Ezek. 37:22

There can be seen two critical doctrinal innovations in these passages: (1) *__now__*, with the advent of the apostolic GOSPEL EVANGELISTIC missions—commanded and commissioned by Jesus Christ [cf. Matt. 28:19-20]—multiple thousands of Israelites [from the theretofore forsaken and scattered NORTHERN tribes] would come into the High Calling of God in Christ Jesus, as per Phil. 3:14; and (2) *__now__*, instead of these northern Israelites [i.e. the "Gentiles" of the New Testament]—because they lived wicked, idolatrous lives in foreign lands—going into *spirit imprisonment*[114] when they died, they would be immediately reincarnated and taken into their tribal borders in Paradise above. This doctrine is seen in the thief's going into Paradise immediately upon *his* death (see Luke 23:43).

(Luke 3: 30)

THY SALVATION—This means the High Calling Salvation Rank [see Phil. 3:14], the components of which were: (a) being born again; (b) coming into everlasting life; (c) becoming an heir of the kingdom of God; and (d) being rewarded with rulership over the cities of Israel in Paradise at Jesus' Second Coming [Luke 19: 17, 19; Phil. 3:14; Heb. 3:1; I Tim. 6:12; and II Tim. 1:9].

(Luke 2: 31)

ALL PEOPLE—This means that "ordained" *__Israelites__*[115] ["Gentiles"] *from all twelve of their tribes*[116] could now enter into everlasting life and the kingdom of God, not just those "called"[117] among the Jews—i.e. descendants of Judah, Benjamin, and Levi.

---

[114] See I Pet. 3:19.
[115] We know that the words "all people" in this instance cannot be interpreted to include true Gentiles from the four corners of the world because the promises and covenants of God pertained ONLY to Israelites—i.e. descendants of the "fathers" Abraham, Isaac, and Jacob (see Rom. 9:4-5).
[116] See Matt. 19:28 and Acts 13:48; 26:7.
[117] See Acts 2:39.

The Church Age [Christ's Adult-time Generation] – AD 29-69

I. TIME LINE FOR THE SEVENTY WEEKS [490 YEARS] THAT JEHOVAH "DETERMINED" FOR THE JEWS,
A.K.A. "TO THE JEWS FIRST" (DAN. 9:24-27; CF. MARK 1:15; JOHN 1:11; 4:22; ACTS 3:26; 13:46a; ROM. 1:16)

(1) 457 BC [483 OF THE 490 YEARS ELAPSE]	(2) AD 26 [the first 3½ years or the 70th week elapse]	(3) AD 29 [3½ more years elapse, ending the 70th week]
Artaxerxes' Decree (Ezra 7:11-26; Dan. 9:25a)	**Messiah appears and "confirms" the 70th week remaining in the 70 Weeks "Covenant"** (Dan. 9:27a; cf. Mark 1:15; John 1:11; 4:22; Acts 13:46a; Rom. 1:16).	**On Passover Day the Messiah is "cut off" or crucified which was "in the midst of the [70th] week"** (Dan. 9:26a, 27b)

(Synchronized with the Second, Third, & Fourth Kingdoms of Dan. 2 and 7):

PERSIAN KINGDOM: GREEK KINGDOM: ROMAN KINGDOM

(Synchronized with the Third Toe/Horn – i.e. Roman Caesar – of Daniel's Fourth Kingdom [Dan. 2:41-42; 7:8, 20, 24]):

Tiberius

II. TIME LINE FOR THE CONVERSION OF "THE LOST SHEEP OF THE HOUSE OF ISRAEL,"
A.K.A. "THE TIMES OF THE GENTILES" (MATT. 10:6; LUKE 21:24; ACTS 9:15; 13:46b; ROM. 11:25)

(4) AD 33	(5) AD 40	(6) AD 62-69	(7) AD 69	(8) AD 69-72	(9) AD 72 [midsummer]
Saul became Paul in Damascus, Syria, and Jesus appointed Him the "Apostle to the Gentiles" (Acts 9:1-20; cf. Gal. 2:8; Rom. 11:13).	**The Uncircumcised Roman Centurion Cornelius was converted by Peter, becoming the first "Gentile" convert** (Acts 10:25-28, 34, 45, 48).	**Great Commission Gradually Became Fulfilled** (cf. Acts 24:5; Rom. 16:26; Col. 1:6, 23)	**The Abomination of Desolation was set up in Asia, ending the church age** (Matt. 24:14-15)	**The Great Tribulation and the "Little Horn" [Antichrist] continue for 3½ years in Asia** (Daniel 7:8, 20, 24-25; Rev. 11:2-3; 12:6, 14)	**The last trumpet: Jesus appears; the still-living elect caught up into Heaven; the elect rewarded; New Jerusalem descends to Paradise; Saints inherit the Kingdom of God** (I Cor. 15:51-52; Matt. 24:30; I Thess. 4:17; Matt. 16:27-28; Rev. 21:2; II Tim. 4:1)

(Synchronized with the Fourth Kingdom of Dan. 2 and 7):

ROMAN KINGDOM

(Synchronized with the Last Eight Toes/Horns – i.e. Roman Caesars – of Daniel's Fourth Kingdom [Dan. 2:41-42; 7:8, 20, 24]):

Tiberius	Caligula	Claudius	Nero	Galba, Otho, & Vitellius	Vespasian

W. H. Hogue, July, 2007

THE PROPHET DANIEL & THE END TIME

Nebuchadnezzar's Dreamed Image

Da 2:28-35

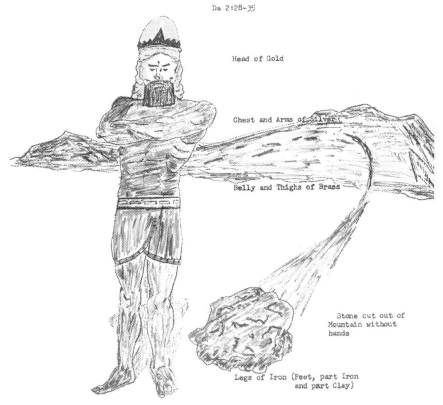

Head of Gold

Chest and Arms of Silver

Belly and Thighs of Brass

Stone cut out of
Mountain without
hands

Legs of Iron (Feet, part Iron
and part Clay)

Artist: Jeffery Dean Hogue

119

"A Woman Clothed with the Sun..."

And there appeared a great wonder in heaven; a woman clothed with the sun, and the moon under her feet, and upon her head a crown of twelve stars. And being with child cried, travailing in birth, and pained to be delivered. – Rev. 12:1-2

"And a Great Red Dragon"

And there appeared another wonder in heaven; and behold a great red dragon, having seven heads and ten horns... – Rev. 12:3

And his tail drew the third part of the stars of heaven, and did cast them to the earth. – Rev. 12:4a

The Dragon Waited to Attack.

And the dragon stood before the woman which was ready to be delivered, for to devour her child as soon as it was born. – Rev. 12:4b

"The Woman Fled into the Wilderness"

And there was war in heaven: Michael and his angels fought against the dragon; and the dragon fought and his angels, And prevailed not; neither was their place found any more in heaven. And the great dragon was cast out, that old serpent, called the Devil, and Satan, Which deceiveth the whole world: he was cast out into the earth, and his angels were cast out with him...And when the dragon saw that he was cast unto the earth, he persecuted the woman which brought forth the man *child*. And to the woman were given two wings of a great eagle, that she might fly into the wilderness, into her place, where she is nourished for a time, and times, and half a time, from the face of the serpent. — Rev. 12:7-9, 13-14

The Dragon Devours
The Woman's Child (i.e.
Devours the Martyrs
Of the First Martyrdom
Episode)!

And she brought forth A
man child, who was to
Rule all nations with a
Rod of iron. – Rev. 12:5a

The Woman's Child Was Caught up to Heaven.

And her child was caught up unto God,
and to his throne. – Rev. 12:5b

God the Father on His Throne,
Surrounded by the four beasts
And a myriad of holy angels
See: Rev. 4:2, 6 and 5:11

Artist: Janice (Hogue) Asher

Satan is "the god of this world."

II Cor. 4:4

Michael Asher

Therefore, this is the sad state of planet earth today.

The Holy Spirit, Jehovah and Jesus are the God of Paradise.

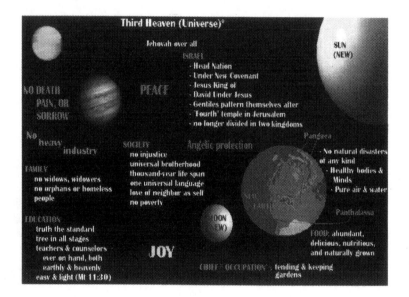

Artist: Michael Asher

Therefore, this is what Paradise is like today.

II Pet. 3:13

(Verse 32a)

THE GENTILES—i.e. descendants of the tribes of Israel that had once comprised the northern kingdom of Israel. In New Testament days they were called "Gentiles" because they had adopted and adapted to Gentile ways; that is, they were *acculturated* "Gentiles."

(Verse 32b

THY PEOPLE ISRAEL—i.e. Jews only. God was also about to elect in High Calling salvation 36,000 Jews: 12,000 from Judah, 12,000 from Levi, and 12,000 from Benjamin. When Simeon foretold this only the Jews were still being reckoned as God's people ["**THY**"] people." Hosea has God saying of all descendants from the northern tribes: "Loruhamah: for I will no more have mercy upon the house of Israel"; and "Loammi: for ye *are* not my people" (Hos. 1:6, 9). The Israelites of the northern tribes became God's people once more, however [through faith in Christ Jesus], when "the times of the Gentiles" commenced in AD 45.

Verse 34)

THE FALL AND RISING AGAIN OF MANY IN ISRAEL—With these words Simeon foretold the Restoration [the lesser ranking salvation] of Palestinian Jewry. First they would **FALL** [Gk. crash]; that is, Titus and Roman troops would kill them during the First Jewish Revolt [AD 66-70]. Then, they would **RISE AGAIN**; that is, God would immediately resurrect them [i.e. reincarnate them] and take them into Paradise [also in AD 66-70].

(Summation)

Let's look at the whole picture. Either on or somewhat before the day of Jesus' circumcision God had revealed to the prophet Simeon two salvation ranks to be had because of Jesus Christ's death for all sin: (1) the High Calling rank, and (2) the lesser Restoration rank.

Regarding High Calling salvation God was about to elect [during Jesus' generation] 12,000 people from each of the twelve tribes of Israel [see Rev. 7:4-8]. All told, God elected 144,000 Israelites to have everlasting life and inheritance in the kingdom. God chose them for the purpose of installing them on His throne in Heaven—i.e. to rule over multiple millions of Israelites from their twelve tribes living in the flesh in Paradise in AD 72. This doctrine is largely seen in Jesus' words: "because thou [i.e. any elect Israelite] hast been faithful in a very little, have thou authority over ten cities [i.e. in the Land of Israel in Paradise]," and "Be thou also [ruler] over five cities [i.e. in the Land of Israel in Paradise]—Luke 19:17, 19.

As for Restoration salvation God was about to save [i.e. reincarnate the slain of] "all Israel"—i.e. the Jewry of Jesus' generation that fell [Gk. crashed] in the First Jewish Revolt at the hands of Titus and his Roman troops [AD 66-70]—and bring them up into Paradise. And this happened to them, according to Rom. 11:25-26, after "the times of the Gentiles" in AD 70 (the "times of the Gentiles" ended in AD 69 and Jerusalem and the Temple were destroyed in AD 70, precisely in that order, just as Paul prophesied in Rom. 11:25-26!).

By this interpretation, then, we can see that it was truly Simeon, not **_Simon_** Peter, that "**FIRST**" foretold God's salvation [both in High Calling and Restoration ranks] of the "Gentiles." So let us see, by reading now what Paul wrote, whether or not Simeon's consolation was fulfilled during Jesus' generation and by Jesus' death for mankind.

After the church was on earth for many years we find that, indeed, the Jews and "Gentiles" were joined together in the church as one fold, reunited as one "nation" (cf. Matt. 21:43 and Eph. 2:11-22). Paul reported that in Christ Jesus God had already joined together as "one" the "called" Israelite descendants of the northern kingdom [i.e. "Gentiles"] with the "called" Israelite descendants of the southern kingdom [i.e. Jews]. Here are Paul's words:

> Wherefore remember, that ye [the "called" of the northern kingdom] *being* in time past **GENTILES** in the flesh [meaning: uncircumcised in the flesh], who are called **UNCIRCUMCISION** by that which is called the **CIRCUMCISION** in the flesh made by hands [meaning the Jews]; That at that time ye ["Gentiles"] were without Christ, being **ALIENS** from the **COMMONWEALTH OF ISRAEL** (the northern kingdom), and **STRANGERS** from the covenants of promise, having no hope, and without God in the world: But now in Christ Jesus ye who sometimes were **FAR**

OFF [the scattered "Gentiles"] are made **NIGH** [to the Father] by the blood of Christ [i.e. no longer through the Law]. For he [Christ Jesus] is our peace, who hath made both one, and hath broken down the middle wall of partition *between us*; Having abolished in his flesh the enmity, *even* the law of commandments *contained* in ordinances; for to make in himself of twain one new man, *so* making peace; And that he might reconcile both unto God in one body by the cross, having slain the enmity thereby; And came and preached peace to you which were afar off, and to them that were nigh. For through him we both have access by one Spirit unto the Father. Now therefore ye ["Gentiles"] are no more strangers and foreigners, but fellow-citizens with **THE SAINTS**, and of the household of God—Eph. 2:11-19

Note that in Pauline parlance the called from the northern kingdom were referred to as:

- "broken off—" & "grafted branches,"[118]
- "Gentiles,"
- "uncircumcision,"
- "strangers,"
- "aliens,"
- "commonwealth of Israel"
- those "far off"
- "foreigners," and
- "fellow-citizens" [i.e. after their conversion]

. . . and the "called" from the southern kingdom were referred to as:

- "the Circumcision,"
- "natural branches,"[119]
- those "nigh," and
- "the saints"

---

[118] See Rom. 11:17, 19, and 24.
[119] See Rom. 11:21.

Thus, we see clearly that the prophecy of Simeon was fulfilled in the church of Jesus' generation. Christ brought together, through Christ's shed blood, the "Gentiles" and the Jews, RESTORING them as one nation.

PART 2
(The Tabernacle of David
Is Restored as in Former Times.)

14 Simeon hath declared how God at the first did visit **THE GENTILES, TO TAKE OUT OF THEM A PEOPLE FOR HIS NAME.**

15 And to this agree the words of the prophets; as it is written,

16 After this I will return, and will build again **THE TABERNACLE OF DAVID**, which is fallen down; and I will build again the ruins thereof, and I will set it up:

17 That **THE RESIDUE OF MEN** might seek after the Lord, and all the **GENTILES, UPON WHOM MY NAME IS CALLED**, saith the Lord, who doeth all these things.—Acts 15

God's "people" were, are, and always will be the people of the twelve tribes of Israel, and none other. Paul, remember, pointed out that it was to Israel that God's promises pertained—i.e. people descended from the "fathers" Abraham, Isaac, and Jacob (see Rom. 9:4-5; cf. Acts 13:31-33). Therefore, the only correct interpretation of the word "Gentiles" (vv. 14 & 17) is *descendants of the tribes of Israel from the "fallen down" northern kingdom.*

The phrase "take out of them" is a reference to the doctrines of predestination and election. That is, God pre-selected or predestinated a prescribed number of them to become church-member *candidates* [i.e. "persons of interest"] for High Calling salvation. Thus, these *Israelites* [during Christ's generation], upon hearing the gospel, believed on Jesus. They were baptized with the Holy Spirit, and became bona fide church members. Luke put it this way: "as many as were ORDAINED [i.e. pre-selected/predestined] to eternal life believed" (Acts 13:48). Paul referred to such "Gentile" believers as "predestined . . . unto the adoption of children by Jesus Christ . . . according to the good pleasure of his will" (Eph. 1:5).

Note that as these "Gentile" converts came into the church, God was thereby "building again" **THE TABERNACLE OF DAVID** (v. 16). This is none other than saying that "Gentile" converts [from the northern tribes] were added to Jewish converts to raise up David's tabernacle. Thus, David's "tabernacle" cannot here signify a temple built by hands, such as Solomon's Temple, made up of quarry stones, gold, silver, and cedar wood from Lebanon. This time the "building stones" were *human* beings—i.e. predestined Jews and "Gentiles" of Jesus' generation—called by Peter the "lively stones" making up "a spiritual house [i.e. temple] . . . to offer up spiritual sacrifices, acceptable to God by Jesus Christ" the "chief corner stone, elect, precious" (I Pet. 2:5-6).

In this vein Paul declared that the ***CHURCH*** was David's Tabernacle: "What?" Paul asked the believers at Corinth, "know ye not that your body is the temple of the Holy Ghost *which is* in you, which ye have of God, and ye are not your own?" (I Cor. 6:19; cf. I Cor. 3:16-17).

David's tabernacle, in order to be built again, therefore, required "Gentile" participants [descendants of the tribes of the northern kingdom of Israel], not just Jewish converts of the southern kingdom of Israel. This makes sense in that when David ruled over Israel he ruled over the northern AND southern tribes of Israel—i.e. ***all twelve tribes***.

These truths are foundational to understanding what the Jerusalem Conference was all about. They are essential to defining just what David's "tabernacle" means. All Christian commentators today who think, believe, and teach that the word "Gentiles" mentioned throughout Acts 15[120] means TRUE Gentiles [i.e. peoples not descended from the twelve tribes of Israel] need to ***rethink*** their whole understanding of the first-century Church and the ***Israelite*** nature of its membership. If they start out with this doctrine—i.e. it was **DAVID'S** Tabernacle—they cannot but be led aright in figuring out who the "Gentiles" were. The word **DAVID** governs and puts immovable limits on defining the "Gentiles" that came into church membership during Jesus' generation. The only definition that will do is that they were descendants of Israel from the ancient but fallen northern kingdom of

---

[120]   See vv. 3, 7, 12, 14, 17, 19, and 23.

Israel. David's Tabernacle was not comprised of Jews only, but also of "Gentiles"; that is, of *ALL TWELVE TRIBES OF ISRAEL*.

To this the prophets testify. Jeremiah, for example, stated that God would raise [i.e. glorify] David as king over a future *reunited* Israel—"Israel" with "Judah":

> For, lo, the days come, saith the LORD, that I will bring again the captivity of my people Israel and Judah, saith the lord; and I will cause them to return to the land that I gave to their **fathers**,[121] and they shall possess it . . . [and] I will raise David their king up unto them.—Jer. 30:3, 9

Likewise Ezekiel, after foretelling the reunification of the two houses of Israel, said:

> And I will make them one nation in the land upon the mountains of Israel: and one king [i.e. David] shall be king to them all: and they shall be no more two nations, neither shall they be divided into two kingdoms any more at all.—Ezek. 37:22

No wonder, then, that James quoted a certain phrase from Amos 9:12 in his concluding remarks at the Jerusalem Conference: **"GENTILES UPON WHOM MY NAME IS CALLED."** This phrase defines the "Gentiles" as Isra**el**ites from the northern kingdom. Part of the name Isra**el** contains God's name—i.e. EL [the Hebrew word [singular] standing for Jehovah].

PART 3
(Hosea's "NOT MY PEOPLE" and Paul's "Gentiles"
Are the Same Identical People as those I Have Frequently Called
"Acculturated Gentiles" in this Book.)

24 Even us, whom he hath called, not of the Jews only, but also of the **GENTILES**?

---

[121] See **Appendix B**: "The Land that God Gave to the Fathers," pp. 246-263.

25 As he saith also in Osee [i.e. Hosea], I will call **THEM** [i.e. the "<u>GENTILES</u>" of v. 24] my people, which were **NOT MY PEOPLE**; and her beloved, which was not beloved.

26 And it shall come to pass, *that* **IN THE PLACE where it was said unto them** [the "Gentiles" or descendants of Israel's northern tribes]**, YE** *ARE* **NOT MY PEOPLE; there shall they be called the children of the living God.**—Rom. 9

Note that Paul's topic is "Gentiles" (v. 24). Note also in v. 25 that these "Gentiles" have a specific identity found only in the Old Testament prophet "Osee" [i.e. Hosea]. Let us read from Hosea:

> Yet the number of **THE CHILDREN OF ISRAEL** shall be as the sand of the sea, which cannot be measured nor numbered; and it shall come to pass, *that* **IN THE PLACE** where it was said unto **THEM** [i.e. "the children of Israel"]**, ye** *are* **NOT MY PEOPLE,** *there* **it shall be said unto THEM** [i.e. "the children of Israel" that]**,** Ye *are* the sons of the living God**.**—Hos. 1:10

By comparing what Paul said [Rom. 9:25-26] with what Hosea said in the above passage we can see that we have a definite connection of context. *Both Paul and Hosea are talking about the same people*. Rom. 9:26 is almost a direct quote from part of Hos. 1:10! Moreover, Paul calls them "Gentiles" (v. 24) which is critical to understand.

If we do a little "stare-step" reasoning we should see, therefore, that Hosea's "my people" and "not my people" are the same as Paul's "Gentiles." O reader, if this confuses you, please go back and read the two passages now, and again after you have proceeded through the four steps below. Please be a *careful* reader of Scripture.

STEP ONE: In Hos. 1:10 [above] it should be clear in the mind of the *careful* reader that Hosea's words "children of Israel" and "them" ("them" is used twice in the passage) refer to *one and the same* "people."

STEP TWO: Paul's "Gentiles" and Hosea's "my people," "not my people," and "the children of Israel" *all have the same exact identity*.

STEP THREE: Paul's "Gentiles" and "my people," and Hosea's "not my people" and "the children of Israel" <u>all have the same exact meaning and identity.</u>

STEP FOUR: All the terms just discussed in these steps have the same identical meaning as the "acculturated Gentiles" that I mention frequently in this book—i.e. descendants of the northern tribes of Israel. Over the centuries of living among Gentile peoples [from 721 BC to AD 33] they themselves eventually adapted to and adopted Gentile ways of eating and worshiping.

("They Shall Be Called the Children of the Living God"!) Hos. 1:10 is the "PLACE" [i.e. an Old Testament **_verse_** of Scripture] where we **_FIRST_** read[122] the following combination of thoughts: "the children of Israel" as "NOT MY PEOPLE" and then immediately also as, "the sons of the living God"—i.e. all in the same verse or "place."

Now let's go back to Paul's words in Rom. 9:24-26 [quoted above]. What was Paul saying, considering his statement's contextual relationship with Hos. 1:10 [also quoted above]? If my analyses above are correct [see Steps One through Four, above] Paul's doctrine is that (1) the "Gentiles" he speaks of are none other than the multiple thousands of **_predestined_**[123] Israelites—i.e. predestined unto **_High Calling Salvation_**—Phil. 3:14; Heb. 1:3. (2) He is also saying that those predestined had not been God's people[124] for many past centuries:—i.e. from the Assyrian destruction of Samaria [i.e. capital of the northern kingdom] in 721 BC to the beginning year of the "times of the Gentiles" [AD 45]. (3) Finally, Paul is saying that Jehovah redeemed them both [Jew and "Gentile"] through the death of Christ, and that now through Jesus ONLY—through faith in His name—will He save either of them. This carries the important implication that God was not saving Jews or "Gentiles"—i.e. in the High-Calling

---

[122]   Until Paul wrote Rom. 9:26, Hos. 1:10 was the *only* "PLACE" in Scripture where these words and the thought they contain could be found [in such explicit terms]. However, the Holy Spirit in inspiring Hosea to write this passage in ancient times knew that in the future [i.e. during the messianic generation] there would live a saint that would quote it. The Holy Spirit, therefore, could safely and correctly inspire Paul to refer to Hos. 1:10 as the *only* "PLACE" these words could be found.

[123]   Rom. 8:29; Eph. 1:4-5, 11

[124]   i.e. That is because Jehovah had "put her away, and given her [i.e. the northern kingdom of Israel] a bill of divorce" during those centuries (Jer. 3:8a)!

salvation rank—by the works of the Law. These three conclusions Paul articulated perfectly in the following passage:

> Even when we [i.e. Jews and "Gentiles"] were dead in sins, [God] hath quickened us together with Christ, (by grace ye are saved;) And hath raised *us* up together, and made *us* sit together in heavenly *places* in Christ Jesus; That in the ages to come he might shew the exceeding riches of his grace in *his* kindness toward us through Christ Jesus. For by grace are ye saved through faith; and that not of yourselves: *it is* the gift of God: Not of works [works of the Law: e.g. circumcision], lest any man should boast. For we are his workmanship, created in Christ Jesus unto good works, which God hath before ordained that we should walk in them. Wherefore remember, that ye *being* in time past Gentiles in the flesh (the "Gentile" Christians were uncircumcised), who are called Uncircumcision by that which is called the Circumcision in the flesh made by hands (the Jews); That at that time ye [i.e. "Gentile" Christians] were without Christ, being aliens from the commonwealth of Israel [i.e. the Northern Kingdom], and strangers from the covenants of promise, having no hope, and without God in the world. But now in Christ Jesus ye [i.e. "Gentile" Christians] who sometimes [i.e. for seven centuries] were far off [i.e. divorced from Jehovah[125]] are made nigh by the blood of Christ. For he is our peace, who hath made both [i.e. Jews and "Gentiles"] one, and hath broken down the middle wall of partition *between us;* Having abolished in his flesh the enmity, *even* the law of commandments *contained* in ordinances; for to make in himself of twain one new man, *so* making peace; And that he might reconcile both unto God in one body by the cross, having slain the enmity thereby: And came and preached peace to you which were afar off [i.e. "Gentile" Christians], and to them that were nigh [i.e. Jewish Christians]. For through him we both [i.e. First-century Jewish and "Gentile" Christians] have access by one Spirit unto the Father. Now therefore ye [i.e. "Gentile" Christians] are no more strangers and foreigners, but fellow-citizens with the saints [i.e. Jewish Christians], and of the household of God; And are built upon the foundation of the apostles and prophets, Jesus Christ himself being the chief corner

---

125   Is. 50:1

stone; In whom all the building fitly framed together groweth unto an holy temple in the Lord: In whom ye also [i.e. "Gentile" Christians] are builded together [i.e. with Jewish Christians] for an habitation of God through the Spirit.—Eph 2:5-22

PART 4

(The <u>Israelite</u> Identity of the "Gentiles"
In Galatians Is Now More
Easily Explained.)

The first point I would like to make here is that Paul addressed **"*Gentile*"** Christians in his epistle to the Galatians; that is, he addressed it to Christian **<u>Israelites</u>** whom God had predestined to High Calling Salvation. In short, he addressed predestinated descendants from the tribes of Israel whose fathers once comprised the Northern Kingdom of Israel. In the tersest words Paul was **not** addressing Jewish Christians in Galatians. However, this is not to say that the Jews [especially those called Judaizers] could not have greatly benefited from studying this epistle in depth.

Why? Because Paul wrote some scary things about the Judaizers—i.e. that they were "accursed" if they did not cease trying to persuade the "Gentile" Christians in Galatia to be circumcised:

> . . . there be some [i.e. legalistic Jews; Judaizers] that trouble you ["Gentile" converts], and would pervert the gospel of Christ. But though we, or an angel from heaven, preach any other gospel unto you than that which we have preached unto you, let him be accursed. As we said before, so say I now again, If any *man* preach any other gospel unto you than that ye have received, let him be accursed.—Gal. 1:7-9

> Behold, I Paul say unto you, that if ye be circumcised, Christ shall profit you nothing. For I testify again to every man that is circumcised, that he is a debtor to do the whole law. Christ is become of no effect unto you, whosoever of you are justified by the law; ye are fallen from grace.—Gal. 5:2-4

Exactly what was it that caused the Judaizers to fall into their "accursed" error—i.e. to insist that "Gentile" Christians be circumcised to be saved? I can see two reasons.

(A) God called **_THEM_** first—i.e. Jews circumcised from infancy—to faith, from which fact they drew the erroneous conclusion that God would save ONLY circumcised believers. They thought God intended their conversion to point the way for *anyone else* to be converted. These Judaizers were first heard of in Acts. They stressed to Paul's "Gentile" converts that, "Except ye be circumcised after the manner of Moses, ye cannot be saved" (Acts 15:1). So zealous were they of this doctrine that they [apparently] dogged Paul's heels and preached "another gospel" [i.e. one that would "frustrate"—Gk. *disannul*—grace and faith (Gal. 2:21)].

(B) They preached circumcision to them because they knew that they were descendants of Abraham. Why did this matter? It mattered because God told Abraham that "He that is born in thy house, and he that is bought with thy money, must needs be circumcised: and my covenant shall be in your flesh for an **EVERLASTING** covenant" (Gen. 17:13). It was this word "everlasting" they found in the ancient Circumcision Covenant with Abraham that was compelling them to insist on "Gentile" circumcision. Paul's "Gentile" converts were Abraham's descendants, so they had to be circumcised. It was that simple. They honestly believed that there was no way around circumcision.

(Why Were the Judaizers Wrong?) There were four critical concepts the Judaizers were not taking into account. First, they were not taking into account that God imputed "righteousness" to Abraham *while he was as yet uncircumcised himself* (see Rom.4:9b, 10).

Second, they did not understand that circumcision was merely a "seal" of Abraham's "righteousness" that God had *already* imputed to him (see Rom. 4:11; cf. Gen. 15:6).

Third, they did not understand that circumcision was a required practice and condition for Israel's possession of the ***earthly*** **Canaan**" (Gen. 17:8-10). That is a far cry from saying that circumcision was also a condition for inheritance of ***the kingdom of Heaven***.

Fourth, they were obtuse about salvation by grace, that it freed both Jew and "Gentile" from the *bondage* to the Law, as Paul wrote elsewhere:

> *There is* therefore now no condemnation to them which are in Christ Jesus, who walk not after the flesh [i.e. the Law], but after the Spirit. For the law of the Spirit of life in Christ Jesus hath made me free from the law of sin and death.—Rom. 8:1-2

> . . . Israel [i.e. the Jews], which followed after the law of righteousness, hath not attained to the law of rightiousness. Wherefore? Because *they sought it* not by faith, but . . . by the works of the law. For they stumbled at that stumblingstone [i.e. Jesus Christ].—Rom. 9:31-32

> Do we then make void the law through faith? God forbid: yea, we establish the law.—Rom. 3:31

Paul established that the deeds of the Law were for worldly salvation, not spiritual salvation [i.e. High Calling Salvation]. For the Jews, worldly salvation meant:

- possession of Canaan (Gen. 17:8-10);
- success in business ventures and farm yields (Deut. 28:3-5);
- healthy humans and livestock (Deut. 28:4a, 11);
- plentiful food and peaceful family relationships (Deut. 28:5-6);
- military and political power over enemy nations (Deut. 28:1, 10, 13); and
- a long physical life in Canaan (Ex. 20:12 and Deut. 5:16).

The High Calling Salvation [i.e. salvation by grace], on the other hand, had *heavenly* rewards, chiefly eternal life and an inheritance in the kingdom of God, and demanded totally different requirements on the part of God and the believer.

(The Things God Had to Do)

He had to (a) "foreknow" and "predestine" the person—Rom. 8:29; (b) spiritually "draw" the person—John 6:44; (c) ordain and send an evangelist to "go" to the person—Matt. 28:19-20 & Rom. 10:15; (d) "call" the person by the "hearing of faith" when the gospel was preached—1 Cor. 1:21 & Gal. 3:2, 5; (e) give the person the new birth—John 3:3, 5-8; II Cor. 5:17; James 1:18; Rev. 21:5; (f) baptize the person with the Holy Spirit; (g) give him a church to attend where he and other brethren could have mutual comfort, exhortation, and teaching; (h) catch him up [i.e. rapture him] into Paradise at Jesus' Second Coming—Matt. 24:40-41; I Thess. 4:17; Rev. 21:1-2; and finally (i) "change" the person's temporal physical body to an immortal and incorruptible body at Jesus' Second Coming—I Cor. 15:51-55.

(The Things the Christian Had to Do)

Next, there were certain things the called person had to do: (a) hear and believe the gospel when preached—Rom. 10:14; (b) call on God to save him—Rom. 10:14a; (c) repent from sins—Acts 2:38; James 1:21; I John 1:9; (d) be water baptized—Acts 2:38; (e) confess Christ publicly with his mouth—Matt. 10:32; Rom. 10:9-10; (f) receive the baptism of the Holy Spirit—cf. Acts 19:2, 6; (g) walk according to the Spirit—Gal. 6:18, 22-25; (h) "abstain from meats offered to idols, and from blood, and from things strangled, and from fornication"—Acts 15:29; (i) do good works—Matt. 16:27; 2:7; Rom. 2:6-7; James 1:22; 2:14, 17, 20-24; and finally, (j) "endure to the end"—Matt. 10:22 & 24:13; Heb. 10:23; Rev. 2:25-26.

The Christian's Rewards

Here are the things God gave the Christian who endured in the faith to the end:

- The final "seal" of His Spirit—Rev. 7:4;[126]
- At Jesus' appearing [AD 72] an instantaneous "change" of bodily substance[127] from mortal and corruptible to immortal and incorruptible—I Cor. 15:50-55;
- "Sit" with Christ on His throne in Heaven and be rewarded according to his works—II Cor. 5:10; Rev. 3:21;
- Entrance into the Kingdom of God and the Father's very presence—Matt. 5:3, 8, 10; John 14:3, 6, 12; Heb. 6:19-20; 7:19; II Pet. 1:11; Rev. 21:3-4;
- Eternal life—Matt. 19:16; John 3:16;
- An eternal inheritance[128] in the Kingdom of God—John 14:2; Acts 20:32; Rom. 8:17a, 32; I Cor. 15:50; Gal. 5:21; Eph. 5:5;
- "Fullness of Joy" and "pleasures forevermore"—Psalm 16:11; and
- Subsidiary rule [i.e. under Jesus and David] over Israelite cities and Israelite people in Paradise—Luke 19:17 & 19.

(All the Galatian Christians Were Once Under the Law of Moses.) Any careful reader of Galatians can deduce from certain passages in the epistle that God regarded the "Gentile" Christians there as once having been under the Law of Moses—i.e. before they believed in Christ. Let us look at them.

---

[126] This eschatological "seal" of the Spirit, when given to the enduring Christians in AD 69, made them that they would not deny Christ during the fiery trials of the Great Tribulation. At that point, according to John, "he that is righteous, let him be righteous still; and he that is holy, let him be holy still. And, behold, I come quickly; and my reward *is* with me, to give every man according as his work shall be" (Rev. 22:11b, 12). In other words, dear reader, the receiving of this "seal" brought Christ's elect brethren to a spiritually advanced point or spiritual plateau whereon they *could not* fall away. Only then did they have what the Southern Baptists define as "eternal security."

[127] i.e. the Christian's BORN AGAIN body. It was the Christian's *born-again* body—*not* his Adamic body—that was thus instantaneously "changed" at Jesus' Second Coming in AD 72.

[128] An inheritance in the Kingdom of God would involve such eternal blessings as possession of a "mansion" [John 14:2-3], a throne [Rev. 3:21], a crown (II Tim. 4:8; Rev. 2:10; 11:3; a priesthood (I Pet. 2:9; Rev. 1:6); geographical regions including the Israelite cities [and the inhabitants of those cities].

GAL 3:23-25

> But before faith came [to either Jewish or "Gentile" believers], **we were kept under the law**, shut up unto the faith which should afterwards be revealed [i.e. the Christian faith]. Wherefore **the law [of Moses] was our schoolmaster** *to bring us* unto Christ, that we might be justified by faith. But after that faith is come, **we are no longer under a schoolmaster**.

Not much comment needed here! To any unbiased reader of this passage it can easily be seen that the Galatian "Gentiles" [i.e. Christians] were ***ISRAELITE*** descendants [from the northern kingdom] whose conversion to Christ had freed them from the Law of Moses (see also Gal. 5:1 to follow).

GAL. 5:1

> Stand fast therefore in the liberty wherewith Christ hath made us free [i.e. from the Law], and be not entangled **AGAIN** with the **yoke** of bondage.

The word "AGAIN" proves that the Galatians, though now liberated from the Law through faith in Christ, had remained under it until that faith became theirs. The word "AGAIN" also suggests that if they reverted to Judaism and circumcision that would put them BACK under the Law and its condemnation! That's why Paul warned them, "Christ is become of no effect unto you, whosoever of you are justified by the law; ye are fallen from grace" (Gal. 5:4). That the "yoke" mentioned here refers to the Law of Moses, see Acts 15:10.

It could never have been said of ***TRUE*** Gentiles that they were ever under the Law of Moses. Therefore, the "Gentiles" spoken of in Galatians were ***NOT*** true Gentiles, but ***ACCULTURATED*** "Gentiles" descended from Abraham, Isaac, and Jacob. They were the descendants of their Israelite forefathers who, in the days of Moses, contracted with Jehovah at Sinai to observe and do everything that the Law commanded them. After Moses went over the Law with the twelve tribes of Israel, the people said:

ALL THE WORDS WHICH THE LORD HATH SAID WILL WE DO.—Ex. 24:3

All twelve tribes said that. In saying it in the presence of three witnesses—Jehovah, Moses, and the angels—the Law of Moses became a perpetual covenant between Israel and God.

(Freed from the Law Covenant) The destruction of Samaria [721 BC] did not end the Law Covenant for the northern tribes of Israel. Despite their subsequent scattered condition they, together with the Jews in the south, remained under the Law of Moses from its inception at Sinai to the destruction of Jerusalem and the Temple in AD 70. Beginning with Pentecost however [AD 29] all who believed on Christ and were Spirit baptized were freed from the Law:

> *There is* therefore NOW [i.e. since Pentecost] no condemnation [i.e. for transgressions of the Law] to them which are in Christ Jesus, who walk not after the flesh [i.e. circumcision and the works of the Law], but after the Spirit. For the law of the Spirit of life in Christ Jesus hath made me free from the law of sin and death.—Rom. 8:1-2

> Seeing then that we [Jewish or "Gentile" Christians] have such hope [in Christ], we use great plainness of speech: And not as Moses, *which* put a veil over his face, that the children of Israel could not stedfastly look to the end of that [i.e. the Law Covenant] which is [by Christ's blood] abolished: But their minds were blinded: for until this day (the Temple still stood in Jerusalem), when Moses is read, the veil is upon their heart. Nevertheless when it [i.e. the Jewish people] shall turn to the Lord, the veil shall be taken away. Now the Lord [Christ] is that Spirit: and where the Spirit of the Lord *is*, there is liberty.—II Cor. 3:12-17

CONCLUSION: The "Gentiles" of Galatians—descendants of Abraham—had remained under the Law Covenant until faith came in Christ Jesus. Therefore, if the Judaizers mentioned in Gal. 1:7 persuaded them to go over to Judaism [i.e. accept circumcision and Law observance] they would have AGAIN come under the Law and its condemnation. Thus, the word "AGAIN" has meaning only if the Galatian Christians were descendants of Abraham, Isaac, and Jacob, and had Israelite fathers as did the Jews when Israel covenanted with Jehovah [at Sinai] to "do" all that is written in the Law [Ex. 24:3].

GAL. 3:16; Cf. John 3:16

> Now to Abraham **and his seed** were the promises made. He saith not, And to seeds, as of many [i.e. all Abraham's descendants]; but as of one, And to thy seed, which is Christ.—Gal. 3:16

Note in this passage that Paul equated the word "seed" with "Christ." What does this mean? If we take it literally, Jehovah gave the promises to only two people, Abraham and Jesus Christ. Is it possible that Jehovah promised ONLY these two persons salvation? All the Bible tells us that this is not so.

For example, in Rom. 9:4 Paul said that the promises of God pertained to the "Israelites," clearly speaking of the whole nation, and indicating "many" descendants of Abraham. Then he wrote: "the children of the promise are counted for the seed" (v. 8). From these passages in Romans we can confidently know that Abraham's "seed" amounts to multiple thousands of Israelites, not just to Abraham himself, and also Jesus Christ. In Rev. 7:4-8 for example we learn that there were 144,000 Israelites who received the promises of God.

Moreover, on Pentecost three thousand Jews [i.e. Israelites] came to God through Jesus Christ, and a few days later five thousand more (Acts 2:41; 4:4). Thus, it is illogical and absolutely wrong to believe that only Abraham and Jesus would be saved by the promises of God.

How, then, are we to interpret Gal. 3:16? I have already shown that the Galatian Christians, of whom there must have been many hundreds of men and women, were all Israelites [called "Gentiles" in the epistle] whose fathers at Sinai put them perpetually under the Law of Moses. In short, the study of Galatians shows that the "Gentiles" in Galatians were NOT **true** Gentiles (**true** Gentiles are peoples NOT descended from Jacob).

(Today's Prevailing Interpretation) All Galatian commentators today interpret the Gentiles in the epistle as *true* Gentiles whom God reckoned to be the "children of Abraham" purely in a *spiritual* sense [in the sense that they believe on Jesus Christ, Abraham's single "seed"]. But what warrant have they for this decision? I know their answer. They find support in certain words, such as "world," "nations," "Gentiles," and "whosoever."

("World" and "Whosoever" in John 3:16)

But these words are tricky by themselves. They need an interpretation that harmonizes with the whole Bible teaching [from Genesis to Revelation]. Let's take the words "world" and "whosoever" for example. They are both used in a very famous passage: "For God so loved the **WORLD**, that he gave his only begotten Son, that **WHOSOEVER** believeth in him should not perish, but have everlasting life" (John 3:16).

There are several critical Bible doctrines to take into consideration before we can settle on the definition of these words.

First, how is it that the "world" in John 3:16 must mean the ***planet Earth*** when elsewhere in Scripture we read that God's end time theater of salvation was limited to the historic Roman Empire and then only during the time of its first ten Caesars (Dan. 2:44 & 7:8, 19, and 24)?

Second, how can John 3:16 mean that by Christ's blood God planned to forgive the sins of just any race of people when for the first 3½ years following Christ's crucifixion God was "determined" to deal only with the Jews and not yet with one descendant of the northern tribes (Dan. 9:24)? What do we do with Scripture saying Jesus' death was only "for the transgressions of **MY** people"—i.e. Israelites (Is. 53:8)? Can this passage in any way be made to mean that Jesus' blood was shed for the forgiveness of the sins of all other nations on earth as well? Peter repeated this limitation of forgiveness when he told a large crowd of Jews at the Temple that "God exalted [Jesus] with his right hand *to be* a Prince and a Saviour, for to give repentance to **ISRAEL**, and forgiveness of sins" (Acts 5:31). Don't forget also that Gabriel told Joseph to take Mary as his wife, and to name her child "JESUS: for he shall save **HIS PEOPLE** from their sins" (Matt. 1:21). Finally, God imputed "sins" only to Israelites because they only were under covenant with Him to "do" all that He commanded them (Ex. 24:3). See also Rom. 5:13 & I John 3:4. If Israelites were the only people to whom God ***imputed*** "sins," then theirs were the only sins He **could** forgive.

(The Greek Language) The Greek word for world in John 3:16 is κοσμόν [Eng. "cosmos"], and it has a small range of possible translations. Dr. James Strong's Greek Dictionary defines it as "orderly arrangement," or "decoration," or "world in a wide or narrow sense, including its inhabitants" (#2889). This is important to know because it shows us that there is no reason why it cannot mean either the planet earth, or the Roman Empire, or just the Israelite people. It would all depend upon the Biblical context surrounding it. We can therefore, based on Dr. Strong's expertise in Biblical Greek, safely say that "world" in John 3:16 might well mean Israelites—i.e. descendants from the twelve tribes of Jacob. With this interpretation I fully concur.

Summation

The word **"WORLD"** in John 3:16, according to all that we have pointed out above, quite definitely should be limited to mean Israelites [i.e. this would include the "world" or "cosmos" of the church]. In Biblical Greek "world" does not have to mean the entire world with all of its varied lands and nations and peoples; in fact, it *rarely* means that. Most of the time it means a nation, a people, or a kingdom as apart or different from other nations, peoples, or kingdoms. Thus the Jewish or the Israelite "world" is a totally viable and acceptable meaning for Cosmos in John 3:16.

("WHOSOEVER" in John 3:16)

According to certain things Jesus taught we must take care how we interpret "whosoever" in John 3:16. For example, consider His words: "No man can come to me, except the Father which hath sent me draw him" (John 6:44). Also, consider that the promises of God pertain only to the children of Israel. Might this explain why we learn from John in Revelation that 140,000 **ISRAELITES** were elected [i.e. chosen] to High Calling Salvation (and this over a period of forty years[129])? See

---

[129]   See Heb. 3:9, 17; cf. I Cor. 10:11.

also Rev. 7:4-8. Don't forget also that Jesus once said: ". . . strait *is* the gate, and narrow *is* the way, which leadeth unto life, and **FEW** there be that find it" (Matt. 7:14).

Consider, moreover, that of the "many" that God *called* unto High Calling Salvation [i.e. 210,000] He finally "chose" a "few" of them [i.e. 140,000]: "For **many** are called, but **few** *are* chosen" (Matt. 22:14). It seems clear to me that the reason for this is twofold.

First, God needed to train only a comparative "few" Israelites to enter the kingdom with Jesus and become co-rulers with Him over the multiple millions of Israelites He resurrected into Paradise on the day Jesus died (i.e. Nisan 14, AD 29). See Matt. 27:51-53; I Pet. 3:18-20.

Second, God "chose" only the "few" Christians He did, apparently, because their faith endured to the end (Matt. 24:13), and that of others [i.e. the "many antichrists"—I John 2:18] did not. Hence, Jesus' teaching: "For the Son of man shall come in the glory of his Father with his angels; and then he shall reward every man according to his works"—Matt. 16:28. We see, then, that apostasy disqualified many Christians from entering the kingdom of God.

These considerations coincide with Jesus' parable of the "net" fishermen, in which He explained:

> Again, the kingdom of heaven is like unto a net, that was cast into the sea, and gathered of every kind: Which, when it was full, they drew to shore, and sat down, and gathered the good into vessels, but cast the bad away. So shall it be at the end of the world [Greek: *age*[130]]: the angels shall come forth, and sever the wicked from among the just, And shall cast them into the furnace of fire: there shall be wailing and gnashing of teeth.—Matt. 13:47-50

In conclusion we see that it was not that easy for just anyone who thought he wanted to, to become one of the "whosoevers" of John 3:16. Matthew wrote of an incident of a rich man who desired to be a disciple of Jesus, but turned and walked away sorrowfully when Jesus told him what he had to do: "go *and* sell that thou hast, and give to the poor" (Matt. 19:21). When the man found out just how hard it was to

---

[130]   i.e. Jesus' adult-time generation was the same as the church "age."

follow Jesus, and walked sorrowfully away, Jesus said to His disciples: "a rich man shall hardly enter into the kingdom of Heaven. And . . . I say unto you, It is easier for a camel to go through the eye of a needle, than for a rich man to enter into the kingdom of God"—vv. 23-24.

Summation

When we come to understand that in the High Calling Salvation rank [see Phil. 3:14; Heb. 3:1] God's plan was (1) to elect **_only_** 144,000 people, who incidentally (2) had to be Israelites, and that (3) this had to be done BEFORE Jesus' generation ended, we begin to understand [and accept] why (a) the Great Commission was able to be fulfilled in just one generation, and why (b) **"WHOSOEVER"** in John 3:16 cannot be interpreted to mean just anyone who casually and without the power of the Holy Spirit decided to believe on Jesus.

We see also from this that John 3:16 has been anachronistic ever since Jesus' generation ended in the first century CE. To be frank [but Biblical and honest with you, O reader], when people today come to believe on Jesus, that no longer means that they are born again or heirs to the kingdom of God.

Note that in Greek John 3:16 reads much differently than in the KJV: "For thus God loves the world, so that He gives His only-begotten Son, that everyone who is believing in Him should not be perishing, but may be having life eonian" (_Concordant Literal New Testament_). This translation is truer to the Greek, and is quite "user-friendly" to my doctrine that God's offer of High Calling Salvation was limited to Israelites[131] during the time of Jesus' generation.

Whenever Jesus or His apostles spoke, either orally or in writing, they always spoke in the present tense—i.e. their own generation. This is a powerful argument that they did not intend that the eternal blessings they promised Christians, or the vengeance they warned that God would inflict upon the antichrists, was to happen in some distant and unknowable future time. RATHER, THEY WOULD HAPPEN

---

[131] "limited to Israelites"—Thus we can better understand why Paul ended Galatians with the words: "And as many as walk according to this rule, peace _be_ on them, and mercy, and upon the **ISRAEL** of God (Gal. 6:16)!

WITHIN THEIR LIFE TIME, ***BEFORE*** THEIR GENERATION PASSED AWAY.

Thus, they were in complete agreement and harmony with Jesus who put everything He said within the context of His own generation, even ***BEFORE*** it would "pass away" (Luke 21:32; cf. Matt. 24:34).

There is one other point that deserves to be mentioned in this vein, and that is what Jesus told Pilate: "My kingdom is not of this world" (John 18:36). Yet Jesus taught that "The time is fulfilled, and the kingdom of God is at hand"—i.e. "at hand" during ***HIS*** generation (see Mark 1:15).

In combining John 18:36 with Mark 1:15 we conclude that just because God's kingdom appears nowhere on this earth doesn't mean that it IS nowhere to be found, or that it was not established **BEFORE** Jesus' generation ended, *just as He said*. The answer to the dilemma is that it was established in Paradise above.

Naturally, we cannot see it *up there* while we still live *in this world*. But we accept that it's there by faith SINCE JESUS DEFINITELY TAUGHT THAT THE KINGDOM WAS "AT HAND" IN HIS GENERATION. Thus, it had to be established SOMEWHERE before His generation ended, and the only other *possible* place in all creation is Paradise above.

O reader, remember Paul's words: ". . . we [believers] look not at the things which are seen [on this earth], but at the things which are not seen [i.e. because they are out of man's sight]: for the things which are seen *are* temporal; but the things which are not seen *are* eternal" (II Cor. 4:18). It is natural for us to WANT God's kingdom to be here on earth, but we back off on that when we realize that it could not be ETERNAL if it were. Let's let it be where the Bible teaches that it exists, "above" in a place we CANNOT see, and where it may indeed be ETERNAL. See Col. 3:1-2.

CONCLUSION

The more time passes without Jesus Christ coming again [to this earth], the more foolish Catholic and Protestant eschatologists look in the eyes of the world. Christ's alleged delay in coming back [for about two millennia now] adds fuel to the negative thinking of unbelievers [i.e. atheists and/or agnostics] such as the late English philosopher

Bertrand Russell (1872-1970) and Oxford evolutionary biologist Richard Dawkins (born 1941). A prime religious reason Russell gave for his atheism, for example, was that Jesus did **not** [as he erroneously understood it] come back before His generation passed away, *as He said He would*. It is sad and too bad that Russell did not have the knowledge explained in this book! Since he did not, please note how he was able to minimize and marginalize Jesus and make light of some Christian teachers of his day who were continuing to teach Jesus' imminent Second Coming:

> "For one thing, He [Jesus] certainly thought that His second coming would occur in clouds of glory before the death of all the people who were living at that time. There are a great many texts that prove that. He says, for instance, 'Ye shall not have gone over the cities of Israel till the Son of Man be come.' Then He says, 'There are some standing here which shall not taste death till the Son of Man comes into His kingdom'; and there are a lot of places where it is quite clear that He believed that His second coming would happen during the lifetime of many then living. That was the belief of His earlier followers, and it was the basis of a good deal of His moral teaching. When He said, 'Take no thought for the morrow,' and things of that sort, it was very largely because He thought that the second coming was going to be very soon, and that all ordinary mundane affairs did not count. I have, as a matter of fact, known some Christians who did believe that the second coming was imminent. I knew a parson who frightened his congregation terribly by telling them that the second coming was very imminent indeed, but they were much consoled when they found that he was planting trees in his garden. The early Christians did really believe it, and they did abstain from such things as planting trees in their gardens, because they did accept from Christ the belief that the second coming was imminent. In that respect, clearly He [Jesus] was not so wise as some other people have been, and He was certainly not superlatively wise."[132]—*brackets added*

---

[132] See *Bertrand Russell, Why I Am Not a Christian and Other Essays on Religion and Related Subjects*, edited by Paul Edwards; pub. Simon & Schuster, 1957; p. 16.

Talking about negativism, let us take note of Richard Dawkin's view of Jehovah of Hosts:

> "The god [sic] of the Old Testament has got to be the most unpleasant character in all fiction: jealous and proud of it, petty, vindictive, unjust, unforgiving, racist, an ethnic-cleanser urging his people on to acts of genocide." [133]

(My Reply to Dr. Richard Dawkins)

I do not quote these men to bring hate in our hearts towards them, dear reader, for considering all the evil that is and always has been in this world since Adam sinned in the Garden—e.g. death and destruction everywhere (even in the pages of the Bible)—their take on "reality" is actually understandable and compelling. Did Jesus Himself not call His own pre-Pentecost disciples "evil" (see Matt. 7:11)?

My reply to Dr. Dawkins is one of love and respect. I respect him for standing up and speaking out for his beliefs, and truly I can see why he believes what he does. I would also tell him, however, that he has grossly misunderstood Jehovah and His acts in the Old Testament, and I challenge him to reread [or read for the first time] the Old Testament and try to see things from Jehovah's point of view. I would ask him to consider what the Bible says about God's eschatological purpose for man, and how He is "the Saviour of all men" (I Tim. 4:10). As importantly, also, I would assure Dr. Dawkins that in the future when he dies and God judges him in Paradise, he will be so thankful for and understanding of everything Jehovah did and said in the Old Testament, and probably really embarrassed by what he said in the above quote.

(A Fit Message Ending this Chapter)

Dear Reader, if you have understood the things that I have said in this book, and have come to believe them, you will agree that it is not for us who believe to sit in judgment on the atheists and agnostics of this world. We can explain and defend our beliefs to them, but our

---

[133]   http://en.wikipedia.org/The_ Root_ of_ All_Evil%3F—p. 7 of 9, 2/5/2009

main message to them should be that God loves them and has saved them despite their insults and untrue statements against Him. God is that gracious that He has devised, through Jesus Christ, a way to save them along with any among us who may falsely think we are more righteous than they.

Remember the gracious words of St. Paul towards the Christians of his day: "God commendeth his love toward us, in that, while we were yet sinners, Christ died for us" (Rom. 5:8). As to any who would judge non-believers, He says: "For all have sinned, and come short of the glory of God" (Rom. 3:23); and again: "There is none righteous, no, not one" (Rom. 3:10); and brethren, these truths apply to you and me.

Finally, let us not forget that Jesus was compassionate and positive even to the wicked thief who **_deserved_** to die [according to his own confession—see Luke 23:40-41]. He said to him, "Verily I say unto thee, To-day shalt thou be with me in paradise" (Luke 23:43). What good will Jesus had even toward sinners! It makes me think of what the angel of God said to the Bethlehem shepherds on the day Jesus was born: "I bring you **GOOD TIDINGS** of great joy, which shall be to **ALL PEOPLE** [even atheists and criminals]. For unto you is born this day in the city of David a Saviour, which is Christ the Lord" (Luke 2:10-11).

NOTES

Chapter Five

REVELATION

<u>Introduction</u>

So far, and unfortunately for today's Christians, a plateau of agreement among eschatologists concerning the meaning of Revelation has never come about. This is no surprise considering that most of them simply don't *believe* the things written in Revelation. If Revelation is ever to be understood, the following things must be believed without any caviling:

FIRST, the *writer* of Revelation was the apostle John, son of Zebedee.

SECOND, John wrote Revelation ca. AD 67-68, a little before Jesus' Second Coming in AD 72.

THIRD, everything in Revelation was to happen "shortly" before Jesus' coming.

FOURTH, Jesus' "servants" were only the members of "the seven churches of Asia," not Christians living after AD 72.

FIFTH, the seven churches do not represent seven church ages.

SIXTH, the 70th Week of Daniel was fulfilled from Jesus' baptism to the conversion of Paul in AD 33. Revelation has absolutely nothing to do with the 70th week.

SEVENTH, chapters 2 & 3 of Revelation are about (1) the Falling Away, (2) repentance of church apostates before the deadline, (3) Jesus' soon coming, and (4) the judgment of the nations—see Matt. 25:32 and Rev. 11:18.

EIGHTH, John's entering the door to Heaven in Rev. 4:1 is not about the Rapture of the church.

NINTH, at no point in Revelation does the prophetic topic switch from the Christians in the seven churches of Asia to an alleged 144,000 Jewish evangelists who are to preach Christ to the world after He raptures the Christian church.

TENTH, The thousand years in Rev. 20 are not literal, but signify the church age from AD 29-69, a period of forty years [cf. Heb. 3:9, 17].

Here are some things I highly recommend you do, dear reader, to arrive at the correct understanding of Revelation:

(1) Set a goal to understand Revelation thoroughly, from chapter 1 through chapter 22.

(2) Ask God *earnestly* for wisdom [Matt. 7:7; James 1:5; cf. Rev. 13:18; 17:9].

(3) Think: *There is only one correct way to understand Revelation.* Commit yourself to finding it as if it is more precious than all the gold in the world.

(4) Read this chapter thoroughly and thoughtfully, and even more so examine the many Bible references provided.

<><><><><><><>

How to Study Revelation

Dear reader, in all humility I feel that I can help you understand Revelation. I would not have included this final chapter if I didn't honestly believe that.

Study this chapter, don't just read it. In other words do all the things that a good *student* would do to facilitate learning. Have your Bible at your fingertips. Don't just read this chapter, but read the entire Book of Revelation also.

Don't read either of them too fast. Meditate on both as, and after, you read them. Meditation means two things: (1) you thinking hard on everything you read, and (2) God giving you understanding. Don't naively accept what I say in this chapter. Compare what I say with Revelation, and the Bible. Be like the noble Bereans who gladly received Paul's teaching, but then turned to the Scriptures for corroboration:

> These [i.e. Bereans: Jews and "Gentile" proselytes] were more noble than those in Thessalonica, in that they received the word with all readiness of mind, and searched the scriptures daily, whether those things were so.—Acts 17:11

Next, keep in mind that Revelation contains mental pictures, scenarios, symbols, metaphors, similes and other literary comparison devices. This is the meaning of the word "signified" in Rev. 1:1.

Realize that God still seeks people who will worship Him with **_truth_** in their heart and mind:

> . . . the hour cometh, and now is, when the true worshippers shall worship the Father in spirit and in truth: for the Father seeketh such to worship him. God *is* a Spirit: and they that worship him must worship *him* in spirit and in truth.— John 4:23-24

Therefore, you are not only seeking God, but God is also seeking you. He wants you to learn **_truth_** and approach Him with sound doctrine.

As God enlightens you betimes, tell Him that you love Him for it. Tell Him that you adore Him! Always give Him thanks! God is love. He not only gives love to you, but He wants you to love Him back. Think of God as your Teacher and you His student. Strive to make all A's! When you pray to Him think of it as if you are asking your Teacher for further explanation. Know that when you pray to Him in earnest He **_hears_** you. A sincere student always enlivens the Teacher, and He **_will_** teach you as only He can, and fill your heart with satisfaction:

> . . . when he, the Spirit of truth, is come, he will guide you into all truth: for he shall not speak of himself; but whatsoever he shall hear, *that* shall he speak: and he will shew you things to come.—John 16:13

Finally, don't stop with Revelation as if it is the only thing you need to know about God, the end times of long ago, or your present Christian experience. Hopefully, as you come to know what Revelation is all about, you will be inspired to pursue Biblical knowledge and understanding for the rest of your days on earth.

Your goal should be to *grow* in knowledge and in truth and never stop doing so. When you reach the point that you just can't do without getting to know God better and better, you will know your frame of mind and view of life is enlightened and just where God wants it.

Dear reader, one day God will call you to your new home in Paradise and reward you according to your works. He will start by begetting you unto Himself with new, non-Adamic flesh, free of the Adamic curse.

Then He will graciously restore unto you all the wonderful benefits and blessings He intended people to have "from the beginning."

<u>Outline of This Chapter</u>

SECTION I:
APOSTASY IN THE
SEVEN CHURCHES OF ASIA

Let's look at all "seven churches of Asia" at the same time. They were the only viable local churches on earth when John wrote Revelation. Collectively, they were *the* church [singular] at this time because great masses of Christians had gathered in Asia to await Jesus' Second Coming and the Rapture. They knew that Jesus would come for them "shortly"[134]—i.e. *before* His generation passed away [Matt. 24:34]. One reason they knew this is because of the sickening apostasy that was taking place among Christians daily in the seven churches. Apostasy was one of the signs Jesus gave in His Olivet Prophecy:

> Take heed that no man **deceive** you. For many shall come in my name, saying, I am Christ; and shall **deceive** many [Christians of Jesus' generation] . . . And many false prophets shall rise, and shall **deceive** many. And because iniquity shall abound, the love of many shall wax cold.—Matt. 24:4b, 5, 11-12

Any church member that became *deceived so much as to deny Christ publicly* had committed apostasy, and apostasy for a Christian meant the forfeiture of a glorified [i.e. immortal] body and an inheritance in the kingdom of God. Jesus warned:

> Whosoever therefore shall confess me before men, him will I confess also before my Father which is in heaven. But whosoever shall deny me before men, him will I also deny before my Father which is in heaven.—Matt. 10:32-33

Recall also that the apostle Paul foretold a "falling away" [i.e. an apostasy] in the church:

---

[134] See Rev. 1:1 (also: Rev. 22:6). Our English word **"SHORTLY"** in these passages means *"in haste"* = soon or quickly or speedily. See *Strong's Concordance,* Greek Dictionary, #5034.

> Let no man deceive you by any means: for that day shall not come, except there come a **falling away** first—II Thess. 2:3

Thus, many Christians in Asia publicly "denied" Jesus Christ (see II Pet. 2:1-3).

(The Many Blessings of Salvation in the High Calling Rank)

Who could commit apostasy? The simplest answer is: Only first-century, born-again Christians; that is, Christ's disciples of His generation called unto and saved in the "high calling" salvation rank [see Phil. 3:14; cf. II Tim. 1:9; Heb. 2:3 and 3:1]. This salvation assured the following blessings and promises to the Christians living in Asia at that time.

- a born-again body [usually given at the time of water baptism] that was no longer made of "cursed" Adamic flesh;
- the baptism of the Holy Spirit;
- the promise of being instantaneously "changed" from mortality and corruption to immortality and incorruption—i.e. being given a glorified body at Jesus' appearing (I Cor. 15:49-55);
- the gift and possession of everlasting life *while still living on this earth*;
- the promise of an inheritance in the kingdom of heaven at Jesus' appearing;
- the promise of co-rulership with Christ in Paradise at the time of Jesus' coming;
- the promise of ruling over "cities" in Paradise soon after Jesus' appearing and the Rapture (Luke 19:17, 19);
- the promise of ascending to the Father at Christ's Second Coming [cf. John 20:17];
- the promise of sitting with Christ on His throne sometime before *His* generation passed away (Rev. 3:21);
- the wonder and mystery of becoming a part of Christ's Bride;
- the promise of being "arrayed in fine linen, clean and white" if martyred, or at Jesus' coming (Rev. 19:8);

- the promise of eating "the marriage supper of the Lamb" shortly after Jesus' Second Coming (Rev. 19:9); and
- the promise of having a mansion in the Father's [i.e. Jehovah's] house prepared for them by their Lord and Savior Jesus Christ—see John 14:2-3.

(Can Today's Christians Fall Away from These Blessings?)

The answer to this question is No! This is because no man since Christ's generation, Christian or otherwise, can claim [as *yet*] any of these blessings and promises of God. Any Christian today who thinks he will [at Jesus' coming or upon dying] receive one or more of them errs. No man not up on the high mountain of the High Calling can fall away from it. God stopped calling Israelites [on *this* earth] into that rank of High Calling Salvation ca. Jan. 15, AD 69 at the time of the abomination of desolation and Great Tribulation.

(True Biblical Apostasy Took Place in the Seven Churches of Asia.)

The things I just wrote above hopefully do not unsettle or frighten anyone reading this book to this point (my assumption is that my readers have been at least *tentatively* receptive to most or all of what has been said). Please remember two things, dear reader: (1) Revelation was written only to Christians who lived during Jesus' generation; and (2) only they could receive or reject any of the blessings and promises listed above.

Jesus' letters to the seven churches [see Rev. 2 & 3] definitely show that the true [i.e. Biblically prophesied] Apostasy was taking place in those seven churches ca. AD 67-68. This time period is in harmony with Jesus' warning to His disciples that before His generation ended "many" born-again disciples would fall away from Him and the Gospel faith:

For many ["antichrists"[135]] shall come in my name, saying, I am Christ; and shall deceive many . . . Verily I say unto you, This [i.e. Christ's] generation shall not pass, till all these things be fulfilled.—Matt. 24:5, 34

In full harmony with Jesus' timing for the apostasy John wrote [ca. AD 67-68]:

Little children, **it is [i.e. John's present tense, not ours] the last time**: and as ye have heard that antichrist shall come, **even now are there many antichrists; whereby we know that it is the last time**.—I John 2:18

Note, also, how the very first verse in Revelation harmonizes with Jesus' "this generation" prophesy:

The Revelation of Jesus Christ, which God gave unto him, to shew unto his servants things which must **shortly** come to pass . . . **the time is at hand**.—Rev. 1:1a, 3b

Let us look now at the undeniable, advanced and growing apostasy that was taking place in the seven churches of Asia in Jesus' generation. To each of the churches Jesus dictated to John a special epistle exhorting the apostates to "overcome" while they still had "a space to repent" (cf. Rev. 2:21).

- ➢ EPHESUS: "Thou hast left thy first love" (2:4); and they were tolerating and accommodating the presence of the "Nicolaitans" in their midst (2:6).
- ➢ SMYRNA: Many members were deceitfully claiming to be Jews (2:9).
- ➢ PERGAMOS: ". . . thou hast there them that hold the doctrine of Balaam, who taught Balac to cast a stumblingblock before

---

135 In full harmony with Jesus' timing for the apostasy [i.e., **before** His own generation ended] John wrote to the Christians gathered in Asia: "Little children, it is the last time: and as ye have heard that antichrist shall come, even now are there many antichrists; whereby we know that it is the last time" (I John 2:18; cf. Rev. 17:10).

the children of Israel, to eat things sacrificed unto idols, and to commit fornication. So hast thou also them that hold the doctrine of the Nicolaitans, which thing I hate" (2:14-15).

➤ THYATIRA: ". . . thou sufferest that woman Jezebel, which calleth herself a prophetess, to teach and to seduce my servants to commit fornication, and to eat things sacrificed unto idols" (2:20).

➤ SARDIS: "thou hast a name that thou livest, and art dead . . . I have not found thy works perfect before God" (3:1b, 2b). Also, (1) they were not "watching" for Jesus' coming—3:3; and (2) they had defiled their garments—3:4.

➤ PHILADELPHIA: Many members were of "the synagogue of Satan" having publicly claimed to be Jews (3:9).

➤ LAODICEA: ". . . thou art neither cold nor hot" (3:16); ". . . thou sayest, I am rich, and increased with goods, and have need of nothing; and knowest not that thou art wretched, and miserable, and poor, and blind, and naked" (3:17b).

(The First Five Heads of the Beast Having Seven Heads)

We should correctly call all these sins just listed in the seven churches "sins of apostasy," because any one of them was an abomination to God and "lethal" to eternal life [i.e. an apostate's forfeiture of High Calling Salvation].

Though they were "lethal," *yet the guilty still had an opportunity to "overcome" them so long as they did so before the deadline of ca. Jan. 15, AD 69.*

That is why at the end of each church letter we find the words "he that overcometh . . . etc."

For example, we note that the apostates at Sardis were in danger of having God "blot out" their names from "the book of life"; but notice that Jesus then extended this hope to them: "He that overcometh, the same shall be clothed in white raiment; and I will not blot out his name out of the book of life, but I will confess his name before my Father, and before his angels" (Rev. 3:5; cf. Matt. 18:10).

In other words, Jesus gave them "space to repent" (cf. Rev. 2:21), which if they did **_before_** the deadline they could again "lay hold on eternal life, whereunto thou art also called" (I Tim. 6:12).

We can safely conclude that all the apostates in the seven churches, at the time John's Revelation reached them from Patmos [i.e. AD 67-68], were the ones (by the multiple thousands) that John meant when he wrote: "five are fallen" (Rev. 17:10). That is, these thousands were members of five distinct waves or movements of apostasy (Jesus called them "mountains"—Rev. 17:9) that had already abominated the seven churches of Asia in AD 67-68.

As just said, however, they still had time to "overcome," but only a **_short_** time [cf. Rev. 1:1, 3]. If they failed to overcome before the empowerment[136] of the beast's 6th head [i.e. the "first beast"—Rev. 13:4, 12], it was too late. They had passed over the deadline for repentance [ca. Jan. 15, AD 69]. Then,

> He that is unjust [i.e. apostate], let him be unjust still [i.e. to Jesus' appearing]: and he which is filthy, let him be filthy still.—Rev. 22:11a

Thus, the first five heads of the seven-headed beast were formed. The following passage is about the final two heads of the beast:

> . . . one is [i.e. the 6th head of the seven-headed beast], *and* the other [i.e. the 7th head] is not yet come; and when he cometh, he must continue a short space.—Rev. 17:10b

SECTION II:
THE ABOMINATION
OF DESOLATION

Each word, "abomination" and "desolation," must be understood separately. Let us look first at the "abomination."

---

136 ". . . and the dragon gave him his power, and his seat, and great authority" (Rev. 13:2).

THE ABOMINATION

One very important thing to grasp in discussing the abomination is that *it happened to and within the seven churches of Asia in the latter years of Jesus' generation.* Paul foretold it as "a falling away" [i.e. of Christians]:

> Let no man deceive you by any means: for *that day*[137] *shall not come,* except there **come a falling away first**, and that man of sin be revealed, the son of perdition—II Thess. 2:3

This "falling away" of Christians is defined as their departure from "the faith which was once delivered unto the saints" (Jude 3). They began abandoning that faith after the great fire of Rome in AD 64, which may be called the "latter years" or "last days" of Jesus' generation when the church was nearing its fortieth year of existence on earth (cf. Heb. 3:9, 17).

When Nero accused the Christians in Rome of starting the fire, he began persecuting them and slaying many. This sudden pressure on Christians terrorized them and triggered the great Falling Away in the church. All Christians who fell did so in order to save their lives; also, to keep their jobs, houses and belongings, and [if parents] give their children a chance for life on earth. It is obvious that they had lost their first love [i.e. for Christ and the brethren], and were thinking just like the lovers of this world. They had forgotten Jesus' warning to His disciples not to look back or fear man:

> And Jesus said . . . No man, having put his hand to the plough, and looking back, is fit for the kingdom of God. —Luke 9:62

> . . . fear not them which kill the body, but are not able to kill the soul: but rather, fear him which is able to destroy both soul and body in hell [Gk. in Gehenna] . . . Whosoever therefore shall confess me before men, him will I confess also before my Father which is in heaven. But whosoever shall deny me before men, him will I also deny before my Father which is in heaven.—Matt. 10:28, 32-33

---

137   *That day*—i.e. the 3½-year Great Tribulation

. . . whosoever will save his life shall lose it: and whosoever will lose his life for my sake shall find it. For what is a man profited, if he shall gain the whole world, and lose his own soul?—Matt. 16:25-26

Ultimately—when the apostasy reached its zenith the apostates had plummeted to "the depths of Satan" (Rev. 2:24b). They had taken on Satan's foul spirit toward all faithful Christians in the seven churches. They began trodding underfoot Christ's blood and blaspheming the Holy Spirit:

And there was given unto him [i.e. to the apostates of the "first beast" or the sixth head of the seven-headed beast] a mouth speaking great things and blasphemies, and power was given him to continue forty *and* two months . . . And it was given unto him to make war with the saints, and to overcome them: and power was given him over all kindreds, and tongues, and nations.—Rev. 13:5, 7

For the time will come when they [i.e. many Christians] will not endure sound doctrine . . . .—II Tim. 4:3a

Let us therefore fear, lest, a promise being left *us* of entering into his rest, <u>any of you should seem to come short of it.</u>—Heb. 4:1

For *it is* impossible for those who were once enlightened, and have tasted of the heavenly gift, and were made partakers of the Holy Ghost, And have tasted the good word of God, and the powers of the world to come, If they shall fall away, to renew them again unto repentance; seeing they crucify to themselves the Son of God afresh, and put *him* to an open shame.—Heb. 6:4-6

For if we sin willfully[138] after that we have received the knowledge of the truth, there remaineth no more sacrifice for

---

[138] Sin willfully—In the context in which this passage is written, the willful "sin" is apostasy—the falling away from Christ. When apostates denied Christ's blood, God had already turned His back on all the animal sacrifices in Jerusalem, so that apostates had nowhere to turn for forgiveness of their sins.

sins,[139] But a certain fearful looking for of judgment and fiery indignation, which shall devour the adversaries [i.e. the antichrists]. He that despised Moses' law died without mercy under two or three witnesses: Of how much sorer punishment, suppose ye, shall he [i.e. any Christian] be thought worthy, who hath trodden under foot the Son of God, and hath counted the blood of the covenant, wherewith he was sanctified, an unholy thing, and hath done despite unto the Spirit of grace?—Heb. 10:27-29

For if after they have escaped the pollutions of the world through the knowledge of the Lord and Saviour Jesus Christ, they are again entangled therein, and overcome, the latter end is worse with them than the beginning. For it had been better for them not to have known the way of righteousness, than, after they have known *it*, to turn from the holy commandment delivered unto them. But it is happened unto them according to the true proverb, The dog *is* turned to his own vomit again; and the sow that was washed to her wallowing in the mire. —II Pet. 2:20-22

They went out from us, but they were not of us;[140] for if they had been of us,[141] they would *no doubt* have continued with us: but *they went out*, that they might be made manifest[142] that they were not all of us.—I John 2:19

THE DESOLATION

The word "desolation" refers to the destruction or "perdition"[143] [Gk. "come to nought"; "despoliation"[144]] of the Christian apostates **_AND_** of the church that they abominated with their spiritual

---

[139] Sins—i.e. "transgressions" against the Law (see I John 3:4)

[140] They were not of Christ's brethren who had firmly determined to "endure unto the end" even if it meant persecution and martyrdom (see Matt. 24:13).

[141] "If they had been of us"—i.e. of us Christians who had determined **_not_** to deny Christ . . .

[142] "That they might be made manifest"—The apostates committed apostasy to avoid persecution and martyrdom. Therefore, they WANTED everybody to see that they were no longer Christians.

[143] See II Thess. 2:3.

[144] See *Strong's Concordance*, "Greek Dictionary": #s 2049 & 2050.

fornication[145] and doctrinal deception. In other words, we are talking about the defilement of the "temple of God" (I Cor. 3:17). Revelation makes it clear that the apostates in the seven churches fell into three general groups: i.e. those who sought to fake themselves as:

1. apostles (cf. Rev. 2:2); or
2. pagans (cf. Rev. 2:14, 20); or
3. Jews (cf. Rev. 2:9 & 3:9).

All three kinds of apostates, in effect, were committing spiritual "fornication." In other words, they were turning from Christ (to whom they were "espoused" [i.e. betrothed; promised]),[146] and were teaching the doctrines of Judaism and Paganism. The False Prophet, that is, had become like a lewd woman—i.e. "whore"—that stood in a public place alluring strangers [i.e. Christians] to come lie with her:

> . . . thou [i.e. any godless usurper of authority in one of the seven churches] sufferest that woman Jezebel, which calleth herself a prophetess, to teach and to seduce my servants to commit fornication, and to eat things sacrificed unto idols. And I gave her space to repent of her fornication; and she repented not. Behold, I will cast her into a bed, and them that commit adultery with her into great tribulation, except they repent of their deeds.—Rev. 2:20-22

Any Christian in Asia at that time, by submitting himself to these ungodly teachers, and their "ungodly" [147] deeds and doctrines, committed spiritual fornication or adultery with **"the great whore,"** and stood to share the same damnation she was about to receive in the "great white throne" judgment:

---

145 "Spiritual fornication"—Revelation makes it clear that any Christian that fell from Christ in order to become a pagan or a Jew [by religion] had committed "fornication." The Antichrist comprised thousands of apostates that had become—or sought to become—"Jews" or "pagans."
146 See II Cor. 11:2.
147 Cf. Jude 15.

Come hither [John]; I will shew unto thee the judgment [Gk. damnation] of the great whore that sitteth upon many waters: With whom the kings of the earth[148] have committed fornication, and the inhabitants of the earth have been made drunk with the wine of her fornication . . . And upon her forehead *was* a name written, MYSTERY, <u>BABYLON</u> THE GREAT, THE MOTHER OF <u>HARLOTS</u> AND ABOMINATIONS OF THE EARTH . . . And the ten horns which thou sawest upon the beast, these shall hate the whore [i.e. "BABYLON/ MOTHER OF HARLOTS"], and shall make her desolate and naked, and shall eat her flesh, and burn her with fire [cf. Lake of fire]—Rev. 17:1-2, 16

(The Desolation of the Apostates)

Thus, the apostates [i.e. the "many antichrists" of I John 2:18] went into perdition, as described frequently in the New Testament:

Know **YE** not that **YE** are the temple of God, and *that* the Spirit of God dwelleth in **YOU**? **If any man** [i.e. any of "ye/ you"] **defile the temple of God, HIM shall God destroy**; for the temple of God is holy, which *temple* <u>YE</u> are.—I Cor. 3:16-17

He that despised Moses' law died without mercy under two or three witnesses: Of how much sorer punishment, suppose **YE**, shall **HE** be thought worthy [i.e. any Christian apostate], who hath trodden under foot the Son of God, and hath counted the blood of the covenant, **wherewith HE was sanctified,** an unholy thing, and hath done despite unto the Spirit of grace? For **WE** know him that hath said, Vengeance *belongeth* unto me, I will recompense, saith the Lord. And again, The Lord shall judge **his people** [i.e. the church apostates—cf. I Pet. 4:17]. *It is* **a fearful thing to fall into the hands of the living God**.—Heb. 10:28-31

But there were false prophets also among the people [i.e. the children of Israel], even as there shall be false teachers [cf. the

---

148 "Kings of the earth"—i.e. either faithful or fallen Christians, depending upon the context [see Rev. 1:5-6; 5:10; 6:15; 10:11; 17:10; 18:3, 9; 19:18-19; 21:24].

False Prophet] among **YOU** [among you Christians in Asia] who privily shall bring in damnable heresies, even denying the Lord that bought **THEM, and bring upon THEMSELVES swift destruction [i.e. desolation].**—II Pet. 2:1

But the heavens and the earth which are **NOW**,[149] by the same word are kept in store, **reserved unto fire against the day of judgment and perdition of ungodly men** . . . the day of the Lord will come as a thief in the night; in the which **the heavens shall pass away with a great noise [See p. 101 (FN#100 c3)], and the elements shall melt with fervent heat, the earth also and the works that are therein shall be burned up.**—II Pet. 3:7, 10

Behold, I will cast her [i.e. Jezebel] into a bed, and them that commit adultery with her into great tribulation, except they repent of their deeds. And **I will kill her children with death**.—Rev. 2:22, 23a

And the ten horns which thou sawest upon the beast, these shall hate the [great] whore [i.e. the apostates of the 7th head], and shall **make her desolate and naked, and shall eat her flesh, and burn her with fire.**—Rev. 17:16

And I saw a great white throne, and him that sat on it, from whose face **the earth and the heaven** [i.e. the Beast and the False Prophet[150]] fled away; and there was found no place for them. And I saw **the dead, small and great**,[151] stand before God; and the books were opened: and another book was opened, which is

---

149 "The heavens and the earth which are **NOW**"—i.e. the false teachers [collectively, "the great whore" or False Prophet] and those Christians whom they deceived (cf. II Pet. 2:1-2).

150 The 6th head [cf. the "first beast" of Rev. 13:3, 12] issued no prophecy or teaching, but merely slew Christians; thus, its work was earthy, dirty. The 7th head apostates [i.e. collectively, the False Prophet] was spiritual—i.e. doctrinal; heavenly [e.g. he sought "to change times and laws"—Dan. 7:25; he "opposeth and exalteth himself above all that is called God, or that is worshipped, shewing himself that he is God"—II Thess. 2:4; ". . . deceiveth them that dwell on the earth"—Rev. 13:14a]. In sum "earth" was the 6th head and "heavens" the 7th head of the seven-headed beast. Cf. II Pet. 3:7, 10 & 12.

151 I.e. the apostates comprising the first five heads of the seven-headed beast

the book of life: and the **dead** (i.e. the apostates were ***spiritually*** dead—cf. Matt. 8:22) were judged out of those things which were written in the books, according to their works. And the sea gave up the dead which were in it; and death and hell delivered up the dead which were in them: and they were judged every man according to their works. And **death and hell** [i.e. the "many antichrists" of I John 2:18] **were cast into the lake of fire.** This is the second death. And whosoever was **not found written in the book of life** [i.e. any Christian apostate—cf. Rev. 3:5] was **cast into the lake of fire**.—Rev. 20:11-15

(The Desolation of Great Babylon:
I.e. The Abominated Church)

The desolation [destruction; judgment] of the once Christian and Holy church is certainly taught in Revelation. In its fallen state the church is called Babylon (cf. Rev. 18:2). The term "Babylon the great," depending on context, can mean either the entire seven-headed beast, or "THE GREAT MOTHER OF HARLOTS" a.k.a. "the great whore" (see Rev. 17:1-5). Importantly, "the great whore" also refers to the 7th head of the seven-headed beast; that is, the False Prophet. With this prompting in mind, read carefully the following passages:

> ***Babylon*** the great is fallen, is fallen,[152] and is **become** the habitation of devils, and the hold of every foul spirit, and a cage of every unclean and hateful bird.—Rev. 18:2

> And there came one of the seven angels which had the seven vials, and talked with me, saying unto me, Come hither; I will shew unto thee the judgment of **the great whore** [i.e. the False Prophet] that sitteth upon many waters:[153] With whom the kings of the earth [apostate Christians] have committed fornication,

---

[152] "Is fallen, is fallen"—i.e. the church "institution" was now totally apostate, with no elect brethren remaining. The elect by ca. Jan. 15, AD 69 had fled to the "wilderness" where "they" fed and nourished her for the next 3½ years—see Rev. 12:6, 14.

[153] "Many waters"—Here "many waters" means the same as John's "many antichrists" in I John 2:18]. In the apocalyptic genre words like "waters," "sea," "mountains," and "nations" are synonymous. In Revelation they symbolize the 7-headed

and the inhabitants of the earth have been made drunk with the wine of her fornication.—Rev. 17:1-2

God commanded Christ's faithful brethren to depart from her [i.e. from "Babylon," or the church now called "the <u>habitation</u> of devils, and the <u>hold</u> of every foul spirit, and a <u>cage</u> of every unclean and hateful bird"—Rev. 18:2]:

> And I heard another voice from heaven, saying, Come out of her, my people, that ye be not partakers of her sins, and that ye receive not of her plagues. For her sins have reached unto heaven, and God hath remembered her iniquities.—Rev. 18:4-5

On the day and hour of Jesus' coming in AD 72, Babylon or the "great whore" was destroyed:

> Therefore shall her [the whore's] plagues come in one day, death, and mourning, and famine; and she shall be utterly burned with fire: for strong *is* the Lord God who judgeth her. And the kings of the earth, who have committed fornication and lived deliciously with her, shall bewail her, and lament for her, when they shall see the smoke of her burning, Standing afar off for the fear of her torment, saying, Alas, alas that great city Babylon, that mighty city! for in one hour is thy judgment [i.e. destruction] come.—Rev. 18:8-10

SUMMARY

In the briefest terms the abomination of desolation was the first-century abomination of [i.e. Satan's ruination of—cf. Rev. 20:7-8] thousands of Asian church members by false teachers. Thus, God desolated the church [for example, took away its true teachers and Christians] and soon burned up the antichrists that commandeered it:

---

beast. The False Prophet [i.e. the "great whore"] sat on seven "mountains," thus *controlling* all seven heads of the Beast. See Rev. 17:3, 7, 9, 15, and 18.

And whosoever [i.e. any apostate Christian from the seven churches of Asia] was not found written in the book of life was cast into the lake of fire.—Rev. 20:15

But that which beareth thorns and briers is rejected, and *is* nigh unto cursing; whose end *is* to be burned.—Heb. 6:8

But a certain fearful [i.e. the Antichrist] looking for of judgment and fiery indignation, which shall devour the adversaries [i.e. the "many antichrists"—I John 2:18]—Heb. 10:27

All Christians in Asia that remained faithful to Christ were neither abominated nor desolated, even though thousands of them were persecuted and ultimately martyred. The reason we can't call that "desolation" for them is because God immediately raised them in the First Resurrection Rank, which involved giving them the fantastic rewards of eternal life and an eternal inheritance in His everlasting kingdom.

Likewise, the desolation of the antichrists was not merely their temporal loss of human life, but the temporal[154] loss of their ***eternal*** life in Christ [cf. I John 5:12] and their temporal ***disinheritance*** in the kingdom of God.

Temporal? Yes, temporal. The Bible says that eventually the antichrists were reincarnated and brought into Paradise [cf. Rev. 3:9] because of the love and power of God who is "not willing that any should [eternally] perish, but that all should [eventually] come to repentance" (II Pet. 3:9).

In this same vein Paul wrote:

. . . God our Saviour . . . will have all men to be saved, and to come unto the knowledge of the truth. For *there is* one God, and one mediator between God and men, the man Christ Jesus; **Who gave himself a ransom for all, to be testified in due time**.—I Tim. 2:3b, 4-6

---

154 The judgment of God against an antichrist was not to make him extinct forever. Paul wrote that, "he [i.e. any Christian apostate] shall suffer loss . . . but he himself shall be saved; yet so as by fire" (I Cor. 3:15).

SECTION III:
THE TEN HORNS

The first thing to point out here is that the ten horns in Daniel [see Dan. 7:7, 20, 24] are not the same thing as the ten horns in Revelation [see Rev. 12:3; 13:1; 17:3, 12-13, 16].

(The Ten Horns in Daniel)

In the 7th chapter of Daniel we learn of four beasts that arise out of the sea. Nearly all eschatologists agree that these four beasts point out the historical fact that from Daniel's time the Middle East/Fertile Crescent part of the world had a succession of four kingdoms or empires:

1. Babylonian (605-539 BC)
2. Medo-Persian (539-331 BC)
3. Grecian (331-168 BC)
4. Roman (prophetic period: 49 BC to AD 79)

Daniel said:

> Then I would know the truth of the **FOURTH BEAST**, which was diverse from all the others, exceeding dreadful, whose teeth *were of* iron, and his nails *of* brass; *which* devoured, brake in pieces, and stamped the residue with his feet; **And of the TEN HORNS that *were* in his head**.—Dan. 7:19, 20a

To Daniel's thinking, while the first three kingdoms were of importance, the fourth kingdom [Roman Empire] went right to the heart of the prophecy. The Roman Empire interested Daniel the most because he knew that IT WOULD BE DURING THAT FOURTH KINGDOM THAT GOD WOULD GIVE POSESSION OF HIS KINGDOM TO THE SAINTS:

> And the kingdom and dominion, and the greatness of the kingdom under the whole heaven, shall be given to the people of **the saints of the most High**, whose kingdom *is* an everlasting

kingdom, and all dominions shall serve and obey him.
—Dan. 7:27

The meaning of the four beasts Daniel knew, but he did not understand the ten horns that were on the head of the fourth beast. After asking God to explain them to him, God answered:

> . . . the ten horns out of this kingdom *are* ten **KINGS** [Caesars[155]] *that* shall arise.—Dan. 7:24a

Reader, you will remember that in the first chapter of this book I interpreted these ten kings as the first ten Caesars of the Roman Empire. Please review that chapter at this time if you need to.

(An Important Point)

Remember, God's answer to Daniel's query about the identity of the ten horns on the fourth beast was that they were "kings." Note Daniel's question:

> Then I would know the truth of the fourth beast . . . And of the ten horns that were in his head.—Dan. 7:19a, 20a

Here was God's answer:

> . . . the ten horns out of this kingdom *are* ten **KINGS** *that* shall arise.—Dan. 7:24a

Dear reader, what we should understand here is a very important point: i.e. **KINGS** who have rule over a **KINGDOM** [e.g. here THE ROMAN EMPIRE] do not all rule at the same time, but ***successively, one after the other***. Julius Caesar ruled first. When he died Augustus took over and when Augustus died Tiberius ascended the throne, and

---

155   Daniel would not have understood the word *Caesars* in his day, so God used "**kings.**" However, in John's day, when there were **Caesars** in the Roman Empire it was easy for John to know that they were the "kings" God spoke of to Daniel.

when Tiberius died Claudius reigned . . . etc . . . until all ten Caesars had ruled.

This succession is very important because it takes a long time for ten kings to rule one after another. With Julius Caesar, therefore, end time prophetic fulfillment began. From Jesus' birth in the days of Augustus to the "last days" [including the first 2½ years of Vespasian's rule] we see the prophetic length of Jesus' generation—4 BC to AD 72. In that generation **"all things which are written"**[156] [i.e. all things concerning end time prophecy] were fulfilled.

It is noteworthy that virtually all things "written" in the Old Testament and in the New Testament concerning the last days [i.e. end time prophecy] are spoken of as either fulfilled or about to be fulfilled during Jesus' generation. A thorough reading of the New Testament shows this to be so.

From Matthew's Gospel to Revelation we read of Jesus' birth; His miracles; His preaching the gospel of the kingdom of Heaven; His death, burial, and resurrection; His ascension unto the Father; the outpouring of the Holy Spirit on Pentecost; the founding of the church; the end time "falling away" and blasphemies against God by the Antichrist [i.e. "another little horn]; the Second Coming of Jesus Christ; the perdition of the Christian apostates; the ascension of Christ's elect brethren to the throne of God; and their inheritance in the Kingdom of **Heaven.**

In short, as Revelation words it, we see in the New Testament **"the Alpha and Omega, beginning and the end, the first and the last"**—Rev. 22:13.

*(We See the Succession of
Nine Caesars in the
New Testament)*

In the New Testament three Caesars—i.e. Augustus, Tiberius and Claudius—are mentioned by name:

---

[156] See Luke 21:22.

And it came to pass in those days, that there went out a decree from **CAESAR AUGUSTUS**, that all the world should be taxed.—Luke 2:1

Now in the fifteenth year of the reign of **TIBERIUS CAESAR**, Pontius Pilate being governor of Judea, and Herod being tetrarch of Galilee, and his brother Philip tetrarch of Iturea and of the region of Trachonitis, and Lysanias the tetrarch of Abilene—Luke 3:1

And in these days came prophets from Jerusalem unto Antioch. And there stood up one of them named Agabus, and signified by the Spirit that there should be great dearth throughout all the world: which came to pass in the days of **CLAUDIUS CAESAR**.—Acts 11:27-28

After these things Paul departed from Athens, and came to Corinth; And found a certain Jew named Aquila, born in Pontus, lately come from Italy, with his wife Pricilla; (because that **CLAUDIUS** had commanded all Jews to depart from Rome:) and came unto them.—Acts 18:1-2

Not understood by most Bible scholars is that the 6th Caesar, Nero, is *alluded to* in Paul's second epistle to the Thessalonians:

For the mystery of iniquity doth already work: only **he [NERO] who now letteth**[157] *will let,* until he be taken out of the way.—II Thess. 2:7

The apostle John and most Christians of his day—i.e. those not martyred—had to have lived long enough on earth to see the rise of nine

---

[157] "Letteth" [Gk. hindereth]: i.e. hinders the Antichrist from arising in the church. Nero was the last emperor before the rise of the "man of sin . . . son of perdition" [i.e. Antichrist]. Soon after his death "three of the first horns"; that is, Galba, Otho, and Vitellius, were "plucked up by the roots" [see Dan. 7:8] all in the year AD 69. We can easily see, then, why this passage contains the allusion to Nero. Before the Antichrist could arise **Nero** had to "be taken out of the way" [i.e. die]. It is a historical fact that Nero WAS taken out of the way before the rise of the Antichrist. On June 9, AD 68 Nero committed suicide, and Galba succeeded him about five months later.

"horns" or Caesars in the head of Daniel's fourth beast [see Dan. 7:7, 24]. Only Julius Caesar, antedating their time, was not *seen* of them.

In the last days of Jesus' generation they "saw," and *suffered* under, the last five Caesars: Nero, Galba, Otho, Vitellius, and Vespasian. The last four of these reigned one after another during the 3½-year Great Tribulation period [i.e. starting Jan., AD 69 and ending midsummer of 72].

In the single year AD 69 the three Caesars Galba, Otho, and Vitellius were "plucked up by the roots" [died without leaving an heir—see Dan. 7:8, 20, and 24]. That, of course, was the year of the rise of "another little horn" [i.e. the Antichrist] under the aegis, allowance, and short-lived protection of the Roman throne.[158]

> I considered the horns, and, behold, there came up among them another little horn, **before whom there were three of the first horns** [i.e. Galba, Otho, and Vitellius] **plucked up by the roots**: and, behold, in this horn *were* eyes like the eyes of man, and a mouth speaking great things [i.e. "blasphemies"—see Rev. 13:5-6]. I beheld till the thrones were cast down [i.e. till the reigns of Galba, Otho, and Vitellius were uprooted], and the Ancient of days did sit . . . judgment was set, and the books were opened.[159] I beheld *even* till **THE BEAST**[160] was slain, and his body destroyed, and given to the burning flame.—Dan. 7:8, 9a, 10d; 11b

(The Ten Horns in Revelation)

The policy of Rome toward religious diversity was very liberal, in that it gave people freedom of worship, providing they also participated

---

158 Thus, the Little Horn was called "diverse" from the first ten horns (Dan. 7:24). Rome protected it by the "power" of the ten horns (i.e. the ten Roman magistrates of Rev. 17:12-13) for only the 3½ years of the Great Tribulation. Then the ten magistrates or horns burned them up "with fire" (Rev. 17:16).

159 "The books were opened"—cf. Rev. 20:12.

160 **"THE BEAST"**—i.e. the Little Horn. The Little Horn no doubt was the same as "the beast having seven heads and ten horns" of Revelation (Rev. 13:1), the collective "antichrists" which "the Ancient of days" sentenced to be cast into the Lake of Fire [Dan. 7:9, 26; Rev. 20:15].

in the Caesar cult. Except for that, Roman freedom of religion was not unlike America's today.

This Caesar-worship was expected from all the people except the Jews, as a reward for their strategic cooperation with Rome in various Judean conflicts in the days of Pompey, Julius Caesar, and Octavian. Rome viewed the later Christian religion as a faction of Judaism, and thus extended to Christians the same special privileges earlier given to the Jews, such as the right to practice their religion, and exemption from the draft.

Thus, the Roman government did not mind the growth of Christ's disciples and the church at first. In fact, it appears that the laws of Rome protected any Christian who happened to also be a citizen of Rome, Paul for example. Twice Paul used his Roman citizenship to escape persecution, once at Philippi in AD 53 (Acts 16:36-40), and again seven years later in Jerusalem for allegedly bringing "Greeks . . . into the Temple" (Acts 21:28; 22:25). The Jews would have stoned him, but the Roman "chief captain" came and rescued him and, upon learning Paul was a Roman citizen waived having him scourged.

(The Pivotal Great Fire of Rome)

However, Rome abruptly canceled all Christian privileges after the Great Fire of Rome in AD 64. Nero caused this change when he accused Christians of setting the fire. Thus from that time writings about Christians, by both secular[161] and New Testament authors (i.e. Luke, Paul, Peter, and John), contain many allusions to intense persecution of Christians. Modern historians in this vein speak of "the *Neronian Persecution*," which I personally define as a Roman *policy of Christian extermination* that started with Nero and finally ended with Constantine's ascension in AD 313.

However, in this chapter we are interested in the period of Christian persecution that took place only in the reigns of Nero, Galba, Otho, Vitellius, and Vespasian [i.e. from AD 64-69]. About AD 64-65 Nero put Paul under house arrest in Rome, and soon had him beheaded

---

[161]   E.g. *The Life and Works of Flavius Josephus*, published in the interval of AD 75-79. Josephus (b. AD 37/38, Jerusalem—d. ca. AD 100, Rome)

[ca. AD 67]. John was apprehended in Ephesus for continuing to preach the gospel and sent as a philosophical/political antagonist to Patmos, the prison-island in the Aegean Sea. Meanwhile, Peter was exiled to Babylon on the eastern frontier of the empire—I Pet. 5:13; cf. John 20:18.

*(The Commissioning of Ten, Ad Hoc
Roman Magistrates in Asia to Oversee the Extermination of Christianity)*

Because of Nero's spreading terrorization and murder of Christians in Rome, thousands of survivors fled into Asia. Almost simultaneously, because of the Roman/Jewish war[162] taking place in the Holy Land beginning AD 66, many more thousands of Christians—*Jewish* Christians—fled their homeland and also aimed for Asia [I Pet. 1:1; James 1:1; cf. Luke 21:20-21].

Knowing this, Nero saw a chance to exterminate Christians from the earth once and for all. It was an obtainable goal since all Christians were cooping themselves up in Asia. He commanded that ten additional magistrates go to or be set up in Asia to bolster the existing court(s) there. By AD 69 the magistrates ordered the massacring of the "woman's man child" (this was the First Martyrdom Episode) rather like Hitler mass-murdered Jews in Europe during WWII. And the "woman" fled into the wilderness (Rev. 12:6, 14).

In the Book of Revelation John referred to these ten extra courts or Roman magistrates as "ten horns." *These* ten horns are not the same as the ten **horns** [i.e. **Caesars**] Daniel spoke of in Dan. 7:7. Daniel's ten *Caesars* succeeded each other, but John's ten magistrates worked in unison *at the same time*, as John said, in ". . . one hour" (Rev. 17:12). If they all exercised power in just "one hour," that hardly allows for John's ten horns to succeed each other, as did Daniel's ten "kings/Caesars" (see Dan. 7:24). Note in I Pet. 2:17 that Peter called Nero "the king"!

John wrote of the magistrates, "These have one mind, and shall give their power and strength unto the beast" (v. 13). We know from history that the ten Roman Caesars did not manifest "one mind." Each Caesar ruled the Empire in his own way, having different situations,

---

162 I.e. the First Jewish Revolt [AD 66-70]

problems, personalities, and relationships with many different people and countries. They each had their own, peculiar personality, and manner of ruling.

Revelation's ten horns worked in unison at the same time and dealt with the same people [e.g. the Christians in Asia]. It didn't matter whether or not they had different personalities because they were all following the orders of Nero who appointed them. Their work did not continue for over a century, only for the 3½-year period of the Great Tribulation. They did not deal with the problems of the entire empire, only with the "Christian problem" in Asia.

Moreover, Revelation's "beast . . . having seven heads and ten horns" collectively constituted Daniel's "another little horn" [cf. John's "antichrist," I John 2:18] which rose up in Asia in AD 69 to "change times" and persecute Christ's elect brethren for "a time, and times, and the dividing of time" (Dan. 7:25). Since the seven-headed beast comprised only powerless apostates it could not have acted without the Ten Horns that "received power as kings [i.e. magistrates] one hour with the beast" (i.e. with the Antichrist, Rev. 17:12).

Therefore, empowered by Nero's ten magistrates [i.e. Revelation's "ten horns"], the Antichrist in Asia amounted to a "little" Caesar [cf. "little horn" [163]] analogous to the ten "first" Caesars in Rome. But it exercised power on a much smaller scale—only in Asia—than that of the first ten Caesars who ruled over the entire Roman Empire. This is why the Holy Spirit called it "another **little** *horn*" or *Caesar* (Dan. 7:8). Interestingly, however, the Little Horn had a stouter "look" than the Caesars then reigning in Rome:

> And of the ten horns that *were* in his head, and *of* the other which came up, and before whom three fell; even *of* that horn that had eyes, and a mouth that spake very great things, whose look *was* more stout **than his fellows**.—Dan. 7:20

The Antichrist looked stouter to the Christians in Asia because: (1) his **"fellow"** Caesars then reigning in Rome—Galba, Otho, and Vitellius—were weak rulers about to be plucked up by the roots; and

---

[163] "Little horn"—i.e. See Dan. 7:8 for this expression.

(2) the Antichrist had the uninhibited power to ban *them* from the market places, and to kill them for not having the 666 tattoo on their right hand or on their forehead.

The Confiscation of Christian and Mammon Property, Goods, and Valuables

Christ looked forward to receiving His **_bride_** in Heaven shortly. Meantime, Satan had a *whore*, which John called "the great whore" whom he rewarded with great riches:

> And the woman was arrayed in purple and scarlet colour, and decked with gold and precious stones and pearls . . .
> —Rev. 17:4a

From whence did Satan get such rich gifts to give to this immoral woman? Undoubtedly he got them from two sources.

First, they came from the Christian martyrs—i.e. their real estate and furniture, clothing, tools, foodstuffs, and cooking utensils, just to name a few of their costly belongings]. The martyrs—martyrs from both the First and Second martyrdom Episodes—numbered 35,000 souls. Though they had not been rich people, yet all their collective properties and possessions, when confiscated and put into one place, amounted to a substantial little treasure.

The second and much greater source no doubt came from the Mammon who had departed their city properties and businesses in order to nourish the woman in the Asian wilderness (Rev. 12, 6, 14). The Ten Horns confiscated all that the Mammon had left behind in the cities—e.g. their considerable real-estate, homes, personal belongings, shops, stores, warehouses, all no doubt amounting to a king's ransom.

All these goods and products, from both the Christians and the Mammon are described in Rev. 18:11-13. The following is a categorized list of the kinds of costly valuables they left behind:

- "gold, and silver, and precious stones, and . . . pearls" (Rev. 18:12a);
- "fine linen, and purple, and silk, and scarlet" (v. 12b);

- "thyine wood, and all manner vessels of ivory, and all manner vessels of most precious wood, and of brass, and iron, and marble" (v. 12c);
- "cinnamon, and odours, and ointments, and frankincense" (13a);
- "wine, and oil, and fine flour, and wheat" (v. 13b);
- "beasts, and sheep, and horses, and chariots" (v. 13c);
- "slaves, and souls of men" (v. 13d).

But Satan had deceived the whore, so that she did not enjoy these luxuries for very long. Note what happened to her:

> And the ten horns which thou sawest upon the beast, these shall hate the whore, and shall make her desolate and naked, and shall eat her flesh, and burn her with fire.—Rev. 17:16

"The great whore" was like a mistress to the collective membership of the seven-headed beast, all of whom had committed "spiritual" fornication with her.

The Holy Spirit gave her the elaborate moniker of "MYSTERY, BABYLON THE GREAT, THE MOTHER OF HARLOTS AND ABOMINATIONS OF THE EARTH" (Rev. 17:5).

Jesus described her in His letter to the church at Thyatira as "that woman Jezebel, which calleth herself a prophetess, to teach and to seduce my servants to commit fornication and to eat things sacrificed unto idols" (Rev. 2:20). She, along with "the beast" is finally cast into the Lake of Fire (Rev. 20:10, 14-15).

God moved the Ten Horns—the same Ten Horns that had earlier empowered the whore—to suddenly turn against her and burn her with fire. [164]

God did not Punish the Ten Horns

Yes, the Ten Horns began to "hate" Babylon, "that great city" and "the great whore," and set her on fire, destroying her during one hour

---

[164]   See Rev. 17:12, 16.

of one day (Rev. 18:8, 10). All who had been made rich by her—merchants, shipmasters, sailors, and likely also the Roman court officials—stood:

> . . . afar off for the fear of her torment, weeping and wailing, And saying, Alas, alas, that great city [i.e. "Babylon"], that was clothed in fine linen, and purple, and scarlet, and decked with gold, and precious stones, and pearls! For in one hour so great riches is come to nought. And every shipmaster, and all the company in ships, and sailors, and as many as trade by sea, stood afar off, And cried when they saw the smoke of her burning, saying, What city is like unto this great city?—Rev. 18:15-18

But what became of the Ten Horns? Did God punish them too? No, Revelation is not about God punishing worldly people. Thus, each of the ten horns lived out his normal life span on earth, then died.

Also, Revelation is not about the end of this world, but the end of the church on earth and God's punishment of the 70,000 church members that fell away from Christ in the years of AD 64-68.

Their punishment was threefold. First, they lost their High-Calling salvation [i.e. their eternal life and their inheritance in the kingdom of Heaven]. Second, they died a horrible death in the Lake of Fire [Rev. 17:16; cf. 20:14-15]. I'll tell you the third way after you read the next paragraph.

Though God cast them into the Lake of Fire, don't forget! Afterward God reincarnated them and took them into Paradise to teach them the paths of righteousness [Heb. 12:6-11]. There they lived out their millennial life span God intended for all men.

But this meant a third way God punished them [i.e. "the kings of the earth"[165]]. By making them wait nearly a thousand years before glorifying them with eternal life and an inheritance in His kingdom, the Christian brethren they were with in the past wound up having a millennial advantage over them.

---

[165] "kings of the earth"—See Rev. 6:15; 17:18; 18:1.

Thus, they were one thousand years *behind* Christ's faithful, first-century brethren in Asia—their then contemporaries—that had kept the church *viable*[166] until ca. Jan. 15, AD 69.

Thus, after a thousand years their reward was much less than that of their faithful and once contemporary brethren of a thousand years earlier. Their eternal life was diminished by a thousand years, and their inheritance in the kingdom was diminished by the number of people they would have ruled over had they never apostatized.

SECTION IV:
A WOMAN, A MAN CHILD,
AND THE REMNANT

(1) And there appeared a great wonder in heaven; **a woman** clothed with the sun, and the moon under her feet, and upon her head a crown of twelve stars; (2) And she being with child cried, travailing in birth, and pained to be delivered. (3) And there appeared another wonder in heaven; and behold, a great red dragon, having seven heads and ten horns, and seven crowns upon his heads. (4) And his tail drew the third part of the stars of heaven, and did cast them to the earth: and the dragon stood before the woman which was ready to be delivered, for to devour her child as soon as it was born. (5) And she brought forth **a man child**, who was to rule all nations with a rod of iron: and her child was **caught up unto God**, and *to* his throne . . . (17) And the dragon was wroth with the woman, and went to **make war with the remnant of her seed**, which keep the commandments of God, and have the testimony of Jesus Christ.—Rev. 12:1-5, 17

(The Woman)

The woman in Rev. 12 was the espoused and soon-to-be bride of Jesus Christ. Specifically, she comprised the 105,000 Christian survivors in Asia after the First Martyrdom episode. Her crown of twelve stars shows that the church was made up only of the twelve tribes of Israel

---

166 Viable church. The viable church was the church of Christ while it was still holy—i.e. before the Antichrist entered it and turned it into "the habitation of devils, and the hold of every foul spirit, and a cage of every unclean and hateful bird" (Rev. 18:2).

[cf. Rev. 7:4-8]. The sun, moon, and stars indicate that she was not of this world,[167] but of Heavenly citizenship. Paul, one person not included in the 105,000, emphatically stated that her "conversation" [i.e. citizenship] was in heaven:

> For **OUR** conversation is in heaven; from whence also **WE** look for the Saviour, the Lord Jesus Christ.—Phil. 3:20

Therefore he gave her the following advice:

> If **YE** then be risen with Christ, seek those things which are above, where Christ sitteth on the right hand of God. Set **YOUR** affection on things above [i.e. in Heaven], not on things on the earth.—Col. 3:1-2

The woman went into labor and delivered a man child. Her "labor" represents her troubled and sorrowful soul in anticipation of the "day of the Lord" [cf. II Thess. 2:2]. She knew that her flight into the wilderness was imminent, and that Satan was about to "devour" her man child.

(The Man Child and the Remnant)

The **man child** (v. 5) comprised the martyrs of the First Martyrdom Episode. The "first beast" began martyring them in the First Martyrdom Episode at the beginning of the Great Tribulation [ca. Jan. 15, AD 69]. They also comprised the "great multitude" that "no **MAN**" could count,[168] yet the Holy Spirit **REVEALED** their number as 31,500.

But the Fourth Seal revealed that God allowed Satan to kill a total of 35,000 Christians in Asia—one-fourth of the 140,000 elect ***church*** brethren of Christ that remained faithful to Him during the apostasy years [approx. AD 64-68]:

> And I looked, and behold a pale horse: and his name that sat on him was Death, and Hell followed with him. And power was

---

[167] See John 17:14-18.
[168] See Rev. 7:9.

given unto them over **the fourth part** of the earth, to kill with sword, and with hunger, and with death, and with the beasts of the earth.—Rev. 6:8

If we subtract 31,500 from the total of 35,000 we get 3,500 more Christians yet to be martyred, but in the Second Martyrdom Episode. We learn from Rev. 11 that the Holy Spirit called these 3,500 martyrs the **"two witnesses"** that were slain for Christ's name's sake just three and one half days before Christ's Second Coming (see Rev. 11:9 & 11; & p. 269, FN#292; & Appendix E, pp. 293-295).

Thus, we may also equate these 3,500 martyrs with both the woman's *"remnant"* and with Christ's martyrs killed in the Second Martyrdom Episode (Rev. 6:11).

But there is more to say about the identity of the **remnant** (the "remnant" is mentioned in Rev. 12:17). Jesus foretold this remnant in His Olivet Prophecy:

> But before all these, they shall lay their hands on you, and persecute *you*, delivering *you* up to the synagogues, and into prisons, being **brought before kings** and rulers for my name's sake. And **it shall turn to you for a testimony**. Settle *it* therefore in your hearts, **not to meditate before what ye shall answer:**[169] For I will give you a mouth and wisdom, which all your adversaries shall not be able to gainsay nor resist. And ye shall be betrayed both by parents, and brethren, and kinsfolks, and friends; and *some* of you shall they cause to be put to death. And ye shall be hated of all *men* for my name's sake. But **there shall not an hair of your head perish**.—Luke 21:12-18

---

[169] "not to meditate before what ye shall answer" (Luke 21:14). In Rev. 10 the **"little book open"** (v. 2) contained the words that the Holy Spirit would soon put into the mouths of Jesus' martyrs [in Asia] in their defense before the Ten Horns. John heard the words in the "seven thunders" and would have written them in Revelation, but "a voice" from Heaven forbade it (v. 4). Had John written them the martyrs would have studied them and broken Jesus' command **NOT** to premeditate on what they might "answer" their accusers. (See also Matt. 10:17-20 & Luke 12:11).

Note the words ". . . there shall not an hair of your head perish." This is an important clue that Jesus was foretelling Revelation's Two Witnesses in this passage. No wonder not a hair of their head perished! Jesus appeared and resurrected them just three and a half days after they died, certainly not enough time for any part of their bodies to begin decaying, not even a hair of their head:

> **And after three days and an half the Spirit of life from God entered into them, and they stood upon their feet**; and great fear fell upon them which saw them. And they heard a great voice from heaven saying unto them, Come up hither. And they ascended up to heaven in a cloud; and their enemies beheld them.[170]—Rev. 11:11-12

The Fifth Seal Is About Both the Man Child and the Remnant.

In the Fifth Seal we see both the *man child* and the *remnant* of the woman. We see that there were going to be **two different episodes** of Christian martyrdom in Asia. The dragon's devouring of the man child was the First Martyrdom Episode and the killing of their brethren [i.e. "the remnant" of Rev. 12:17] a "little season" later was the Second Martyrdom Episode:

> And when he [Jesus] had opened the fifth seal, I saw under the altar the souls of them [**i.e. the man child**] that were slain for the word of God, and for the testimony which they held: And they cried with a loud voice, saying, How long, O Lord, holy and true, dost thou not judge and avenge our blood on them that dwell on the earth? And white robes were given unto every one of them; and it was said unto them, that they should rest yet for a little season, until their fellow-servants also and their brethren, that should be killed as they were [**i.e. the remnant**], should be fulfilled.—Rev. 6:9-11

---

[170] "and their enemies beheld them"—See Rev. 1:7.

SECTION V:
"THE REST OF THE DEAD"

> But **the rest of the dead** lived not again until the thousand years were finished. This *is* the first resurrection. Blessed and holy is he that hath part in the first resurrection: on such the second death hath no power.—Rev. 20:5

Few have *carefully* read this passage. It says that "the rest of the dead" were to have part in "the first resurrection." That is, they were to have eternal life and inherit the kingdom of God. This being so their names were certainly found written in the Book of Life and God could not have cast them into the Lake of Fire (see Rev. 20:15).

With whom were they to have part in the first resurrection? Answer: the 14**0**,000 church elect. The rest of the dead, numbering 4,000 and added to the 140,000, brought Jesus' full number of elect brethren to 14**4**,000.

> And I heard the number of them which were sealed: *and there were* sealed an hundred *and* forty *and* **four thousand** of all the tribes of the children of Israel.—Rev. 7:4

These extra 4,000 **very rich** elect brethren, however, were never church members but were elected by Jesus during the Great Tribulation *after* the church age [i.e. the "thousand years"] had ended on earth [ca. Jan. 15, AD 69]. It was at that time that about 105,000 church elect had to flee into the wilderness to escape the Beast, False Prophet, and Ten Horns. They fled hastily, taking nothing with them, in obedience to Christ's command:

> Then let them which be in Judea[171] [i.e. defined here as Jesus' elect brethren in Asia] flee into the mountains: Let him

---

[171] Apocalyptic: "Judea," viz., Christ's church elect in Asia. The reason the Christians in Asia could be symbolized by the word "Judea" is because they constituted the "body" of Jesus [see e.g. Rom. 12:5; I Cor. 6:19; 12:27; Eph. 1:22-23], the Jew who saved them: "salvation is of the Jews" (John 4:22). Also, they were the true "Jerusalem," as revealed in Scripture (see Gal. 4:26 & Heb. 12:22), the capital city of ***Judea***.

which is on the housetop not come down to take any thing out
of his house: Neither let him which is in the field return back to
take his clothes.—Matt. 24:16-18

Thus they entered the wilderness with hardly anything more than
the clothes they had on. How were they to survive in the wilderness
for 3½ years? Who had the resources to feed and nourish 105,000
people for three and a half long years: to keep them supplied with
food, drink, medicine, clothing, and shelter? (Jesus called [elected]
"the rest of the dead"—***very rich men;*** that is, "***MAMMON***"[172]—to do
just that). These 105,000 church elect constituted the woman in the
wilderness (Rev. 12:6, 14), and "the rest of the dead" were the **"they"**
in the following verse:

> And the woman fled into the wilderness, where she hath
> a place prepared of God, that **THEY** should feed her there a
> thousand two hundred *and* threescore days.—Rev. 12:6

Also, dear reader, remember that "the rest of the dead" are alluded
to numerous times in the New Testament. They were the helpers (Matt.
10:40-42); the eleventh-hour hires (Matt. 20:6, 9); the sheep (Matt.
25:32); and the Mammon (Luke 16:9).

SECTION VI:
"THE HEAVENS AND EARTH
WHICH ARE NOW"

In his Second Epistle, chapter three, Peter's language is largely
apocalyptic and is based partly on the flood of Noah and partly on
Jesus' end-time teachings (i.e. His Olivet Discourse).

Note right off that Peter's context is the "last days." Remember that
the last days came to pass during the latter years of Jesus' generation:

> Knowing this first, that there shall come **in the LAST DAYS**
> scoffers, walking after their own lusts, And saying, Where is
> the promise of his coming? for since the fathers fell asleep, all

---

[172] See Luke 16:9.

things continue as they were from the beginning of the creation.
—II Pet. 3:3-4

Here the words "shall come" speak of things on the verge of happening to Christians during Jesus' generation—i.e. to Peter and to the very first readers of his two epistles. I know this because the Holy Spirit inspired Peter to declare it in the plainest possible language, and to do so several times! Since God's Spirit stressed this truth so firmly and consistently, if the things he told Peter to write did not come to pass during Jesus' generation, the Holy Spirit Himself was at fault.

Please note what the Holy Spirit inspired Peter to write in *the most unambiguous language possible to the human tongue*:

> Receiving the end of your faith, even the salvation of your souls. Of which salvation the prophets have inquired and searched diligently, who prophesied of the grace that should come unto YOU: Searching what, or what manner of TIME the Spirit of Christ which was in them did signify, when it testified beforehand the sufferings of Christ, and the glory that should follow [i.e. soon follow, not centuries later]. Unto whom it was revealed, that not unto themselves, but unto US they did minister the things, which are NOW reported unto YOU by them [Christ's apostles] that have preached the gospel unto you with the HOLY GHOST sent down from heaven; which things the angels desire to look into. Wherefore gird up the loins of YOUR mind, be sober, and hope to THE END for the grace that is to be brought unto YOU at the revelation [i.e. Second Coming] of Jesus Christ.—I Pet. 1:9-13

> Forasmuch as ye know that ye were not redeemed with corruptible things, as silver and gold, from your vain conversation received by tradition from your fathers; But with the precious blood of Christ, as of a lamb without blemish and without spot: Who verily was foreordained before the foundation of the world, but was manifest in THESE last times for YOU.—I Pet. 1:18-20

> . . . THE END or all things is AT HAND: be YE therefore sober, and watch unto prayer.—I Pet. 4:7

For the TIME is come that judgment must begin at the house of God.—I Pet. 4:17

Conclusion: Anyone who can read these Scriptures and still hold that the LAST DAYS and Jesus Christ's SECOND COMING could still be in **OUR** future is simply not getting Peter's meaning. Either that or he is *unbelieving* of Holy Scripture. See John 20:27; Rom. 15:13; I Pet. 1:8.

A Closer Look at "Shall Come" by Comparing II Pet. 3:3 with II Pet. 2:1-3

O reader, do not be unbelieving, but believing. Do you not now see that "shall come" in II Pet. 3:3 is not to be interpreted to mean any future time beyond Christ's or Peter's generation? In fact, Peter's "shall come" does not refer to the Last Days, as if the last days themselves were still to come, because he makes it plain that they were ALREADY ongoing. The words, rather, pertain to "scoffers." In other words it was the **"*scoffers*"** that "shall come," and not the last days.

We can see this by looking at the *chronology* of prophetic events. Chronologists tell us that Peter wrote his epistles ca. AD 64-65, somewhat *before* AD 69, or the time [according to Daniel] that the Antichrist would bully his way into the "temple of God"; that is, *into the first-century church of Christ.* See II Thess. 2:4; cf. I Cor. 3:16.

Thus, the Last Days were already ongoing, but the **scoffers** [false teachers] had not yet arrived in the churches. Proof of this is seen in the future tense helping verb "shall" in the following passage:

> But there were false prophets also among the people [i.e. among Israelites in Old Testament days], even as there **SHALL** be false teachers [i.e. scoffers] among you, who privily **SHALL** bring in damnable heresies, even denying the Lord that bought them, and bring upon themselves swift [Gk. soon] destruction. And many [Christians] **SHALL** follow their pernicious ways; by reason of whom the way of truth **SHALL** be evil spoken of [i.e. scoffed].—II Pet. 2:1-2

Dear reader, having said all this, we should know now that the Second Coming of Jesus, the "end" of the church age [or, church **cosmos**], the appearing of the Antichrist [scoffers], and the Last

Judgment all happened before Jesus' generation passed away, just like Jesus said events would happen:

> Verily I say unto you, This generation [i.e. His own] shall not pass away, till all [end time events] be fulfilled.—Luke 21:32

We understand, then, that because everything Peter foretold in his epistles took place before Jesus' generation ended, that this effectively refutes the futurists who say Jesus has **_yet_** to come, and that the literal "heavens and the earth which are now" (II Pet. 3:7) are **_yet_** to be destroyed. If they were not *literally* destroyed **_before_** Jesus' generation ended, is that not absolute proof that the *literal interpretation* of them is false?

(An Incontrovertible Basis
Upon Which to Interpret
All Events Peter Spoke of in
II Peter Three)

Dear reader, as believers of Scripture, we are bound to likewise accept that Jesus Christ's Second Coming and all other end time prophetic events came to pass nearly two thousand years ago. I have shown over and over again in this book that this is an **_incontrovertible_** Biblical teaching. Both Jesus and His apostles agreed upon this truth in all that they spoke or wrote. I am compelled, therefore, to interpret and paraphrase each of the following verses according to this irrefutable _REVELATION_ OF THE HOLY SPIRIT.

Interpreting II Pet. 3:5-13 by Paraphrase

Dear reader, what follows are my paraphrases of all nine verses in II Pet. 3:5-13. The passage on its surface seems to say that the literal heavens and earth were soon to be destroyed by fire. But when we know from the Holy Spirit that all end time prophesies were to be fulfilled *before* Jesus' generation passed away, it *follows* that an interpreter must look at the words "heavens" and "earth" symbolically, not literally. Whatever they symbolize God was about to pour out His wrath upon them in Peter's day.

We must ask this question, therefore: WHAT CAN WE POINT TO, REVEALED IN THE BIBLE, THAT GOD COULD HAVE BEEN SO SET ON DESTROYING, AND SO SOON? Whatever we find that answers that question is the true meaning of Peter's "heaven" and "earth."

Reader, it was the church apostates ("many antichrists"—I John 2:18) that God was about to destroy with fire. Jesus, Paul, the Hebrews author, Jude, and John made that very plain:

> The Son of man shall send forth his angels, and they shall gather out of his kingdom all things [i.e. Christian apostates] that offend, and them which do iniquity; And shall **cast them into a furnace of fire:** there shall be wailing and gnashing of teeth.—Matt. 13:41

> So shall it be at the end of the world: the angels shall come forth, and sever the wicked [i.e. Christian apostates] from among the just, And shall cast them into the furnace of fire: there shall be wailing and gnashing of teeth.—Matt. 13:49-50

> For *it is* impossible for those [i.e. apostate Christians] who were once enlightened, and have tasted of the heavenly gift, and were made partakers of the Holy Ghost, And have tasted the good word of God, and the powers of the world to come, If they [church members in Jesus' generation] shall fall away, to renew them again unto repentance; seeing they crucify to themselves the Son of God afresh, and put *him* to an open shame. For the earth [cf. first-century church membership] which drinketh in the rain [cf. Holy Spirit] that cometh oft upon it, and bringeth forth herbs meet for them by whom it is dressed, receiveth blessing from God: But that which beareth thorns and briers [e.g. fear, disobedience, apostasy, etc.] *is* rejected, and *is* **nigh unto cursing; whose end** *is* **["shortly"—Rev. 1:1] to be burned.**—Heb. 6:4-8

> For if **WE** [Christians during Jesus' generation] sin willfully [apostatize] after that **WE** have received the knowledge of the truth, there remaineth no more sacrifice for sins, But a certain fearful looking for of judgment **and fiery indignation, which shall devour the adversaries**.—Heb. 10:26-27

Every man's [i.e. Christian's] work shall be made manifest: for the day shall declare it, because it shall be revealed by *fire*; and **the fire shall try every man's work** of what sort it is. If any man's work abide which he hath built thereupon, he shall receive a reward. **If any man's work shall be burned**, he shall suffer loss: but he himself shall be saved; **yet so as by fire**. —I Cor. 3:13-15

And to you who are troubled rest with us, when the Lord Jesus shall be revealed from heaven with his mighty angels, In flaming fire taking vengeance on them that know not God, and that obey not the gospel of our Lord Jesus Christ. **Who shall be punished with everlasting destruction** from the presence of the Lord, and from the glory of his power—II Thess. 1:7-9

And then shall that Wicked [i.e. "man of sin" (II Thess. 2:3)] be revealed, **whom the Lord shall consume** with the spirit of his mouth, and shall destroy with the brightness of his coming —II Thess. 2:8

And others save with fear, **pulling *them* out of the fire**; hating even the garment spotted by the flesh.—Jude 23

And the beast was taken, and with him the false prophet that wrought miracles before him, with which he deceived them that had received the mark of the beast, and them that worshipped his image. **These both were cast alive into the lake of fire burning with brimstone**.—Rev. 19:20

And they [Gog and Magog; i.e. Christian apostates in Asia] went up on the breadth of the earth, and compassed the camp of the saints about, and the beloved city: **and fire came down from God out of heaven, and devoured them**.—Rev. 20:9

And whosoever was not found written in the book of life was cast into the lake of fire.—Rev. 20:15

Reader, note that everywhere in God's holy word it is PEOPLE ["many antichrists"—I John 2:18] that are destroyed by fire and brimstone, not the literal heavens and earth. Yes, Peter's writing genre makes many Christians today think that the literal heavens and earth are yet to be burned up. However, Peter wasn't trying to mislead anybody. It is too clear that he expected his FIRST reading audience to understand his *apocalyptic* language and its imminent *time setting*.

Now John also spoke of God judging the heavens and earth, but note how he spoke of them:

> And I saw a great white throne, and he that sat on it, from whose face **the earth and the heaven fled away; and there was found no place for them.**—Rev. 20:11

Here John speaks of the heaven and earth as Peter did. However, note that John says they "fled away" from the Judge sitting on the Great White Throne. Is it logical to think that the material, morally-neutral earth could fear God or that heavenly bodies would flee away from Him? No, it is against all theology and human reason (to say nothing of physics) to think this.

Reader, doesn't both common sense and Scripture tell us that it was the _Antichrist_ that fled from the Judge on the Throne because they feared His wrath?

> And said [i.e. John's "many antichrists" of I John 2:18 said] to the mountains and rocks, Fall on us, and hide us from the face of him that sitteth on the throne, and from the wrath of the Lamb: For the great day of his wrath is come; and who shall be able to stand?—Rev. 6:16-17

Doesn't this suggest that in the apocalyptic genre it is fitting to equate "the heavens and the earth" with the Beast and False Prophet (cf. Matt. 24:29, 35; Rev. 12:7-9)?

In support of this, note that it was said of the heaven and earth, that they "fled away" and that "there was found no **place** for them." Scripture uses the word "place" to indicate one's having a "part" in; that is, a "habitation" in or an "inheritance" in the kingdom of Heaven (cf. Dan. 2:35; Acts 1:20, 25; Rev. 20:11).

PARAPHRASES

The following paraphrases of II Pet. 3:5-13 will show a sensible, theological interpretation of God's wrath against the "heaven" and the "earth." Remember, dear reader, the incontrovertible truth that all end time prophecies were fulfilled **_before_** Jesus' generation passed away (Luke 21:22, 32). This irrefutable truth is a basic rationale by which all Scripture dealing with the end time must be interpreted. Thus, the following paraphrases reflect that rationale:

> For this they willingly are ignorant of, that by the word of God the heavens were of old, and the earth standing out of the water and in the water:—II Pet. 3:5 (KJV)
> The scoffers are conveniently forgetful that God sent the Flood in Noah's day and . . .—II Pet. 3:5 paraphrased

> Whereby the world that then was, being overflowed with water, perished.—II Pet. 3:6 (KJV)
> . . . flooded the antediluvian world, drowning untold millions of wicked people.—II Pet. 3:6 paraphrased

> But the heavens and the earth, which are now, by the same word are kept in store, reserved unto fire against the day of judgment and perdition of ungodly men.—II Pet. 3:7 (KJV)
> But today it is the "world" of the scoffers and antichrists that God is reserving for imminent destruction on judgment day. II Pet. 3:7 paraphrased

> But, beloved, be not ignorant of this one thing, that one day _is_ with the Lord as a thousand years, and a thousand years as one day.—II Pet. 3:8 (KJV)
> But beloved, don't be ignorant that God counts Jesus Christ's generation as a thousand years, and "the thousand years" as Christ's generation. II Pet. 3:8 paraphrased

> The Lord is not slack concerning his promise, as some men count slackness; but is longsuffering to us-ward, not willing that any should perish, but that all should come to repentance.—II Pet. 3:9 (KJV)
> God is not forgetful of Jesus' Second Coming as the antichrists are speculating, but is giving them a little more time to repent. II Pet. 3:9 paraphrased

But the day of the Lord will come as a thief in the night; in the which the heavens shall pass away with a great noise, and the elements shall melt with fervent heat, the earth also and the works that are therein shall be burned up.—II Pet. 3:10 (KJV)

But Jesus' Second Coming will overtake them as a thief in the night, and they will scream out loudly for mercy. Every element of their bodies will melt as they (here symbolized as "heaven") burn at the stake. Moreover, their works will burn up with them. II Pet. 3:10 paraphrased

Seeing then *that* all these things shall be dissolved, what manner *of persons* ought ye to be in *all* holy conversation and godliness,—II Pet. 3:11 (KJV)

Seeing then that all antichrists and their works shall go up in flames, what manner of holiness and godliness ought you to maintain . . . II Pet. 3:11 paraphrased

Looking for and hasting unto the coming of the day of God, wherein the heavens being on fire shall be dissolved, and the elements shall melt with fervent heat?—II Pet. 3:12 (KJV)

. . . as you watch expectantly for Christ's coming, when the antichrists' very bodily elements will dissolve in intense heat? II Pet. 3:12 paraphrased

Nevertheless we, according to his promise, look for new heavens and a new earth, wherein dwelleth righteousness.—II Pet. 3:13

We, however, according to God's promise, look for Bephzibah in Beulah Land [i.e. restored Jerusalem in Paradise] wherein only righteousness dwells. II Pet. 3:13 paraphrased. Cf. Is. 1:26 and 62:4.

SECTION VII:
THE "NEW HEAVENS
AND A NEW EARTH"

A careful and in-depth study of the new heavens and earth leads to a remarkable conclusion: *the new heavens and new earth have been in existence ever since Adam's generation!* Five Biblical truths considered together show that this must be true:

(A. God's "In the Beginning" Truth)

God's eternal purpose is plainly discerned by the wonderful things God gave and did for Adam and Eve "in the beginning"—e.g. life itself, and the paradisiacal Garden of Eden. Jesus taught this truth to the Pharisees who had asked Him whether or not Moses' Law allowed them to divorce their wives "for every cause" (Matt. 19:3). Jesus answered in the negative by pointing out to them what God's **_original_** purpose in marriage was. He said to them:

> Have ye not read, that he which made *them* **at the beginning** made them male and female, And said, For this cause shall a man leave father and mother, and shall cleave to his wife: and they twain shall be one flesh? Wherefore they are no more twain, but one flesh. What therefore God hath joined together, let not man put asunder.—Matt. 19:4-6

Then Jesus added:

> . . . from the beginning it [i.e. divorce] was not so. —Matt. 19:8b

In this saying we see a **_basic truth_** by which soteriologists[173] can correctly understand the full extent of God's salvation of mankind: i.e. *that ALL the good things God gave and planned for men "in the beginning"* [seen in Gen. 1-11] *now belong to mankind again through Jesus' death.*

---

[173] Soteriologists are theologians that specialize in the study of God's salvation of man.

Soteriologists by this principle may now correctly define God's salvation of man as follows: ***The restoring to <u>all</u> men <u>all</u> the things God gave and did for Adam and Eve in the Garden of Eden.***

Peter received understanding of this truth after God baptized him with the Holy Spirit on the day of Pentecost. He now understood the *universal salvation* underway in Paradise above:

> Jesus Christ . . . whom the **heaven** [Paradise] must receive [hold; keep] until **the times of RESTITUTION OF ALL THINGS [in Paradise],** which God hath spoken by the mouth of all his holy prophets **since the world began**.
> —Acts 3:20-21

In other words Peter said that Jesus Christ had begun on that very day [i.e. of Pentecost], by the power His Father had given Him on His throne,[174] to restore to mankind all the original gifts and blessings clearly purposed by God from the beginning.

When He finished restoring all things He would "come again"[175] with "his angels"[176] and collect His elect brethren "from one end of heaven to the other."[177] These same angels would catch them up[178] into "the clouds/air"[179] and Jesus would "receive" them unto Himself[180] *as the New Jerusalem and His Bride* (Rev. 21:2). Thus, He did not "receive" them on this earth, but in Paradise, and in Heaven to their Father (cf. John 14:3, 6, 12c, and 20:17).

This means that from the air Jesus and the elect would ***ascend*** to the Father's presence [cf. the Tabernacle's or Temple's innermost room called the Holy of Holies, or the Holiest Place].[181] At that time their name would be "the city of my God, *which is* new Jerusalem."[182]

---

[174] See Rev. 3:21.
[175] John 14:3; Acts 3:19-20; Heb. 9:28
[176] Matt. 16:27; 24:31; I Thess. 4:16
[177] Matt. 24:31
[178] I.e. in the Rapture (see Matt. 24:40-41; I Thess. 4:17a)
[179] I Thess. 4:17
[180] John 14:3; cf. Psalm 49:15
[181] John 14:12c, 28; Eph. 4:10; Heb. 2:17-18; 4:14; 6:20; 8:1; 9:3, 24
[182] Rev. 3:12; 21:2, 10

In this holy "City" Jesus and His brethren, all 144,000 of them, would sit together at "the marriage supper of the Lamb,"[183] for which event, John wrote, "his wife hath made herself ready,"[184] being "arrayed in fine linen, clean and white." [185] After the supper Jesus would give her to sit with Him on His throne.[186]

Then together they would come "from God [the Father] out of heaven"—i.e. out of *H*eaven (i.e. the "Highest"; see Rev. 21:2; cf. Luke 6:35)—"down" to Paradise [i.e. to "a new heaven and a new earth"—Rev. 21:1]. The Holy Spirit inspired Paul to call the new heaven and earth "the third **heaven**,"[187]and Peter to add: ". . . wherein dwelleth righteousness."[188]

Peter's words "wherein dwelleth righteousness" tell us that he was then expecting Jesus' imminent completion of "the restitution of all things" in Paradise (Acts 3:21), including "all Israel"—i.e. all the Jews of Jesus' generation (Rom. 11:26).

Let me stress that John did not see the New Jerusalem [i.e. Jesus and His Bride] come down out of Heaven to the "former" earth, or to *this* earth. The context forbids us to think this. Rev. 21:1 specifically speaks of the **"new earth,"** meaning the Third Heaven or Paradise (II Cor. 12:2, 4). Verse 4 says that "the former things" [i.e. from the perspective of the 144,000] had "passed away." In English "passed away" is interpretable as *annihilated* or *destroyed*, but in the original language [Greek] the correct meaning is "passed alongside" [i.e. this "former" earth passed <u>alongside</u> the "new earth"]. Also, note that in Rev. 21:1 the "new earth" is firmly established as the correct and only context. So there can be no other conclusion but that the New Jerusalem came down to Paradise, the NEW earth, not to ***this*** earth.

SATAN—originally called "Lucifer" [Is. 14:12]—is the ruler of *this* earth or world (see Matt. 13:22; Luke 4:5-8; John 14:30; 17:14; 18:36; II Cor. 4:4; Col. 3:1-4; Rev. 12:9). That will never change, because

---

183 Rev. 19:9
184 Rev. 19:7
185 Rev. 19:8
186 Rev. 3:21
187 II Cor. 12:2, 4
188 II Pet. 3:13

God is not one to take back what He gives to a being, in this case Lucifer. Paul put it this way:

> God's gifts and God's call are under full warranty—never canceled, never rescinded.—Rom. 11:29, *The Message*

The Creator made him the god of this world "from the beginning," and that is why we see him in the Garden of Eden:

> Thou [i.e. Lucifer, who became Satan] hast been in Eden the Garden of God . . . Thou *wast* perfect in thy ways from the day that thou wast created, till iniquity was found in thee.—Ezek. 28:13a, 15

Why would the Father create new heavens and the new earth and then put Jesus' Bride back in the former earth? There would be constant and endless warfare between good and evil. It is in Paradise that God returns to the inhabitants the "very good"[189] life He intended mankind to have "from the beginning," and continue to do it for all future generations.

Yes, in the New Earth people have the blessings God gave Adam and Eve "in the beginning" [before Adam sinned]. Dear reader, if you will read Gen. 1-11 carefully, you will see the kinds of blessings God will give us all one day when *we* enter Paradise:

- a paradise environment; Gen. 2:8
- water for plant growth without the inconvenience of rain; 2:5-6, 10
- tasty, nutritious food always at arms length; 2:16; cf. 3:6
- no hard labor; 2:16
- a strong, healthy, "very good" flesh-and-blood body or soul; 2:7 [see also 1:31]
- God's presence among men, assuring individual guidance and instruction; 2:16
- true science; 2:19-20 [contrast *false* science—I Tim. 6:20]
- tame, beautiful, and helpful animals around them; 2:19

---

[189] "very good"—See Gen. 1:31.

- for the unmarried, a suitable spouse provided and selected by God Himself; 2:21-22
- God as marriage counselor; 2:24; cf. 3:16c and Matt. 19:3-6
- Wives give birth without pain or sorrow; 1:28a and 3:16
- a proper relationship between husband and wife, and between them and their parents; cf. 2:24 and 3:16c
- marital oneness; 2:24
- centuries of marital fertility;—1:28; cf. 5:1-5
- millennial life span in mortal bodies; 5:1-32
- a universal language; 11:1, 6
- mankind divided into separate nations within separate boundaries; cf. 11:8
- human, fish, fowl, plant, and animal life throughout a Garden-of-Eden habitat; 1:20-28; 9:1-3
- God only is the source of the knowledge of good and evil, not man's eyes or his human reasoning—2:17; 3:1-11

(B. God Is Sovereign and Unchangeable.)

The Bible everywhere teaches that God's will and purpose are eternal and unchangeable:

> Let all the earth fear the LORD: let all the inhabitants of the world stand in awe of him. For he spake, and it was *done;* he commanded, and it stood fast. The LORD bringeth the counsel of the heathen to nought: he maketh the devices of the people of none effect. The counsel of the LORD standeth for ever, the thoughts of his heart to all generations.—Psalm 33:8-11

> And all the inhabitants of the earth *are* reputed as nothing: and he doeth according to HIS will in the army of heaven, and *among* the inhabitants of the earth: and none can stay his hand, or say unto him, What doest thou?—Dan. 4:35

> I [i.e. Darius] make a decree, That in every dominion of my kingdom men tremble and fear before the God of Daniel: for he *is* the living God, and stedfast for ever, and his kingdom *that* which shall not be destroyed, and his dominion *shall be even* unto the end. He delivereth and rescueth, and he worketh signs

and wonders in heaven and in earth, who hath delivered Daniel from the power of the lions.—Dan. 6:26-27

For I *am* the LORD, I change not; therefore ye sons of Jacob are not consumed.—Mal. 3:6

Do not err, my beloved brethren. Every good gift and every perfect gift is from above, and cometh down from the Father of lights, with whom is no variableness, neither shadow of turning.—James 1:16-17

From the principle of God's invariableness and sovereign will and purpose, and that no living being in heaven or earth can stop Him or even dare ask Him "What doest thou?" the following principle may be extrapolated:

IN EVERY GENERATION OF MAN BEFORE CHRIST'S DEATH, AND DESPITE ADAMIC SIN, GOD HAD BEEN REINCARNATING THE RIGHTEOUS DECEASED AND TAKING THEM INTO THE THIRD-HEAVEN OR PARADISE.

But, some will argue that the principle of death and resurrection proves that when men die they must wait until the still-future, end-time Universal Resurrection and Last Judgment before they live again.

I reject this argument for two reasons:

First, Jesus taught that men of faith do not enter into judgment, but are "passed from death unto life":

Verily, verily, I say unto you, He that heareth my word, and believeth on him that sent me, hath everlasting life, and shall not come into condemnation; but is **passed from death unto life**. Verily, verily, I say unto you, The hour is coming, **AND NOW IS**, when the dead shall hear the voice of the Son of God: and they that hear shall live.—John 5:24-25

Jesus saith unto her [Martha], I am the resurrection, and the life: he that believeth in me, though he were dead, yet shall he live: And whosoever liveth and believeth in me **SHALL NEVER DIE**.—John 11:25-26

Note Jesus' words, **"<u>AND NOW IS</u>"** in the first passage. He was talking about His *contemporary* followers and disciples who believed on Him. He said they had "everlasting life" (John 3:16). So long as they kept believing in Him they were **"passed from death unto life"**!

In the second passage Jesus said the same thing to Martha. Those who believed in Him would *never* die. He told her, "I **AM** the resurrection," [i.e. present tense not future tense]. Thus He had the power on earth to raise the dead anytime the Father instructed Him to do so. He did not have to wait until some future time. He did not say to Martha, "I will one day be the resurrection."

The doctrine of the ***immediate reincarnation*** of the faithful deceased inevitably follows from Jesus' words. It is because God reincarnated the faithful when they died that Jesus said to Martha, "I **am** the Resurrection." Reincarnation was in most cases immediate for the righteous upon their death, but not always. For example, God did not resurrect Lazarus until the fourth day after he died (John 11:39). Also, God did not raise the Two Witnesses until three and one-half days after they were martyred (Rev. 11:11). When God *did* reincarnate the dead it surely happened "in a moment, in the twinkling of an eye" (I Cor. 15:52).

Moreover, the doctrine of immediate reincarnation of the faithful deceased necessitates that God began creating Paradise from earliest times [i.e. during Adam's generation]. Otherwise, He could not have raised Abel. Where would He have taken Abel if Paradise was not already available and prepared to receive him?

Second, the apostle Paul unquestionably taught that death was not the end but a new start in life:

> For to me to live *is* Christ, and to die *is* gain. But if I live in the flesh, this *is* the fruit of my labour: yet what I shall choose I wot not. For I am in a strait betwixt two, having a desire to depart, and to be with Christ; which is far better [for me].—Phil. 1:21-23

Christ's death conquered death, provable by His resurrection three days and nights after His crucifixion. He did not conquer it just for Himself, but for all men: not just for saints but also for sinners.

For this *is* good and acceptable in the sight of God our Saviour; Who will have all men to be saved, and to come unto the knowledge of the truth. For *there is* one God, and one mediator between God and men, the man Christ Jesus; Who gave himself a ransom for all, to be testified in due time.—I Tim. 2:3-6

Therefore as by the offence of one *judgment came* upon all men to condemnation; even so by the righteousness of one *the free gift came* upon all men unto justification of life.— Rom. 5:18

For since by man *came* death, by man *came* also the resurrection of the dead. For as in Adam all die, even so in Christ shall all be made alive.—I Cor. 15:21-22

God . . . is the Saviour of all men, specially of those that believe [i.e. hence, even of those that **don't** believe].—I Tim. 4:10, brackets mine

In sum, it is because of God's sovereignty and the unchangeability of His nature and His purpose for man that we know Paradise has existed from earliest times, and that God has been resurrecting [i.e. reincarnating] both the righteous deceased [from creation], and the wicked deceased [from the time of Jesus' crucifixion (Luke 23:43)].

(C. The Principle of "All Things New")

Both Old Testament and New Testament Scripture declares that God is continually ***creating*** [i.e. present-progressive tense] the new heaven and earth:

For, behold, I create [Heb. I am creat***ing***] new heavens and a new earth—Is. 65:17

For as the new heavens and the new earth, which I will make [Heb. which I am mak***ing***], shall remain before me, saith the LORD, so shall your seed and your name remain. Is. 66:22

Behold, I make [Gk. I am mak***ing***] all things new.—Rev. 21:5

But besides this grammatical evidence there are other valid reasons for knowing that God has been creating the new heavens and earth from earliest times; in fact, early in Adam's generation.

God's "In the Beginning Principle" Was Good for the ***Righteous*** *Deceased*

For example, God's "in the beginning" principle was good for the righteous deceased in Old Testament times because God's purpose is eternal, unstoppable, and uninterruptible.[190] The Biblical concept of eternity, therefore, takes us <u>backwards</u> in historical time as well as forward into the <u>future</u>:

> Blessed *be* the LORD God of Israel from everlasting, and to everlasting. Amen, and Amen.—Psalm 41:13

This means that no generation of man has been overlooked or passed over when it comes to God's "very good" things that He did for mankind "from the beginning":

> According to the eternal purpose [Gk. the purpose of the ages, or of all generations] which he purposed in Christ Jesus our Lord—Eph. 3:11

> The counsel of the LORD standeth for ever, the thoughts of his heart to all generations.—Psalm 33:11

> Thy faithfulness *is* unto all generations—Psalm 119:90a

Thus, God did not allow gaps between periods of time, or between generations, either short ones or long ones. His "in the beginning" purpose—that man should be a **"LIVING"** soul [Gen. 2:7] would not allow that. Thus He has guarded and performed His will and purpose faithfully down through the ages to this day!

Jesus taught the Sadducees and Jews, for example, that Abraham, Isaac, and Jacob were alive during the days of Moses and even in Jesus' present generation. No doubt they are still alive to this day, for God is still their God.

---

[190] See Dan. 4:35.

I see a sound doctrinal extrapolation in this, viz., that Jesus' teaching was true of all other righteous people who died in Old Testament days. God resurrected all the righteous as they died. They did not have to wait and be raised *collectively* centuries or millennia later in the Universal Resurrection.

Thus, all other Old Testament saints such as Abel, Seth, David, the prophets, etc. were also alive and in Paradise on the day that Jesus taught this lesson to the Sadducees and Jews.

Yes, they were alive even before Jesus' crucifixion, which was the time of the Universal Resurrection of the wicked. They had not had to wait for the Universal Resurrection to be reincarnated. Let us believe, therefore, dear reader that the following passage was true for all the righteous deceased of Old Testament times, not just for Abraham, Isaac, and Jacob:

> But as touching the resurrection of the [Old Testament righteous] dead, have ye not read that which was spoken unto you by God, saying, I am the God of Abraham, and the God of Isaac, and the God of Jacob? **God is not the God of the dead, but of the LIVING**.—Matt. 22:32

Jesus mentioned only three generations in the Old Testament [i.e. Abraham's, Isaac's, and Jacob's]; however, we know that the righteous deceased of ALL Old Testament generations were also alive as Jesus spoke. Note the reaction of the Jews when they heard Jesus' doctrine:

> And when the multitude heard *this*, they were astonished at his doctrine.—Matt. 22:33

The only difference between the Old and New Testament saints was that the former existed in Paradise and the latter in this world. Otherwise, nothing separated them, as Paul wrote:

> Who shall separate us from the love of Christ? *shall* tribulation, or distress, or persecution, or famine, or nakedness, or peril, or sword? As it is written, For thy sake we are killed all the day long; we are accounted as sheep for the slaughter. Nay, in all these things we are more than conquerors through him that

loved us. For I am persuaded, that neither **DEATH**, nor life, nor angels, nor principalities, nor powers, nor things present, nor things to come, Nor height, nor depth, nor any other creature, shall be able to separate us from the love of God, which is in Christ Jesus our Lord.—Rom. 9:35-39

God's "In the Beginning" Principle Also Meant Resurrection for the *Wicked* Dead of Old Testament Times.

God's "in the beginning" principle also promised continued life for the wicked deceased. God restored their lives to them by reincarnating them in the hour of Jesus' death—i.e. in the Universal Resurrection. We can say, then, that God withheld reincarnating the wicked until the day that Christ shed His blood for all men. Until then the Holy Spirit referred to them as "captives," "prisoners [of death]," "bound," and "bruised":

> The spirit of the Lord GOD *is* upon me [i.e. Jesus declared]; because the LORD hath anointed me to preach good tidings unto the meek; he hath sent me to bind up the brokenhearted, to proclaim liberty to the [Old Testament deceased, wicked] **captives**, and the opening of the **prison** to *them [i.e. the same* "*captives] that are* **bound.**—Is. 61:1, brackets added for clarity

> The Spirit of the Lord *is* upon me, because he hath anointed me to preach the gospel to the poor; he hath sent me to heal the brokenhearted, to preach deliverance to the captives, and recovering of sight to the blind, to set at liberty them that are **bruised**.—Luke 4:18

On the day Jesus died God took Him by spirit to preach the gospel to all the wicked dead[191] who had been held captive in the prison house of death—some only recently, some for centuries, and others for millennia. How were they so held? It was their personal angels that held them (their personal angels were like their prisons or jail cells![192]). *This all changed as Jesus' body lay entombed in the earth for three days and nights.*[193]

---

[191]   See I Pet. 4:6.
[192]   See Matt. 18:10; cf. Acts 12:15; Heb. 1:13-14.
[193]   See Matt. 12:39-40; I Pet. 3:18-19.

Upon hearing God's command[194] [on the day Jesus died for sin] these jail-house angels set their spirit-captives free. Many came forth from their graves[195] and remained in Jerusalem for about four days. Not until Jesus ascended to His Father on the fourth day after His crucifixion did God command the angels to take their long-time prisoners—*now released and reincarnated [i.e. born again]*—into Paradise.

Until Jesus' ascension, then, the multiple millions of reincarnated wicked people of past generations waited visibly[196] or invisibly (God knows) until that fourth day—i.e. "the first day of the week" [see John 20:1]. It was a Sunday morning. Jesus ascended to the Father, and on His way up He led[197] the newly liberated captives into Paradise to be restored to the "very good" life that God intended them to have "from the beginning" [Gen. 1:31; cf. Matt. 19:8].

When they entered Paradise the first thing God did to *and for* them was to chastise them:

> For whom the Lord [i.e. Jehovah] loveth he chasteneth, and
> scourgeth every son whom he receiveth.—Heb. 12:6 [cf. NASB]

Their Father chastised them with teachers who taught them to walk in the paths of righteousness.[198] Theirs then, was "the resurrection of damnation [i.e. of judgment]"—John 5:30; cf. Heb. 9:27.

<u>God Treated the Wicked Deceased Differently from the Righteous Deceased.</u> These explanations show us that during Old Testament days God treated the righteous and the unrighteous deceased very differently.

Through inspiration of the Holy Spirit David recognized this, and declared it clearly in one of his psalms:

---

194 Angels don't do anything without first hearing Jehovah's commands for them to act. See Psalm 103:20.
195 See Matt. 27:52-53 and John 5:28-29.
196 Cf. Matt. 27:52-54.
197 He led captivity captive—See Eph. 4:8.
198 E.g. see Is. 30:20-21.

> Like sheep they [the ungodly] are laid in the grave; death shall
> feed on them; and the upright shall have dominion over them
> in the morning [i.e. at the time of the Universal Resurrection
> on Nisan 14, AD 29; cf. John 5:28-29]; and their beauty shall
> consume in the grave from their dwelling. But God will redeem
> **MY** soul from the power of the grave: for he shall **RECEIVE**
> me [i.e. receive my reincarnated spirit (i.e. my born-again spirit)
> into Paradise.]—Psalm 49:14-15

The Adamic bodies of the righteous deceased perished in the
grave, just as did the bodies of the unrighteous [see Job 14:12; Eccles.
3:19-20]. But ***THE RIGHTEOUS*** never lost consciousness because
God ***immediately*** "received" them into Paradise, having reincarnated
their departed spirits.

The wicked deceased, however [i.e. their departed spirits] He put
in prison, having commanded their angels[199] to guard their spirits until
the Universal Resurrection—John 5:28-29. Peter, for example, speaks
of the wicked flood victims as still being in "prison" up to the day of
Christ's crucifixion:

> For Christ also hath once suffered for sins [i.e. for sinful
> men], the just for the unjust, that he might bring us to God,
> being **put to death in the flesh**, but quickened by the Spirit:
> By which also he [i.e. Jesus] went and preached unto the **spirits
> in prison** [i.e. the wicked flood victims]; Which sometime
> were disobedient, when once the longsuffering of God waited
> in the days of Noah *(God gave them 120 years to repent and
> be saved from the coming Flood—Gen. 6:3)*, while the ark was
> a-preparing, wherein few, that is, eight souls were saved by water.
> —I Pet. 3:18-20

Note Jesus' reason for going to the imprisoned flood wicked:—i.e.
to preach the gospel to them, viz., that His shed blood was for them as
well as for the righteous! Thus, Peter added:

---

[199] "Their angels"—Jesus taught that everybody has his own personal angel (see
Matt. 18:10).

For this cause was the gospel preached also to them that are[200] dead, that they might be judged according to men in the flesh, but live according to God in the spirit.—I Pet. 4:6

How Did God Accommodate the Millions and Millions of Wicked People that Suddenly Appeared in Paradise?

So many millions of wicked people entered Paradise, and so suddenly when Jesus ascended to the Father! The question is: How was Paradise able to accommodate them? It seems that at first the godly citizens already there were shocked to see them, and so many of them! Both the millions of newcomers and those that had lived there since Adam's time were cramped for living space. It was probably the newcomers that said to God:

> The place *is* too strait for me: give place to me that I might dwell.—Is. 49:19-20

Now don't you know, dear reader, that God heard their justifiable complaint and request? He answered them by creating the extra space they needed to be comfortable! This helps us better understand why God is constantly creat*ing* the new heavens and earth. I would be surprised if this was not a daily concern and problem in Paradise, so that God is constantly creat*ing* extra land as needed. People enter Paradise every day, not only from those hundreds of thousands dying on earth, but those being born there[201] as well.

This crowding and asking God for more living space evidently took place also in the Promised Land during Joshua's Conquest of Canaan. Gradually, as God gave Israel victory over the "Amorites, and the Hittites, and the Perizzites, the Hivites, and the Jebusites" (see Ex. 23:23), they were cramped for land. Note the prayer of Jabez:

> And Jabez called on the God of Israel, saying, Oh that thou wouldest bless me indeed, and **ENLARGE MY COAST** [i.e.

---

200 "Are" is spurious here in the KJ translation, not being accounted for anywhere in the Greek original. Therefore, the passage should open as follows: "For this cause was the gospel preached to them that *were* dead [e.g. the flood wicked] . . ."

201 "Born there"—Cf. Psalm 87:4-6 and Is. 65:23.

give me more land], and that thine hand might be with me, and that thou wouldest keep *me* from evil, that it [i.e. the crowded condition] may not grieve me! **AND GOD GRANTED HIM THAT WHICH HE REQUESTED**.—I Chr. 4:10

(D. God Took the Righteous Deceased
To Paradise from
Earliest Times.)

When righteous people in Old Testament times died, because God immediately reincarnated them, He had to take them *somewhere*. He couldn't have just taken them into the vacuum of outer space for obvious reasons.

Neither in a reincarnated [i.e. born again] body would Jehovah have brought them into His presence [i.e. His realm] since the Bible teaches that flesh-and-blood cannot live in His presence.[202]

Jacob understood this, and when the angel that wrestled with him wouldn't tell him His name, he assumed that it was God. When he didn't die he was relieved, thankful, nonplused and surprised all at the same time:

> And Jacob called the name of the place Peniel [Heb. the face of God]: for I have seen God face to face, and my life is preserved.—Gen. 32:30

The Bible gives other examples of people thinking an angel they saw was Jehovah, and then became fearful whether or not they could continue to live. I think of Gideon (Judg. 6:22-23); Manoah (Judg. 13:22); Daniel (Dan. 8:17; 10:15); and John (Rev. 1:17; 22:8-9).

Moreover, Paul knew that Christians, so long as they remained in "flesh and blood" bodies, would not be able to enter God's presence or inherit the kingdom of God (I Cor. 15:50). He said that God would remedy this problem at Jesus' Second Coming when He would instantaneously change them [i.e. their born again bodies] into incorruptible, immortal beings—i.e. into "spiritual" or "heavenly" bodies (I Cor. 15:44, 48, 51-54).

---

[202] Cf. I Cor. 15:50.

Thus, the Holy Spirit inspired John to write that "No man hath seen God at any time" (John 1:18; I John 4:12). Jesus told Nicodemus, ". . . no man [i.e. in the flesh] hath _**ascended**_ up to heaven" (John 3:13). In his Pentecost sermon Peter said that not even David had ascended into Heaven:

> For David is not ascended into the heavens—Acts 2:34

It should be understood that the word "ascended" is a regal term, such as when Jesus ascended to his throne at God's right hand. Also, throughout the Bible it is the verb consistently used in connection with men going _**up**_ to Jerusalem or _**up**_ to God in Heaven. Also, both men and angels ASCEND to Jerusalem or to God's Heaven.[203]

Paradise

Dear reader, if God did not take deceased Old Testament saints to celestial orbs in outer space, and if He did not take them up into His abode [i.e. the highest heaven, or heaven of heavens], only one place remains where He could have taken them. That would be Paradise, called also the "third heaven"[204]—II Cor. 12:2, 4.

---

[203] See: Judg. 13:20; Psalm 24:3; 68:18; 139:8; Is. 14:13; Ezek. 38:9; Luke 19:28; John 1:51; 6:62; 20:17; Rom. 10:6; Eph. 4:8, 10; Rev. 8:4; 11:12.

[204] Why is Paradise called the Third Heaven? In Bible parlance the word "heaven" refers not only to the Earth's atmospheric strata, but also to Earth itself. The word "heavens" [plural] refers to three "heavens and earth" REALMS of existence. The Holy Spirit created the "Heaven and Earth" where Jehovah dwells, appropriately called the "Highest," or the "Heaven of heavens" [Luke 2:14; II Chr. 6:18; Psalm 68:33]. Thus we should call that realm the **First Heaven**. Next, Jehovah created our heaven and earth as recorded in Gen. 1, making it the **Second Heaven**. When Adam sinned he and his descendants became both physically and spiritually defiled, their very flesh cursed with death (Gen. 2:7, 17; 3:19). The second heaven became the place of death [Sheol]. Consequently, if God was to fulfill His will for man He was obliged to create yet the **Third Heaven** variously called "new heavens and earth," or "paradise" in the Bible. The ground in Paradise is not cursed, and the people dwelling therein are no longer cursed with death. They are born again, having new and undefiled flesh suitable for the indwelling of the Holy Spirit.

Men or angels, however, are never said in the Bible to *ascend* to Paradise.[205] Why? Is it not because Paradise is not where God's throne is? Only when God rewarded the saints to sit on His throne with Him could they __ascend__ to Him. Two things on earth were analogous to Paradise: (1) the Holy Place in the Tabernacle or the Temple, and (2) the Church on earth during Jesus' generation [and before it was defiled with the Antichrist]. Only at Jesus' Second Coming in AD 72 did any saint ascend to Jehovah in the Holy of Holies: i.e. the Heaven of heavens. It was *there* that God gave them thrones on which to sit and rule Paradise with Him for all eternity.

> And Jesus said unto them [i.e. His twelve disciples], Verily I say unto you, that ye which have followed me, in the regeneration when the Son of man shall sit in the throne of his glory, ye also shall sit upon twelve thrones, judging the twelve tribes of Israel.—Matt. 19:28

> He [i.e. Jesus Christ] said therefore, A certain nobleman [i.e. Himself] went into a far country [i.e. Paradise] to receive for himself a kingdom, and to return. And he called his ten servants [i.e. Christians of Jesus' generation], and said unto them, Occupy till I come. But his citizens [i.e. the Jews of Jesus' generation] hated him, and sent a message after him, saying, We will not have this *man* to reign over us. And it came to pass, that when he [i.e. Jesus Christ] was returned, having received the kingdom, then he commanded these servants [Christians] to be called unto him, to whom he had given the money, that he might know how much every man had gained by trading. Then came the first, saying, Lord, thy pound hath gained ten pounds. And he said unto him, Well, thou good servant: because thou hast been faithful in a very little, have thou authority over ten cities [i.e. of Israel, in Paradise]. And the second came, saying, Lord, thy pound hath gained five pounds. And he said likewise to him, Be thou also over five cities [of Israel in Paradise]. —Luke 19:12-19

---

[205]   Lucifer did not attempt to ascend to Paradise but to the Highest Heaven and to God's throne (see Is. 14:13-14).

To him [i.e. any antichrist in Asia before the deadline] that overcometh will I grant to sit with me in my throne, even as I also overcame, and am set down with my Father in his throne. —Rev. 3:21

As for Paradise the Bible speaks of saints ***going up*** or being ***taken up*** or ***caught up*** [never ascending] into it. See the following examples:

(ENOCH)—And Enoch walked with God: and he *was* not; for God **took** him [i.e. into Paradise].—Gen. 5:24

(ELIJAH)—And it came to pass, as they still went on, and talked, that, behold, *there appeared* a chariot of fire, and horses of fire, and parted them both asunder; and Elijah **went up** by whirlwind into heaven [i.e. into Paradise].—II Kings 2:11

(JESUS)—And while they looked stedfastly toward heaven as **he [i.e. Jesus] went up**, behold, two men stood by them in white apparel; Which also said, Ye men of Galilee, why stand ye gazing up into heaven? this same Jesus, which is **taken up** from you into heaven [i.e. Paradise], shall so come in like manner as ye have seen him **go into** heaven.—Acts 1:10-11

(PAUL)—I knew a man in Christ above fourteen years ago, (whether in the body, I cannot tell; or whether out of the body, I cannot tell: God knoweth;) such an one **caught up** to the third heaven. And I knew such a man, whether in the body, or out of the body, I cannot tell: God knoweth;) How that he was **caught up** into paradise, and heard unspeakable words, which it is not lawful for a man to utter.—II Cor. 12:2-4

Now [After Christ Died] All Men Go into Paradise Upon Dying!

It is because God, throughout Old Testament times, "received"[206] into Paradise all ***righteous*** deceased persons that Jesus was able to tell the thief dying by crucifixion at His side:

---

[206] See Psalm 49:15.

Verily I say unto thee, To-day shalt thou be with me in paradise.—Luke 23:43

Think with me. Seeing Jesus said this to the thief don't we have the authority to believe and teach that Paradise already existed? How could He and the thief go there if it did not exist?

(THE WICKED DECEASED FROM ADAM TO CHRIST)—Here was the new heaven and earth where God had taken all the righteous deceased persons on earth from the time of Adam to Christ. That was an approximate period of 4,037 years.

Because Satan had not ruled ***there*** during that time (his domain was this earth only), only a culture of ***truth*** and ***righteousness*** firmly resulted. Neither [until Christ entered Paradise] had anybody died since arriving in Paradise. The result was that the righteous culture in Paradise had remained secure.

By the time of Christ's generation, therefore, all the people in Paradise were capable of receiving into their midst a sudden arrival of multiple millions of once wicked people that God had just raised [reincarnated] in the Universal Resurrection.

Thus, Paradiseans (sic) had the collective ability, love, knowledge, experience, and will to re-educate and discipline *most* of the wicked! That's why throughout Old Testament times God had, when they died, taken the righteous deceased [generation after generation] into Paradise, so that by the time of His generation and the Universal Resurrection[207] [4,037 years later] not even the sudden influx of millions of wicked people God took into Paradise at that time would be able to corrupt the righteous culture entrenched in Paradise for all past ages.

Not only had the righteous citizens there by the multiple millions been living in Paradise all that time [i.e. 4,037 years], but Jesus had also entered Paradise and taken power over the once wicked newcomers on the day of His crucifixion! After all, that is one major reason Jesus shed His blood on the cross: to save all Adam's descendants, the wicked as well as the righteous. Thus, we recall Jesus' astonishing teaching, viz.,

---

[207] My word "Universal" is implied and authorized by Jesus' word **"ALL"** in the following passage: "Marvel not at this: for the hour is coming, in the which **ALL** that are in the graves shall hear his voice, And shall come forth"—John 5:28, 29**a**.

"**ALL** that are in the graves shall hear his voice, And shall come forth" (John 5:28-29). Then—on "The first day of the week"—Jesus led the "captivity" [i.e. the reincarnated wicked] into Paradise:

> Wherefore he saith, When he ascended up on high, he led captivity captive [i.e. into Paradise], and gave gifts unto men.—Eph. 4:8

Scripture shows that after the wicked enter Paradise godly counselors teach them righteousness "as at the beginning." See e.g. Is. 1:25-27; 2:3; 30:20-22; cf. Ezek. 37:23. Apparently this counseling will frequently include grievous chastisements as seen in Heb. 12:6-11.

(THE THIEF)—Jesus personally led them into Paradise! The thief on the cross is an example, to whom Jesus said: **"To-day shalt thou [a "malefactor"] be with me in paradise"** (see Luke 23:39-43).

Jesus had the power and authority from His Father to be Ruler not only over the wicked in Paradise, but also over Satan and his angels. No more would mankind have to fear Satan, or be deceived by him, or lose their salvation because of him, as seen in the following passages:

> And Jesus came and spake unto them, saying, All power is given unto me in heaven and in earth.—Matt. 28:18

> . . . And Jesus answered and saith unto him [i.e. Satan], Get thee behind me, Satan—Luke 4:8

> And he said unto them [i.e. His disciples], I beheld Satan as lightning fall from heaven.—Luke 10:18 . . . be of good cheer; I have overcome the world.—John 16:33

> *And* having spoiled principalities and powers, he made a shew of them openly, triumphing over them in it.—Col. 2:15

> And there was war made in heaven: Michael and his angels fought against the dragon; and the dragon fought and his angels, And prevailed not; neither was their place found any more in heaven. And the great dragon was cast out, that old serpent, called the Devil, and Satan, which deceiveth the whole world: he was cast out into the earth, and his angels were cast out with him. And I heard a loud voice saying in heaven, Now is come salvation,

and strength, and the kingdom of our God, and the power of his Christ: for the accuser of our brethren is cast down, which accused them before our God day and night.—Rev. 12:7-10

(E. The Principle that God Is Impartial)

Stressed throughout the Bible is the truth that God is impartial, or, as expressed in the KJV, "not a respecter of persons":

> For the LORD your God *is* God of gods, and Lord of lords, a great God, a mighty, and a terrible, which **regardeth not persons**, nor taketh reward—Deut. 10:17

> Wherefore now let the fear of the LORD be upon you; take heed and do *it:* for *there is* no iniquity with the LORD our God, **nor respect of persons**, nor taking of gifts.—II Chr. 19:7

> Then Peter opened *his* mouth, and said, Of a truth I perceive that **God is no respecter of persons**: But in every nation HE THAT FEARETH HIM, AND WORKETH RIGHTEOUSNESS [cap's mine], is accepted with him.—Acts 10:34-35

> For there is **no respect of persons with God**.—Rom. 2:11

> But of these who seemed to be somewhat, (whatsoever they were, it maketh no matter to me: **God accepteth no man's person**:) for they who seemed *to be somewhat* in conference added nothing to me—Gal. 2:6

> And, ye masters, do the same things unto them, forbearing threatening: knowing that your Master also is in heaven; **neither is there respect of persons with him.**—Eph. 6:9

> But he that doeth wrong shall receive for the wrong which he hath done: and **there is no respect of persons**.—Col. 3:25

> And if ye call on **the Father, who without respect of persons** judgeth according to every man's work, pass the time of your sojourning *here* in fear—I Pet. 1:17

The Acts 10:34-35 quote explains an important point: *God CERTAINLY IS partial to <u>anyone</u> who seeks to know Him and obey Him.* Thus, throughout the Bible we see a division between the righteous and the wicked (cf. Psalm 37:9). In Old Testament days God reincarnated the righteous when they died but let the wicked perish [i.e. He did not reincarnate *them* when *they* died (Psalm 49:14-15), but put them in "prison" (cf. I Pet. 3:19)]. The Bible shows many other instances and times in which He was partial towards the righteous.

- God saved Noah and his immediate family, but drowned the wicked. Why did God save Noah and his family? Moses wrote: "And the LORD said unto Noah, Come thou and all thy house into the ark; for thee have I seen righteous before me in this generation" (Gen. 7:1).

- He called Abraham and Sarah to found the nation of Israel over every other couple living on earth at that time. Why? Was it not because He *knew* Abraham was seeking the only true God and would obey Him? See Gen. 18:19.

- God killed everybody in Sodom and Gomorrah, but saved Lot and his two daughters who obeyed Him, feared Him, and trembled at His word.

- He chose Isaac over Ishmael because Abraham's wife Sarah prayed to God to give her husband a son. Hagar bore him a son only because she was commanded to do so.

- God chose Jacob over Esau because Esau trivialized and sold his birthright, and Jacob coveted it dearly. See Rom. 9:13; Heb. 12:16.

- God blessed Jacob over Laban because Laban lied to Jacob about Rachel and gave Jacob inferior sheep as his pay. Also, Jacob was the heir to God's promises through Abraham and Isaac. Jacob also vowed to give God a tenth of his increase upon returning safely to Canaan.

- God promised to bless Israel over all other nations if they would hear His word and obey Him. See Deut. 28:1.

- God favored Elijah's sacrifice of a bullock on the altar over that of Baal's priests on their altar because Elijah prayed to the true God, and Baal's priests prayed to false gods. See I Kings 18:21-40.

And the list could go on.

(God Raptures Righteous People Intermittently.)

Let me now further limit my discussion on the impartiality of God to the topic of the intermittent raptures—i.e. the catchings-up—of saints into Paradise. God's reason for this was to give hope to the righteous and warning to the wicked.

Why God Raptured Enoch

It is apparent that when God caught Enoch up into Paradise it made a lasting impression on the antediluvian world. From generation to generation following the event the patriarchs talked about it to their children and their children's children.

There Were Other Righteous People on Earth Before the Flood.

Jehovah had an important reason for **openly** and ***publicly*** rapturing Enoch. He wanted the righteous to remember Enoch's faith, his name, and his close fellowship with Him. Rapturing him up into heaven was so astounding an event that the righteous people living in later centuries would still know about it, ponder it, discuss it, and increase their faith by it. This is exactly what Jehovah wanted, because by the time of Enoch's rapture, 669 years before the flood, the wickedness of man had already grown great in the earth.

However, because God raptured Enoch and because the patriarchs kept the memory of it alive from one generation to the next, and because the patriarchs were teachers of righteousness [both by word and example], it must be that many righteous people remained on earth up to the time of Noah and the Ark.

As so often is the case, though, the wicked bully the righteous and wind up dictating the moral ambiance of the culture. In the days of Noah man's immoral and violent behavior had grown so gross that Jehovah decided to drown the wicked in a worldwide flood. His purpose in the flood was not just to kill the wicked, but also to give man a new start on earth when the flood was over.

<u>God Saved Other Righteous Antediluvians Besides Noah and His</u>
<u>Family.</u>

There can be no doubt that besides Noah and his family there
were many thousands of other righteous people living on earth in that
generation. But if the flood was to cover the entire earth, how could
the righteous avoid being killed in the flood along with the wicked?
God would not allow that. He does not punish the righteous with the
wicked. Abraham pleaded with God not to destroy the righteous in
Sodom along with the wicked. He said to God:

> That be far from thee to do after this manner, to slay the
> righteous with the wicked: and that the righteous should be as
> the wicked, that be far from thee: Shall not the Judge of all the
> earth do right? And the LORD said, If I find in Sodom fifty
> righteous within the city, then I will spare all the place for their
> sakes.—Gen. 18:25-26

> And they [two angels] smote the men [of Sodom] that *were*
> at the door of the house [of Lot] with blindness, both small and
> great: so that they wearied themselves to find the door. And the
> men [the two angels] said unto Lot, Hast thou here any besides?
> son in law, and thy sons, and thy daughters, and whatsoever
> thou hast in the city, bring *them* out of this place: For we will
> destroy this place, because the cry of them is waxen great before
> the face of the LORD; and the LORD hath sent us to destroy
> it.—Gen. 19:11-13

No, God did not drown the thousands of righteous people alive
on earth in Noah's day. He raptured them as He had Enoch 669 years
earlier! What is our lesson here? See the answer:

> The Lord knoweth how to deliver the godly out of
> temptations, and to reserve the unjust unto the day of judgment
> to be punished—II Pet. 2:9

(God Saved Multiple Thousands of
Righteous Antediluvians by
Rapturing them into Paradise!)

> For the Lord himself shall descend from heaven with a shout, with the voice of the archangel, and with the trump of God: and the dead in Christ shall rise first: Then we which are alive *and* remain shall be **caught up** together with them in the clouds, to meet the Lord in the air: and so shall we ever be with the Lord.—I Thess. 4:17

First, let's clear up, once for all, the meaning of the Rapture of the Church. Note the words "caught up" in this passage. This is our Authorized or King James translation of the Greek word *harpagesometha*. In the Vulgate St. Jerome translated this Greek word with the Latin word *raptus* [anglicized as "rapture"] which means "shall be caught up."

The clear meaning of I Thess. 4:17 is that when Jesus came He would suddenly seize His elect brethren on earth [i.e. in Asia] and take [i.e. rapture] them up to the Father with Him. In this book from cover to cover I have said that this event took place in midsummer of AD 72.

We see a picture then of multiple thousands of Christians in AD 72 being suddenly and powerfully transported [i.e. raptured] from Asia into the "air," only then to *ascend* to the Highest Heaven.

But let's return to our present theme of the flood in the days of Noah. Jehovah had more than one objective in sending the flood. Here are four objectives that I perceive: (1) to keep mankind and the animals from becoming extinct on earth; (2) to temporarily imprison the antediluvian wicked; (3) to rapture the multiple thousands of antediluvian righteous into Paradise; and (4) to let all of us believers today know that Jehovah can and may well rapture US CHRISTIANS as well [in case of an all-destructive WWIII].

ONE

Jehovah's objective in saving Noah and his family in the Ark was to preserve all air-breathing flesh so He could have the means to repopulate the earth after the flood. After the flood Noah would undoubtedly start everything off on a righteous footing. Men therefore would not likely become so universally wicked, and so quickly, again.

TWO

Jehovah wanted to imprison the whole wicked antediluvian population at the same time and in the quickest and most merciful way.

Imprisonment assured that He could and would raise them back up in the Universal Resurrection millennia later. That Resurrection took place on the day of Jesus' crucifixion [Nisan 14, AD 29]. At that time He released them [i.e. their spirits] from "prison" by commanding their personal angels to reincarnate them and bring them into Paradise.

> For Christ also hath once suffered for sins, the just for the unjust, that he might bring us to God, being put to death in the flesh, but quickened by the Spirit: By which also he went and preached unto the spirits in prison; Which sometime were disobedient, when once the longsuffering of God waited in the days of Noah, while the ark was a-preparing, wherein few, that is, eight souls were saved by water [i.e. instead of by a rapture].—I Pet. 3:18-20

By having them all die at the same time and then later resurrecting them all at the same time, all the family and community relationships they had in their former life would be the same as when they died in the flood. This cut down on a lot of confusion and disorientation in getting them started again in the New World. For example, mothers and fathers would see their children next to them. Friends would find their old acquaintances. Little children would find their former playmates. Brothers, sisters, cousins, uncles, aunts, and grandparents came into view once more, still in their former familial relationships. Finally, they could all rejoice and praise God together, and cleanse their minds from their former idolatry and misconceptions. Everybody would gladly submit to God's discipline and learn eternal truth. Life would have purpose to them for the first time. Everything in their new world and life would conform to God's eternal purpose for man. People everywhere would love one another, trust each other, and jettison all their former fears and doubts. In short, life would be "very good" as God intended it to be from the beginning (see Gen. 1:30).

> For this cause was the gospel preached also to them that are[208]dead [Greek: to the dead], that they might be judged

---

[208] The word "are" is not in the original text. Considering that the Universal Resurrection involved only the dead from Adam to Christ [see John 5:28-29]

according to men in the flesh, but live [again] according to God in the spirit.—I Pet. 4:6

THREE

Jehovah's impartiality moved Him to rapture the righteous that lived on earth before the flood. He had saved Enoch from death and taken him into Paradise, so therefore He could do no less for the righteous antediluvians. By rapturing them THEN He insured that they, having lived in Paradise for millennia prior to the Universal Resurrection, would be the natural and rightful teachers and disciplinarians of their once wicked contemporaries that came into Paradise on the day of Jesus' death.

FOUR

Dear reader, it appears that human and animal life will one day, sooner or later, come to an end on this earth, as indicated in the following passage:

> And, Thou, Lord, in the beginning hast laid the foundation of the earth; and the heavens are the works of thine hands: They shall perish; but thou remainest; and they all shall wax old as doth a garment; And as a vesture shalt thou fold them up, and they shall be changed: but thou art the same, and thy years shall not fail.—Heb. 1:10-12

A final war on earth—i.e. a nuclear war—is almost inevitable. This war could start very soon now, depending on whether or not radical Islamic militants try to nuke Israel, or if they dare lob a nuclear-armed ICBM [intercontinental ballistic missile] toward the United States of America, or toward any nation with like nuclear and intercontinental missile capabilities. Such an act would have the potential of triggering an all-out nuclear war in the world. It would be WWIII, a war that would truly end all wars, and end all human and animal life on earth.

---

the word "were" should have been added, not "are." Thus, the first part of the verse should read: "For this cause was the gospel preached also to them that *were* dead . . . etc."

It is my belief however that sometime before this happens God will rapture the righteous *off the earth and bring them into Paradise.* Thus God will see to it that all righteous and innocent persons [including such Muslim people] will escape it. Just as Jehovah raptured Enoch "that he should not see death" (Heb. 11:5), so He will catch the righteous on earth up into Paradise that they [i.e. we?] may not see such horror (II Kings 22:20 and Is. 57:1). Such is the way and will of the great, loving, just, merciful, and impartial Jehovah God.

(Who Will God Rapture in the Future?)

Many will then begin disappearing from earth in a succession of raptures. The question is: Who? Of course, only God will be the final judge of that. Upon what basis He will make that judgment is apparent in the following passages:

> If thou [i.e. Cain] doest well, shalt thou not be accepted? —Gen. 4:7a

> And he [i.e. Abram] believed in the LORD [i.e. JEHOVAH]; and he counted it to him for righteousness.—Gen. 15:6

> ...if from thence thou shalt seek the LORD [i.e. JEHOVAH] thy God, thou shalt find *him*, if thou seek him with all thy heart and with all thy soul.—Deut. 4:29

> ... the LORD looketh on the heart.—I Sam. 16:7

> Learn to do well; seek judgment, relieve the oppressed, judge the fatherless, plead for the widow.—Is. 1:17

> Blessed *are* they which do hunger and thirst after righteousness: for they shall be filled. Blessed *are* the merciful: for they shall obtain mercy. Blessed *are* the pure in heart: for they shall see God. Blessed *are* the peacemakers: for they shall be called the children of God.—Matt. 5:6-9

Let your light so shine before men, that they may see your good works, and glorify your Father which is in heaven.—Matt. 5:16

. . . if ye forgive men their trespasses, your heavenly Father will also forgive you—Matt. 6:14

. . . all things whatsoever ye would that men should do to you, do ye even so to them; for this is the law and the prophets.—Matt. 7:12

. . . Jesus said, Suffer little children, and forbid them not, to come unto me: for of such is the kingdom of heaven. —Matt. 19:14

Jesus said unto him, Thou shalt love the Lord [i.e. LORD] thy God with all thy heart, and with all thy soul, and with all thy mind. This is the first and great commandment. And the second *is* like unto it, Thou shalt love thy neighbour as thyself. On these two commandments hang all the law and the prophets. —Matt. 22:37-40

Finally, brethren, whatsoever things are true, whatsoever things *are* honest, whatsoever things *are* just, whatsoever things *are* pure, whatsoever things *are* lovely, whatsoever things *are* of good report; if *there be* any virtue, and if *there be* any praise, think on these things. Those things, which ye have both learned, and received, and heard, and seen in me, do: and the God of peace shall be with you.—Phil. 4:8-9

. . . without faith *it is* impossible to please *him;* for he that cometh to God must believe that he is, and *that* he a rewarder of them that diligently seek him.—Heb. 11:6

(What Will Happen to the
Wicked on Earth in The Event of WWIII?)

All the wicked [e.g. murderers, thieves, idolaters, adulterers, perjurers, and any other hateful and immoral son of the devil] living during this horrid war will all die in the nuclear conflicts taking place throughout the world. However, remember, God is merciful "according to [His] eternal purpose" which He has had for mankind "from the beginning" (Matt. 19:4, 8; Eph. 3:11a).

Therefore, when these wicked die in WWIII God will immediately bring them reincarnated into Paradise where they will find that God has appointed their righteous contemporaries to rule over them.

In Paradise God makes those that had lived wickedly the "tail" and no longer the "head" in man's society and culture [cf. Deut. 28:13]. God will teach the wicked to weep and repent and to seek Him with all their heart.

Thus we see the wisdom and necessity for people to exert all effort to be followers of God and righteousness in this present, evil world. God will one day rapture the righteous, but will let evil come to its lethal and just consequence with the wicked. Nevertheless, He will save them, too, but only after they have passed through fire [cf. I Cor. 3:15; Heb. 12:29]!

Yes, in Paradise the righteous will be exalted and the wicked made low. When the hearts of the wicked are finally cleansed and right before God, He will urge and expect them to give a heartfelt apology to Him, and also to the righteous ones they had hurt. Consider the following passage:

> Behold, I will make them of the synagogue of Satan, which say they are Jews [cf. righteous], and are not, but do lie; behold, I will make them to come and worship before thy feet, and to know that I have loved thee.—Rev. 3:9

Epilogue

My principal goal in this book is to bring the reader to a *timelier* and therefore a more *accurate* understanding of how WE should interpret the Holy Bible. There are important differences in how the Christians of Jesus' generation and how we in our generation should understand the Bible. Unfortunately, Christians today still see themselves as subject to what is called <u>Orthodox</u> Theology. This book teaches that <u>Biblical Theology</u> is preferable to Orthodox Theology because we are not living during Jesus' generation. Biblical Theology explains how to interpret Bible doctrines *appropriately for our day*. Dear reader, Biblical Theology, in other words, is the TRUTH for us today. It is OUR guide for how WE are to worship God, and how WE should understand Him and His will for us today:

TRUE WORSHIPERS SHALL WORSHIP THE FATHER IN SPIRIT AND IN TRUTH: FOR THE FATHER SEEKETH SUCH TO WORSHIP HIM. GOD *IS* A SPIRIT: AND THEY THAT WORSHIP HIM MUST WORSHIP HIM IN SPRIT AND IN TRUTH.—John 4:23-24

Implicit (and sometimes explicit) teachings in the Bible are seen throughout this book. These teachings have theological terms with which some of my readers may be unfamiliar. Following is a list of those terms, and a brief summary of how this book explains them in the Biblical Theology paradigm:

- **<u>Soteriology</u>: The study of salvation.** In this book I explain that there are two ranks of salvation discernible in the New Testament: (2) *High Calling* and (2) *Universal* or *Restoration*

Salvation.[209] The first rank has to do with eternal life,[210] an inheritance in the kingdom of Heaven, possession of a heavenly mansion,[211] a glorified body,[212] and rule over "cities"[213] in Paradise.[214] Restoration salvation promises a *reincarnated* body[215] and a *millennial life span*[216] in Paradise [the "Third Heaven"[217]], and a restoration of mankind[218] to the blessings God intended man to have on earth "from the beginning" (Gen. 2; cf. Matt. 19:4 and 8).

- **Ecclesiology: The study of the church.** Biblical Theology shows that the *Church of Christ* during Jesus' generation and the later Church founded by the church fathers are two different churches. This is too cumbersome to document in this brief forum, but any church historian, dear reader, can tell you that each church we see on earth today was founded by men. Some men started it and nursed it into existence and growth. According to Solomon, therefore, these churches are in the category of all other earthly things: "vanity of vanities"[219] (cf. Eccles. 1:2). Nonetheless, would it not be refreshing if men of wisdom[220] today could found yet a new church with doctrines greatly more harmonious with Biblical Theology?

- **Pneumatology: The study of spirits.** It is implicit throughout this book that the Holy Spirit is the Original, self-existing God that preexisted creation, including Jehovah [i.e. the "formed"

---

209 See John 3:17; I Cor. 15:21-22; I Tim. 2:4, 6; 4:10.
210 See e.g. John 3:16.
211 See John 14:2-3.
212 See Rom. 8:30; I Cor. 15:51-55; Phil. 3:21.
213 See Luke 19:17, 19.
214 See II Cor. 12:2, 4.
215 I.e. a born-again body. See John 3:3, 7; 1 Cor. 15:38, 44a; II Cor. 5:17.
216 See Gen. 1:1; 5:3, 27; cf. Matt. 19:4, 8.
217 The "third heaven" is the same as "Paradise"—II Cor. 12:2, 4.
218 See "restitution of all things"—Acts 3:21.
219 Solomon's "vanity of vanity" does not mean that these churches are evil or non-beneficial to mankind, but only that they come far short of the power, soteriological, and prophetic significance of the true church built by Jesus Christ and His apostles.
220 Cf. I Cor. 6:5.

Father[221]] and the first-century, glorified Son of God, Jesus Christ. Pneumatology also includes the study of angels [called both "sons of God"[222] and "ministering spirits"[223]]. Moreover, pneumatology involves the study of man's spirit, which God creates "in" him.[224] Next, it involves the truth that Jehovah is called "the Father of spirits."[225] At death the Holy Spirit [i.e. through the ministry of "holy angels"[226]] removes a deceased person's spirit, reincarnates it, and takes it intact, unharmed, and unaltered into Paradise and a reincarnated body.

- **Theology: The study of God [also, of the "gods"—i.e. Elohim]**

  1. **The Holy Spirit**
  2. **Jehovah**, the Father
  3. **Jesus** Son of God (Christ/Messiah)
  4. **Jesus** the First Resurrected or Glorified
  5. **Angelic** sons of God
  6. **Christians** born again [i.e. "sons of God"[227]]
  7. **Christians** glorified[228]

- **Biblical Anthropology, the study of man in the Bible**

  1. **Spirit** in man
  2. **Soul** of man, or man living, thinking, and doing
  3. **Bodies** of man—i.e. the Adamic, the born-again, and the glorified

---

221 Cf. Isa. 43:10.
222 See Gen. 6:2 and Job 1:6 and Job 2:1.
223 See Heb. 1:14; cf. Matt. 4:11 and Luke 22:43.
224 See Zech. 12:1; cf. I Cor. 2:11.
225 See Num. 16:22; Heb. 12:9.
226 See Luke 9:26 and Rev. 14:10.
227 See I John 3:1-2.
228 See Rom. 8:30.

- **Eschatology**: The study of the 'last days'[229] and last events in God's prophetic agenda

1. The Antichrist (I John 2:18; cf. II Thess. 2:3)
2. Abomination of desolation (Matt. 24:15)
3. Great Tribulation: the persecution of Jesus' elect brethren (Matt. 24:9, 21)
4. Election of "the rest of the dead" (Rev. 20:5)
5. Jesus' Second Coming (Heb. 9:28)
6. The First Resurrection and rewarding of the saints (Rev. 20:6; Matt. 16:27)
7. The Last Judgment—i.e. of the wicked[230] (Rev. 20:11-15).

(A Brief Summary of What This Book Says)

This book, *The Second Coming of Jesus—Think Again,* says that Jesus Christ came again in mid-summer of AD 72, "immediately"[231] following the three and one-half year[232] Great Tribulation[233]—*before* Jesus' generation passed away.[234] The Rapture[235] then occurred, in which Christ's 144,000 elect *Israelite* saints[236] [i.e. saved in the High Calling Salvation Rank] ascended into Heaven, sat with Jesus at the Marriage Supper of the Lamb, received their rewards, and came down from God out of Heaven to Paradise where they took up co-rulership with Jesus over "all Israel"[237] (see Rom. 11:26; Rev. 21:1-2). Thus, the

---

[229] The "last days" took place during Jesus' generation. See Heb. 1:2; cf. I Pet. 1:20.

[230] The "Last Judgment" did not affect the saints of God who, as Jesus had taught would not be judged (see John 5:24; 12:31).

[231] "Immediately," Matt. 24:29

[232] See Rev. 3:2-3; 12:6, 14.

[233] See Matt. 10:17-23; 24:9-21; 25:34-40; John 9:4; 16:1-3; Luke 21:10-17; Rev. 6:7-11; 7:14; 11:2-10; 12:2, 7, 12b, 15, 17; 13:7, 12-18; II Tim. 3:1, 12.

[234] See Matt. 10:23; 11:16; 23:36; 24:34; cf. Rom. 13:11-12; Heb. 1:2; 10:37; I Pet. 1:20.

[235] Rapture: Cf. Matt. 24:40-41; John 14:3; Acts 1:11; I Cor. 15:51; I Thess. 4:16; Rev. 11:11-12.

[236] **Israelite** saints: Cf. Matt. 10:23; 28:19; Acts 5:31; 26:7; 28:20; Rom. 9:4-5; Gal. 3:16, 23-24; 6:16; Rev. 7:4-8.

[237] See Rom. 11:26; cf. Matt. 19:28.

Kingdom of God had come, ***not here on earth***[238] but in Paradise;[239] that is, the "new earth" that Peter mentioned in II Pet. 3:13.

This means, dear reader, that the True Church—the one Jesus said He would build in His generation (Matt. 16:18; Col. 2:6-7; 1Pet. 2:4-6) vanished from the earth in the Rapture of AD 72.

(The Anachronic End Time Prophetic Fulfillments)

The big lesson of this book, dear reader, is that the gospel of the kingdom of heaven [i.e. the High Calling Salvation gospel], evangelized by Jesus and His disciples during their generation, is now ***anachronistic*** [i.e. no longer applicable]. Anachronistic also are all other end time prophecies, events, and judgments, such as: (1) the High Calling Salvation Rank; (2) the Second Coming of Jesus;[240] and (3) everything in Revelation[241]—e.g. (a) the falling away;[242] (b) the appearing of Antichrist;[243] (c) the formation of the seven-headed beast having ten horns;[244] (d) the seven seals, trumpets, and plagues; (e) the Two Witnesses;[245] (f) Armageddon;[246] (g) the Rapture;[247] and (g) the Great White Throne Judgment and more.[248]

(What about Us Christians? What Are We to Do?)

Dear reader, I'm sure you have one or more of the following questions in your mind: (1) What about me, I have been baptized, I go to church, am I not a Christian? (2) I believe in Jesus, won't God take

---

[238] Cf. John 18:36; cf. II Pet. 3:13; Rev. 4:1; 11:12; 21:1-5.

[239] Paradise: See II Cor. 12:4.

[240] See Matt. 24:30-34.

[241] See Rev. 1:1, 3.

[242] See Rev. 2 & 3. These two chapters describe the apostasy that was taking place in the seven churches of Asia. See also II Thess. 2:3.

[243] See Rev. 22:7, 12, and 20.

[244] See Rev. 13:1-3, 11; 17:9-12, 16.

[245] See Rev. 11:2.

[246] See Rev. 16:16.

[247] See Rev. 11:12.

[248] See Rev. 20:11.

me to Heaven when I die? (3) Won't non-Christians go to hell when they die? Etc.

Let me see if I can help you with these questions. What is a Christian? Yes, dear reader, if you have believed in Jesus, have been baptized, go to church, take the Lord's Supper, love your neighbor, your family, your children, and try to keep the Ten Commandments, then I'd certainly say you are a Christian. You are doing the right kinds of things for our generation. You are helping to keep Christ and His death, burial, and resurrection known in this world. I wish there were millions more Christians such as you. You teach your children to believe in Jesus and to do the same things you are doing.

You certainly *will* go to Heaven [i.e. Paradise] when you die, as well as all other Christians like you. But is it because you do all the things you do? The answer may surprise you: No, it is not because you do those things, but because Jesus died for "all men:"

> Therefore as by the offence of one *judgment came* upon all men to condemnation; even so by the righteousness of one *the free gift came* upon all men unto justification of life.—Rom. 5:18

> For since by man *came* death, by man *came* also the resurrection of the dead. For as in Adam all die, even so in Christ shall all be made alive.—I Cor. 15:21-22

Thus sinners don't "go to hell" upon dying, but will only be **judged** (i.e. corrected).

> **It is appointed unto men once to die, but after this the judgment**.—Heb. 9:27

Therefore, please keep on being the Christian you are, because when you enter Paradise you will receive, as Jesus put it, "few *stripes*" (Luke 12:48). If you stop doing good and begin to do evil, you will receive "many *stripes*" (Luke 12:47).

Keep in mind also that you are not saved in the High Calling[249] rank, but in the Universal Salvation rank. High Calling

---

[249] See Phil. 3:14.

was a **"special"**[250] salvation that was given only to "called"[251] ISRAELITES of Jesus' generation. At Jesus' coming in AD 72 God raptured them into Heaven [not Paradise] to be with God and the Son, they ate and drank with Jesus at the Marriage Supper of the Lamb, and received a prepared mansion in which to live throughout eternity. The Lord changed their bodies from corruptible and mortal into incorruptible and immortal bodies, for, as Paul put it, "flesh and blood cannot inherit the kingdom of God" (I Cor. 15:50).

Dear reader, since you and I will go into Paradise [not the highest Heaven] when our days on earth are done, this means that we are saved in a lesser rank[252] of salvation than that of the High Calling. We have good and great things waiting for us, too, however, when we enter Paradise. Though we will first be chastised of God (see Heb. 12:6), we will awake in Paradise, such as that Garden of Eden described in Gen. 1 & 2. We will no longer live by the sweat of our face (see Gen. 3:19), but have free food from the abundant trees in Paradise (Gen. 2:9). We will have a life expectancy of approximately one thousand years in Paradise and then God will glorify us and take us into Heaven to be with Him and Jesus and Paul, Peter, and millions of other people who have been living there for thousands of years before us.

Dear reader, to make a long story short, don't worry. You and I and all other people living on earth have a bright future to look forward to "For God is love."[253] We may have complete confidence that in our future there will be eternal life for us, and all the sorrows we have suffered and all the tears we have cried will be taken away:

> And I heard a great voice out of heaven saying, Behold, the tabernacle of God *is* with men, and he will dwell with them, and they shall be his people, and God himself shall be with

---

[250] "God . . . is the Savior of all men [i.e. Universal Salvation], **SPECIALLY** of those that believe [i.e. High Calling].—I Tim. 4:10b

[251] See e.g. **Rom.** 1:6-7; 8:28, 30; 9:24; **1 Cor.** 1:2, 9, 24, 26; **Gal.** 1:6, 15; **I Thess**. 2:12; **II Tim.** 1:9; **Heb.** 5:4; **James** 2:7; **I Pet.** 1:15; 2:9; 5:10; **II Pet.** 1:3; **Rev.** 17:14; 19:9.

[252] Universal Salvation is a lesser ranking salvation than that "special" salvation, called High Calling salvation (Phil. 3:14).

[253] See I John 4:8.

them, *and be* their God. And God shall wipe away all tears from their eyes; and there shall be no more death, neither sorrow, nor crying, neither shall there be any more pain: for the former things are passed away. And he that sat upon the throne said, Behold, I make all things new. And he said unto me, Write: for these words are true and faithful.—Rev. 21:3-5

Appendix A

Regarding "666"

> [N]o MAN might buy or sell, save he that had the **mark**, or the **name** of the beast, or the **number** of his name. Here is **wisdom**. Let him that hath **understanding** count the number of the beast: for it is **the number of a MAN**; and his number *is* **Six hundred threescore *and* six**.—Rev. 13:17-18

The "wisdom" needed for "understanding" the number 666 stems from the following considerations:

- It can be obtained [i.e. figured out] only if we think in terms of the 1st-century Roman Empire—i.e. during Jesus' generation. At that time the word game called isopsephia was in its zenith, being "played" by children as well as by serious philosophers. See pg. 92 (FN#67, c3). In fact, the 1st-century Christian readers of Revelation had to "play" this game in order to figure out what the name of the beast was (see Rev. 13:17-18, above). Since the "wise" [e.g. the scholars; the educated] members of the church read, wrote, and spoke Greek, they no doubt were the ones who put their heads together and solved the 666 puzzle.
- It was the church apostates [i.e. the "many antichrists" of I John 2:18] that, by order of the False Prophet, had to receive [be tattooed with] this number on either their right hand or on their forehead (Rev. 13:14).

- The word "MAN" in the above passage is another example of a unipluralism—a noun that can be understood in either the singular or the plural. Other biblical examples of unipluralistic nouns are "man of God" (I Tim. 6:11; cf. II Tim. 3:17), "man of sin"/"son of perdition" (II Thess. 2:3), and "antichrist"/"antichrists" (I John 2:18).

- All male subjects of Rome had this general name and its number, though they were not the people intended in Rev. 13:17-18. This was probably the "key" the scholars in the church used to figure out the name of the beast and his "666" number.

"Latinos"

Consider, dear reader, that before conversion to Christ all members of the church of Christ—during Jesus' generation—had been subjects of the Roman Empire. The general term for them was Latinos, the same spelling we have yet today to refer to people from south of the border. Webster defines "Latino" as (a) "a native or inhabitant of Latin America," or (b) "a person of Latin-American origin living in the U.S."[254]

Upon conversion to Christianity, however, the word Latinos became a distasteful and untenable name for Christ's disciples. Luke tells us that they soon began calling themselves "Christians" (see Acts 11:26).

Retaining Latinos for self-reference, you see, carried the connotation that they **loved** being known as upstanding [i.e. proud, virtuous, honorable] members of the Latin Kingdom, "the Roman Empire." But the teaching of the Holy Spirit was that His disciples were not of this world. Jesus taught this emphatically:

> They are not of this world, even as I am not of this world.
> —John 17:16

John understood this doctrine to mean that Christians were not to love anything about this world, on grounds that it would mean the rejection of their Father in Heaven:

---

[254] Note that either of these definitions is gender-inclusive, referring to men or women, boys or girls.

> Love not the world, neither the things *that are* in the world.
> If any man love the world, the love of the Father is not in him.
> —I John 2:15

In this vein Paul wrote the following:

> If ye then [i.e. Christ's disciples] be risen with Christ, seek
> those things which are above, where Christ sitteth on the right
> hand of God. Set your affections on things above, not on things
> on the earth. For ye are dead [i.e. to this world and its "things"],
> and your life is hid with Christ in God.—Col. 3:1-3

If they were not of this world, and if loving anything about this world meant the rejection of their Father in Heaven,[255] and if their lives were hidden "with Christ," then the only proper self-reference for Christ's disciples became "Christians," no longer Latinos:

> And the disciples were called Christians first in Antioch.
> (Acts 11:26c)

"Christian" was a name that fit them perfectly, connoting the possession of the anointing of the Holy Spirit [making them "saints"] and their brotherly relationship to Jesus Christ. In His goat-sheep parable Jesus referred to His disciples as "these my brethren" (Matt. 25:40). He once told them:

> Who is my mother? and who are my brethren? . . . Behold
> my mother and my brethren! For whosoever shall do the will of
> my Father which is in heaven, the same is my brother, and sister,
> and mother.—Matt. 12:48-50

Thus, Christians willingly and factually rejected their connection to "this world"—the Latin Kingdom—and became citizens of "the world to come"[256]—i.e. God's kingdom. Before conversion they were

---

[255] Jesus commanded His disciples: ". . . call no *man* your father upon the earth: for one is your Father, which is in heaven."—Matt. 23:9

[256] See Matt. 12:32 and Heb. 2:5.

"of this world,"—i.e. of the Roman Empire [cf. "fourth beast"] that Daniel saw rise up out of the sea (Dan. 7:7).

"The Latin Kingdom"

When Christians departed from their faith instead of any longer being of God's kingdom they became again subjects of the Latin kingdom [the Roman kingdom]. That is, they "automatically" defaulted to their pre-conversion relationship to this world. They willingly and willfully chose to relate to and re-connect with their former worldly citizenship and their love for the things of this world.

Spiritual reattachment to the Latin Kingdom gave them the number 666 because in certain words and titles the Greek letters—due to their numerical equivalents—add up to 666.

Dr. Adam Clarke, in his commentary on Revelation spells this out for us.[257] In Greek "the Latin kingdom" is spelled H (The) Λατινη (Latin) Βασιλεια (Kingdom). Note the numerical equivalent of each of these letters, and that they add up to 666:

H = 8
Λ = 30
α = 1
τ = 300
ι = 10
ν = 50
η = 8
B = 2
α = 1
σ = 200
ι = 10
λ = 30
ε = 5
ι = 10
α = 1

TOTALS 666: the number of "The Latin Kingdom"

---

257 *Clarke's Commentary*, vol. vi, p. 1026

"Lateinos"

The word Lateinos is in the masculine gender (hence, "the number of a **man**") but refers alike to a male or female subject of the Latin kingdom, much as the word "Latino" in today's speech is gender-inclusive in the U.S.

This alternate spelling of Latinos came from the Ante-Nicene church Father Irenaeus [AD 120/140-200/202] in his book *Against Heresies*, [258] and apparently was not challenged or objected to by anybody for thirteen centuries. One reason, no doubt, is that very few people in Europe knew anything about Irenaeus, and even fewer had read his book. The chief reason, however, was no doubt the intellectual passivity that permeated the European culture during the Middle Ages. Individualism, intellectual zeal, and freedom of thought and speech were dangerous characteristics for anyone to exercise in those centuries because of the religious dominance of the Roman Catholic Church and its propensity to sentence heretics to death by burning them at the stake.

Galileo,[259] for example, was forced, on pain of such a death, to "agree" with the Church that the heliocentric doctrine of Copernicus was a mere hypothesis, not a logical and demonstrative conclusion based on scientific observation. Also, though he had seen them with his own eyes through the telescope he perfected, he was compelled by the Church to deny that there were any craters on the surface of the moon. Nevertheless, and often not very privately, Galileo continued to talk about heliocentricity and Moon craters as more than theories. The Church would have burned him at the stake as a heretic had it not been for Bellarmin and other more liberal-thinking churchmen who advised against it.

---

[258] See this entire book in *The Ante-Nicene Fathers*, vol. I, p. 559.

[259] Galileo (b. Feb. 15, 1564, Pisa—d. Jan. 8, 1642, Arcetri, near Florence. At age 25 he became lecturer in mathematics at the University of Pisa, and later professor of mathematics at the University of Padua, where he developed the astronomical telescope through which he discovered craters on the Moon, sunspots, phases of Mercury, and the satellites of Jupiter. He also showed that the Milky Way is composed of stars. (See the *Britannica*, vol. 5, p. 86.)

The Renaissance

The Protestant Reformation and the strong, ongoing spirit of the Renaissance at that time [i.e. humanism], resulted in the beginning of a more liberal Catholic Church [i.e. toward scientific findings]. Works produced in ancient times, especially writings by Greek and Latin churchmen, philosophers, scientists, mathematicians, artists, and historians had become the craze.

The Jesuit Bellarmin,[260] for example, became interested in the Greek church Father Irenaeus and his book *Against Heresies.* Some things in Irenaeus' theology he found threatening to Roman Catholicism. One thing was Irenaeus' use of isopsephia to find the name and "number" of the beast [666]. Irenaeus' had to use an alternate spelling of Latinos [i.e. Lateinos] in order to obtain this 666. That is, he changed the spelling to contain the "ei" diphthong. Bellarmin saw that as unfair tinkering with the known orthography of that word. But Bellarmin, being a staunch and famous Roman Catholic, was obliged and expected to object to Irenaeus' Lateinos solution to Rev. 13:18.

Clarke's Commentary, however, states that down through the generations following Irenaeus' time "almost all commentators" accepted Irenaeus' "ei" diphthong as authoritative and themselves used Lateinos as the only solution to Rev. 13:18.

> Many names have been proposed from time to time as applicable to the beast, and at the same time containing 666. We will only notice one example, viz., that famous one of Irenaeus, which has been approved of by almost all commentators who have given any sort of tolerable exposition of the Revelation. The word alluded to is $\Lambda\alpha\tau\varepsilon\iota\nu o\varsigma$, the letters of which have the following numerical values: λ 30, α 1, τ 300, ε 5, ι 10, ν 50, ο

---

[260] Full name: San Reberto Francesco Romolo Bellarmino (b. Oct. 4, 1542, Montepulciano, Tuscany—d. Sept. 17, 1621). He was the Italian cardinal and theologian that vigorously opposed Protestant doctrines during the Reformation. He actually sympathized with Galileo's teaching the heliocentric Copernican theory, but because Protestantism and Catholicism were embroiled at the time he advised Pope Paul V in 1616 to decree it "false and erroneous." See the *Britannica*, vol. 2, p. 72. See also *Keepers of the Keys*, by Nicolas Cheetham; pub. Charles Scribner Sons, New York, © 1982: pp. 217, 223.

70, ς 200; and if these be added together, the sum will be found to be the equivalent to the number of the beast. [261]

All this being said, Irenaeus still did not seem to "catch on" to the salient idea in Rev. 13:18, that the name Lateinos, *__because of its masculine suffix__*, had "the number of a **man**." Rather, he stressed that the name represented the indictment of the then existing—2nd century—Latin Kingdom [i.e. the Roman Empire] as the beast. He was thinking in terms of his own age, of course. He also saw Rev. 13:18 as tied in with Dan. 7:7-8, where Daniel stressed the notions of (a) the fourth beast, and (b) "another little horn" without the least inkling of the "little horn" having to be limited to any such idea as "the number of a **man**."

> Then also *Lateinos* (ΛΑΤΕΙΝΟΣ) has the number six hundred and sixty-six; and it is a **very probable** [solution], this being the name of the last kingdom [of the four seen by Daniel].[262] (stress added)

Note how the numerical equivalents of the Greek letters in the name—Λατεινος (Eng. Lateinos)—give us the number 666:

Λ = 30
α = 1
τ = 300
ε = 5
ι = 10
ν = 50
ο = 70
ς = 200

TOTALS 666: the number of the name of the beast

Bible commentator Adam Clarke also must have considered Lateinos a possible, if not also a "very probable" solution to Rev. 13:18,

---

261 Op. cit., *Clarke's Commentary*
262 loc. cit., *The Ante-Nicene Fathers*

or he would not have bothered to discuss it at length in his commentary on Revelation [see Rev. 13:18].

"Wisdom" and "Understanding"

I also look very favorably upon this solution. Note the following passage from Revelation:

> Here is **WISDOM**. Let him that hath **UNDERSTANDING** count the number of the beast—Rev. 13:18a

Why would the Holy Spirit have stressed "wisdom" and "understanding" as requirements for arriving at the number 666 unless He knew that some intellectual [or maybe the word should be "picky"] conflict would be associated with it? I see Bellarmin's objection to Irenaeus' diphthong spelling as *conflictive*, but I also understand it to be more *picky* than pertinent: like Jesus put it, "strain at a gnat, and swallow a camel" (Matt. 23:24).

I also see it as what the Holy Spirit had in mind for the need of wisdom and understanding. There is "wisdom" in knowing that 666 would be hard to nail down to a strict orthography, and that variants in the spelling of many words are often universally accepted without question. Why, then, should the "ei" diphthong be an insurmountable obstacle to a truly wise man? I also see the wisdom in believing that John, after his release from Patmos and return to Ephesus, went to the seven churches of Asia to explain this very wisdom. It takes a man of wisdom and understanding to distinguish between reasonable and picky objections.

More Wisdom and Understanding About Spelling Variations At the time of Jesus' generation spelling was a matter of individual choice, depending upon writing experience or lack of it, or education or lack of that. Probably the main combination of reasons for accepting Irenaeus' variant spelling is that (1) it works, and (2) it is the only one of many 666 solutions that meet the requirement of being "the number of a **man**."[263]

---

[263] The variant spelling of certain English surnames today is testimony that in times past even the English people lacked orthographic guidance in their spelling. My own last name, for example [Hogue], has five distinct variants in the Louisville,

Conclusion

Dear reader, there can be no denial over the fact that in the Greek game Isopsephia both "The Latin Kingdom" and "Lateinos" add up to exactly 666. The stronger of these two is "Lateinos," being, as John wrote,

"The number of a <u>man</u>" (Rev. 13:18).

Lateinos is a Greek word in the ***masculine*** gender, which is why John said 666 is "the number of a **man**." Moreover, by associating (a) "the Latin Kingdom" [i.e. the Roman Empire] and (b) "Lateinos," with Daniel's fourth beast [Dan. 7:7]—the Roman Empire—we have incontestable reason to believe that **Lateinos** is the very word the Holy Spirit and John had in mind.

Irenaeus and other Bible scholars knew of several other words and phrases that also added up to 666, but "Lateinos" is the ***ONLY*** one of them that logically "fits" the unique notion of "the number of a ***MAN***."

NOTES

Kentucky telephone directory: Hoag, Hoge, Hogg, Houge, and Hough. Note the diphthongs ["oa" and "ou"] in two of the spellings as opposed to the single-vowel "o" in the other two. All four of these spellings are usually pronounced exactly alike by most people possessing these names. One cannot, in a sane state of mind, claim that only one of the spellings is the "correct" one. By the same wisdom, Iranaeus' "ei" version of Latinos can be neither casually nor studiously dismissed.

Appendix B

"The Land that I Gave to Your Fathers."—Ezek. 36:28

Genesis 13:14-17 is about a "land" that God promised to give Abram and his "seed" [descendants] forever. God said to Abram:

> Lift up now thine eyes, and look **from the place where thou art** northward, and southward, and eastward, and westward: For **all the land which thou seest**, to thee will I give it, and to thy seed **for ever**.—vv. 14-15

Note the three stressed parts of this passage. All three must be correctly interpreted in order to identify the land God had in mind. Let me give you an initial, brief comment on each part:

"FROM THE PLACE WHERE THOU ART"

That would be **Bethel**, about ten miles north-north-west of Jerusalem (Gen. 13:3).

"ALL THE LAND WHICH THOU SEEST"

Two questions here: (1) which land? and (2) how much of it could Abram actually see in the short duration God spoke to him? As to "which land," was it on earth or in heaven?[264]

"FOR EVER"

How are we to understand "for ever" in the context of Gen. 13:14-15 (see quote above)? Would all his descendants live there forever with none of them ever dying? Or, would they live **and** die there throughout their normal succession of generations forever? In the former choice we must acknowledge that the setting would have to be in Paradise where God's people never die; in the latter case, on this earth [i.e. no doubt Canaan] where generations of Israel have historically lived and died.

See the next verse:

> And I will make **thy seed**[265] as **the dust of the earth**: so that if a man can number the dust of the earth, *then* shall thy seed also be numbered.—v. 16

To most interpreters this seems to mean that **a yet future time** will come when Israel's population in today's Holy Land will be as innumerable as the dust of the earth, and the stars of heaven,[266] *and all of them will **continue** living there forever, **without ever dying*** (Gen. 13:15).

The next verse reads:

> Arise, walk through the land in the length of it and in the breadth of it; for I will give it unto thee.—v. 17

Whatever and wherever this land is or was, one thing is for sure: Abram walked throughout its length and breadth in the short while that God spoke to him out of heaven. Let's return to v. 14, where we read, "from the place where thou art" (Gen. 13:14).

---

264   Here's a hint to the answer: The Hebrews author wrote of a **"heavenly"** country—Heb. 11:16.

265   Abram's descendants through Isaac—Gen. 12:21; cf. Rom. 9:7 & Heb. 11:18

266   See Gen. 15:5; cf. Ex. 32:13; Rom. 4:18; Heb. 11:12.

*(Abram Saw and Walked
In the "Land" by
The Power
Of God.)*

But how could Abram have walked throughout this land when his body remained in one place [i.e. implied by God's words, "where thou art"]? If he did not move from that place while he saw the land and walked throughout it, does this not tell us that he did it in his spirit, not in his *natural* body? If this is so, does it mean that the land he saw and walked through was not real but only a kind of "prophetic vision" of a future, real land? Reader, the latter conclusion is not totally *necessary* if the "land" **_really_** existed in Paradise in Abram's day.

If so, therefore, a supernatural feat was involved here. God took Abram into Paradise in an OBE [out-of-body-experience], so that his body remained in Bethel while his spirit did the seeing and the walking. The apostle Paul also indicated that God may well have taken **him** to Paradise in an OBE (see II Cor. 12:1-4).

Evidently the Bible is replete with God's prophets having OBEs. If I correctly understand a *Biblical* OBE, it involves an angel of God taking the prophet's spirit out of his natural body and attaching it to or placing it inside his own body. Then God permits the spirit of the prophet to use or direct the angel as he would himself. Thus, the prophet would see, hear, and act through the angel.

Their OBEs explain how the prophets had the ability to look upon God Himself in all His Majesty, Power, and Glory, and do it without dying. They did not die because they were not technically human while inside the body of the angel. For all practical purposes they were themselves **angels**! Jesus said that His disciples would one day be like the angels of God, neither marrying nor giving in marriage (see Matt. 22:30). Ezekiel, for example, seems to say that God put him into a trance before he saw visions. He wrote:

> And it came to pass in the sixth year, in the sixth *month*, in the fifth *day* of the month, **_as_ I sat in mine house**, and the elders of Judah sat before me, that the hand of the Lord GOD fell there upon me [i.e. put my body to sleep—cf. Gen. 2:21]. Then I [i.e.

my spirit in an angel] beheld, and lo a likeness as the appearance of fire from the appearance of his loins even downward, fire; and from his loins even upward, as the appearance of brightness, as the colour of amber [was this God?]. And he put fourth the form of an hand, and took me by a lock of mine head; and the spirit [of God] lifted me up between the earth and the heaven, and brought me in the visions of God to Jerusalem, to the door of the inner gate that looketh toward the north; where *was* the seat of the image of jealousy, which provoketh to jealousy. **And, behold, the glory of the God** of Israel *was* there, according to the vision that I saw in the plain.—Ezek. 8:1-4

In the five and twentieth year of our captivity, in the beginning of the year, in the tenth *day* of the month, in the fourteenth year after that the city [Jerusalem] was smitten, in the selfsame day the hand of the LORD was upon me [He put my body in a trance/deep sleep—cf. Gen. 2:21] and brought me [i.e. my spirit] thither [to Jerusalem in Paradise]. In the visions of God **brought he me into the land of Israel** [in Paradise], and set me upon a very high mountain, by which was the frame of a city on the south [Jerusalem]. And he brought me thither, and, behold, *there was* a man [angel], whose appearance *was* like the appearance of brass, with a line of flax in his hand, and a measuring reed; and he stood in the gate. And the man said unto me, Son of man, behold with thine eyes, and hear with thine ears, and set thine heart upon all that I shall shew thee; for to the intent that I might shew *them* unto thee *art* thou **BROUGHT**[267] hither: declare all that thou seest to the house of Israel.—Ezek. 40:1-4

John also had an OBE. He wrote about it as follows:

I John, who also am your brother, and companion in tribulation, and in the kingdom and patience of Jesus Christ, was **in the isle that is called Patmos**, for the word of God, and for the testimony of Jesus Christ. I was in the Spirit [i.e. of an angel, out of my own body] on the Lord's day [i.e. the day of

---

[267] So, reader, we see that Ezekiel was **_really_** taken to Jerusalem [in Paradise] inside his angel-body. He was "brought" there!

the Great Tribulation—cf. II Thess. 2:2], and heard behind me a great voice, as of a trumpet, Saying, I am Alpha and Omega, the first and the last [I am God—i.e. Jesus glorified]: and, What thou seest, write in a book, and send it unto the seven churches which are in Asia; unto Ephesus, and unto Smyrna, and unto Pergamos, and unto Thyatira, and unto Sardis, and unto Philadelphia, and unto Laodicea. And I turned to see the voice that spake with me. And being turned, I saw seven golden candlesticks; **And in the midst of the seven candlesticks *one* like unto the Son of man, clothed with a garment down to the foot, and girt about the paps with a golden girdle. His head and *his* hairs *were* white like wool, as white as snow; and his eyes *were* as a flame of fire; And his feet like unto fine brass, as if they burned in a furnace; and his voice as the sound of many waters.**—Rev. 1:9-15

And there came unto me one of the seven angels which had the seven vials full of the seven last plagues, and talked with me, saying, Come hither [i.e. within me], I will shew thee the bride, the Lamb's wife. And he carried me away in the spirit [i.e. John's spirit within the angel] to a great and high mountain, and shewed me that great city, the holy Jerusalem, descending out of heaven from God, having the glory of God: and her light *was* like unto a stone most precious, even like a jasper stone, clear as crystal; And had a wall great and high, *and* had twelve gates, and at the gates twelve angels, and names written thereon, which are *the names* of the twelve tribes of the children of Israel.—Rev. 21:9-12

(The Same Pattern Occurs
In the Prophetic Visions
Of the Bible.)

Reader, do you see the way God showed visions to His prophets? First, the prophet's location is always given, indicating that his body did not move during his vision. In his first vision Ezekiel's body remained in his house (Ezek. 8:1). In the second we see that he [i.e. his spirit] was in the land of Israel [in Paradise] upon a very high mountain (Ezek. 40:2). John's natural body was on the isle of Patmos "for the word of

God, and for the testimony of Jesus Christ"; that is, to receive God's word and Jesus' testimony (Rev. 1:9).

Next we read of the prophet [i.e. his spirit] being caught up moved about by God's hand [i.e. by an angel], and shown visions. An angel grabbed a lock of Ezekiel's hair and lifted him up between the earth and the heaven. The angel's body often serves as a living "chariot," in which the prophet moves about and through which he is able to see, hear, talk, and walk.

Then the prophet sees great and wonderful things that he could not see if he were in his own body. John, for example, saw God sitting on His throne (Rev. 4:2). Had he looked upon God with his own eyes, and not through the angel's eyes, he would have died, for no man has seen God at any time and lived (Ex. 33:20; John 1:18; 5:37; 6:46; I Tim. 6:16; I John 4:12).

Also, the visions are replete with details, such as the gate of the temple Ezekiel stood before, or the kind of garment Jesus wore and what His eyes and hair looked like. It is these details that demonstrate to us that the prophets were in a real time and space setting.

Finally, the visions all have to do with God's chosen people, Israel.

The Interpretation of Gen. 13:14-17

We know that the land God showed Abram was the Land of Israel in Paradise, indicating that Paradise already existed in Abraham's day. Paradise was actually the **"new"** heaven and earth the Bible refers to in such passages as Is. 65:17; 66:22; and Rev. 21:5. The "land" that God showed Abram was literally the *Land of Israel* IN PARADISE. He told Abram that He was going to give *this particular land* [i.e. country], to him and his "seed" [descendants] after him "for ever."

We must realize that Paradise is not just "the land of Israel," but an entire world, an entirely new creation, i.e. the new heaven and earth. Paul called it "the third heaven," and said that God had taken him there—"whether in the body, I cannot tell; or whether out of the body,[268] I cannot tell: God knoweth" (II Cor. 12:1-4). God did not tell Abram that He was giving him and his seed the entire New World [i.e. Paradise], but only the **Land of Israel** in Paradise.

---

[268]   OBE

Just as God gave Israel a particular land—Canaan—on Earth, so He gave Israel a special land in Paradise. Just as Canaan was referred to as "Israel," or the **_country_** of Israel in the Near East—so in Paradise Israel's land is also their **_country_**, and possibly it is in a "Near East" part of Paradise as well.

(The "Land" God Showed
Abram Was Definitely
In Paradise.)

We know also that the land God showed Abram was not Canaan. One reason we know this is because Abram had shown Canaan to himself by "humanly" traveling up and down in it in the first three years he lived there. In contrast, God showed Abram "an heavenly" country in just a few minutes (cf. Luke 4:5). Through the instrumentality of an angel God showed it to him. By this angel Abram *went* to Paradise, and *walked* throughout the Land of Israel there. He saw Paradise through his angel's eyes, and walked throughout it through the angel's legs and feet. I think it was through his own, personal angel[269] [i.e. by its instrumentality] that God showed **Abram** the Land of Israel.

Another reason we know that Canaan was not the land God showed Abram is that Abram, upon dying **_discontinued living in Canaan_** and entered Paradise. But Gen. 13:15 says that the land God promised him would be his "for ever" [i.e. without interruption by death]. How can we say that **Canaan** was his forever since he died and departed **from** it forever?[270] He should still be living in Palestine today if Canaan were the intended land.

Finally, Jesus revealed to the Sadducees that Abraham was living in Paradise:

---

[269] Jesus taught that everybody has an angel that "always" stands for him before the Father in Heaven (Matt. 18:10). Also, in Hebrews we learn that God sends ministering angels to people on earth (Heb. 1:14).

[270] The Bible speaks of only one person who, after death, returned to this world—i.e. Jesus. Nowhere in the Bible do we see the least hint that Abraham or anyone else would ever return to this world once having died and passed into Paradise.

> But as touching the resurrection of the dead, have ye not read that which was spoken unto you by God, saying, I am the God of Abraham, and the God of Isaac, and the God of Jacob? God is not the God of the dead, but of the **LIVING**. —Matt. 22:31-32

If Abraham was then "living," God must have reincarnated his departed spirit [when he died] and put him somewhere **other** than this world. In effect, Jesus was saying to all that heard and understood Him that Abraham had been dwelling in PARADISE! The Bible teaches that there are only three realms of existence: Heaven, Earth, and Paradise. He was not living on Earth, which was obvious to all. He was not living in Heaven [i.e. God's presence] because Jesus said that "no man hath ascended up to heaven" (John 3:13). Therefore, he must have been in Paradise.

("The Land Wherein
Your Fathers Have
Dwelt"—Ezek. 37:25)

> And **they** [i.e. the just-resurrected "whole house of Israel"—Ezek. 37:11] shall dwell in **the land that I have given** [Heb. perfect tense] unto Jacob my servant, **wherein your fathers have dwelt** [Heb. perfect tense]; and **they** shall dwell therein, *even* **they**, and their children, and their children's children for ever: and my servant David *shall be* their prince for ever.—Ezek. 37:25

To correctly understand this passage it is vital that we know two things: (1) the identity of the persons indicated by the pronoun "they," seen thrice in the passage, and (2) the importance of correctly translating the two dependent clauses in the passage, both of which have predicates in the Hebrew perfect tense.

(I) "THEY"

All pronouns have antecedents, and can be understood only by knowing the connection between the pronouns and their antecedents. That is not all. More importantly, the antecedent itself must be *clearly* understood.

Dear reader, "they" in this passage refers to those people Ezekiel called "the whole house of Israel" in Ezek. 37:11. But next we must understand, also, that "the whole house of Israel" refers to the "dry" bones mentioned at the beginning of the chapter (see vv. 1-2). Finally, we must understand to what or to whom the dry bones refer. If we know all these things, we can correctly interpret Ezek. 37, especially v. 25.

Let us attend to this problem now. Ezekiel found himself taken to "the valley which *was* full of bones" (v. 1). This was a real valley, located in Paradise. The bones God created in the valley were His first step in resurrecting [i.e. reincarnating] "the whole house of Israel." Their coming together [i.e. "bone to his bone"—v. 7] was the second step. Note the whole new-creation process:

- God created the bones in the valley—v. 1
- "the bones came together, bone to his bone"—v. 7
- "the sinews and the flesh came up upon them"—v. 8a
- "the skin covered them . . . but *there was* no breath in them"—v. 8b
- "breath came into them"—v. 10a
- "they lived"—v. 10b
- they "stood upon their feet, an exceeding great army"—v. 10c

This Was the Reincarnation of Israel's **Wicked** Dead

Reader, the above are the general steps God took in reincarnating Israel's *wicked* dead on the day of the General Resurrection [i.e. Nisan 14, AD 29]. Notice that God reincarnated a whole "army" of Israelites ["the whole house of Israel"—i.e. that had been "in the graves"—John 5:28-29]! Of course, not only did God resurrect Israelites in the General Resurrection, but also all other descendants of Adam that had died **in wickedness** throughout ancient times [i.e. from Adam to Christ]—see John 5:28-29.

Remember, God had put the wicked deceased in the "prison"[271] of death [angelic imprisonment], and their coming to life again had to wait until Jesus' death for **all** mankind (see Rom. 5:18; I Cor. 15:21-22). But in the context of our present discussion we are talking about Israel only, and the reincarnation [i.e. resurrection] of their wicked dead on the day of Christ's death.

Yes, Ezekiel's vision of the dry bones was prophetic, meaning it did not happen in Ezekiel's day, but was to be fulfilled centuries later in Jesus' generation, at the time of His death, when the General Resurrection took place.

But how do we know that Ezekiel saw the future resurrection only of the WICKED of Israel? Note what those reincarnated said of themselves as soon as they came to life: ". . . our bones are dried, and our hope is lost: we are cut off for our parts" (Ezek. 37:11). Only the wicked would speak of themselves in this downcast, negative manner. Note also what God said about them:

> And say unto them, Thus saith the Lord GOD; Behold, I will take the children of Israel from among the heathen, whither they be gone, and will gather them on every side, and bring them into their own land: And I will make them one nation in the land upon the mountains of Israel; and one king shall be king to them all: and they shall be no more two nations, neither shall they be divided into two kingdoms any more at all: **Neither shall they defile themselves any more with their idols, nor with their detestable things, nor with any of their transgressions**: but I will save them out of all their dwellingplaces, wherein they have sinned, **and will cleanse them**: so shall they be my people, and I will be their God.—Ezek. 37:21-23

If they weren't going to be idolaters **"any more,"** then that proves that during their life time they **had** been idolaters. They died in a wicked state and God raised them with that wickedness still on their mind. But He brought them into Paradise where He chastened them and soon "converted" them into His **righteous** sons and daughters:

---

[271] prison—See Is. 61:1; cf. I Pet. 3:19.

And ye have forgotten the exhortation which speaketh unto you [unto sinners] as unto children, My son, despise not thou the chastening of the Lord, nor faint when thou art rebuked of him: For whom the Lord loveth he chasteneth, and scourgeth every son whom he receiveth . . . Now no chastening for the present seemeth to be joyous, but grievous: nevertheless afterward it yieldeth the peaceable fruit of righteousness unto them which are exercised thereby. Wherefore lift up the hands which hang down, and the feeble knees; And make straight paths for your feet, lest that which is lame [halt, crippled] be turned out of the way; but let it rather be healed. Follow peace with all *men*, and holiness, without which no man shall see the Lord.—Heb. 12:5-6, 11-14

Reader, I have led you through enough of Ezek. 37, I think, to help you see beyond all doubt that the **antecedent** of "they" is the past wicked generations of Israel that God finally resurrected on the day of Christ's death. So now, we should be able to go back and reread Ezek. 37:25 [see at the head of this section] with clear understanding. It is the **past wicked** of the whole house of Israel [i.e. both from the northern kingdom and the southern kingdom] that God resurrected and took into the Land of Israel in Paradise, to live in the presence of their righteous fathers who had been living there from the time of Abraham to Christ.

(II) The Two Hebrew Perfect-tense Clauses in Ezek. 37:25

Notice that Ezek. 37:25 has two dependent clauses: (1) "that I **have** given . . ." and (2) "wherein your fathers **have** dwelt." Grammarians will recognize that both clauses have predicates in the English **present-perfect** tense, indicated by the auxiliary verb "have." In both the Hebrew "perfect tense" and the English present-perfect tense these predicates indicate an action interpretable as one (1) beginning in the past and continuing into the present, or (2) that both began **and** ended in past time. Most of the time, lacking a definitive context, translators will choose the latter sense. Thus, the Hebrew perfect tense and the English present-perfect tense are equally ambiguous in nature. They require a settled ***context*** to help both translators and theologians decide on their correct meaning.

For example, the KJ translators just as easily could have chosen the English **past-perfect** tense: "**had** given" and "**had** dwelt." I know why they didn't, because this English tense is strict and immovable, affording no wriggling—i.e. luxury of ambiguity. It can *only* mean an action that started AND ended *in the past*. Therefore, by choosing the present-perfect tense for the two dependent clauses the KJ translators essentially left the interpretation open for the theologians to settle.

Let's Have Some Theological Reasoning Here

Dear reader, I am one of those theologians left to sort out the meaning of Ezek. 37:25 according to its correct context.

Let me explain to you *why* the KJ translators were correct in choosing the English present-perfect tense translation. There is a great difference in God's saying "I have given" and "I had given," or "fathers have dwelt" and "fathers had dwelt." "Have given" and "have dwelt" allow a theologian to teach the following:

The fathers [i.e. the righteous fathers of Israel, such as Abraham, Isaac, Jacob, David, and the prophets] were still dwelling in the Land of Israel at the time of the General Resurrection on Nisan 14, AD 29 when God brought their wicked descendants [i.e. "they, and their children's children"] into the land with them.

This interpretation is based on the correct context of Ezek. 37:1-11, which is plainly and undeniably about an actual resurrection of the wicked Israelites on the day Christ died on the cross (vv. 1-11). The New Testament teaching of a **resurrection**—a coming to life again of the dead—opts out the teaching and belief, held by present-day premillennialists, that Ezek. 37 is about the May 14th, 1948 "rebirth" of Israel in Palestine. They teach that the "Jews" [inclusive of all twelve tribes of Israel] came "alive" again on that historical date.

Premillennialists simply "invented" this interpretation of Ezek. 37, made convenient to them by recent 20th- and 21st-century Jewish history—e.g. the **emigration** of Jews from many European and Asian countries into Palestine following the Holocaust in WWII. Instead of understanding Ezek. 37:1-11 as a prophesied, *actual* resurrection of the past wicked generations of Israelites [i.e. Israelite generations from the 7th century BC to the 1st century AD], they look at it as a "spiritual" [not an actual] resurrection. In doing so they ignore Bible teaching that all prophecy pertaining to Israel was fulfilled before Jesus' generation passed away. Remember Jesus' teaching to His disciples:

> Verily I say unto you [Jesus' early, 1st-century disciples], This generation shall not pass, till all these things be fulfilled. —Matt. 24:34

> For these be the days of vengeance [i.e. God's judgment of the Jews during Jesus' generation], that all things which are written [pertaining to Israel] may be fulfilled.—Luke 21:22

Both Jesus and the Premillennialists cannot be right, in that their views do not harmonize chronologically or demographically. Jesus was talking about Jews of His own time and generation, and the premillennialists are talking about 20th and 21st-century Jews.

("And **THEY** Shall Dwell Therein, even They") Ezek. 37:25b

These words are very important, yet are mostly misunderstood today. The pronoun **"THEY"** refers first to the idolatrous generation of Israelites "slain"[272] by Shalmaneser king of Assyria in 722 BC;[273] and the other thousands of them deported two years later by Shalmaneser's brother Sargon II.[274] In short, **"THEY"** refers first of all to the Israelites living when Samaria was destroyed and its inhabitants either slain or deported. Of course, by Jesus' time and the General Resurrection on the day of His crucifixion, they were all in their graves.

---

[272] Slain—See Ezek. 37:9.
[273] "Shalmaneser V, the son of Tiglath-pileser III, king of Assyria (727-722)"—*Harper's Bible Dictionary*, p. 932
[274] "The 'king of Assyria' who exiled Israelites from Samaria (2 Kings 17:6a) was Sargon II, who reconquered the city in 720 B.C."—Ibid.

Next, note "**shall,**" the *future-tense* auxiliary. The future of course was seven centuries later, on Wednesday, Nisan 14, AD 29, when Jesus died for the sins of Israel and God raised them to life. Then, the glorified Jesus four days later [on Sunday, Nisan 18] led them into Paradise (cf. John 5:28-29; Matt. 27:52-53; Luke 23:43; Eph. 4:8).

("Their Children, and Their Children's
Children For Ever")
—Ezek. 37:25b

"**THEY**" also refers to the wicked children and grandchildren of the slain and deported generation that had lived and died—where God had scattered them—up to the day of Jesus' crucifixion and the General Resurrection. According to our passage [Ezek. 37:25] they entered the Land of Israel in Paradise at that time, and began to dwell with their righteous fathers[275] who had dwelt their since the days of Abraham. They abode there with them and will abide with them there "for ever" (see Gen. 13:15):

> Behold, O my people [i.e. the wicked deceased of Israel, represented by the dry bones], I will open your graves, and cause you to come up out of your graves, and bring you into the land of Israel [i.e. in Paradise] And ye shall know that I *am* the LORD, when I have opened your graves, O my people, and brought you up out of your graves, And shall put my spirit in you, and ye shall live, and I shall place you in your own land [i.e. in Paradise]: then shall ye know that I the LORD have spoken *it*, and performed *it*, saith the LORD . . . Neither shall they defile themselves any more with their idols, nor with their detestable things, nor with any of their transgressions: but I will save them out of all their dwellingplaces, wherein they have sinned, and will cleanse them: so shall they be my people, and I will be their God. And David my servant *shall be* king over them; and they all shall have one shepherd: they shall also walk in my judgments, and observe my statutes, and do them.—Ezek. 37:12-14, 23-24

---

275   Their righteous fathers then became "kings and priests" that, under David, ruled over them, "in the morning," as the psalmist [David] foretold (see Psalm 49:14; cf. I Pet. 2:5; Rev. 1:6).

("The Heathen Shall Know")

> Moreover I will make a covenant of peace with them; it shall
> be an everlasting covenant with them: and I will place them, and
> multiply them, and will set my sanctuary in the midst of them
> for evermore. My tabernacle also shall be with them: yea, I will be
> their God, and they shall be my people. And **the heathen shall
> know** that I the LORD do sanctify Israel, when my sanctuary
> shall be in the midst of them for evermore.—Ezek. 37:26-28

This passage tells us that even the heathen-deceased [i.e.
Gentile-dead[276]] rose in the General Resurrection and entered Paradise.
Because God is impartial, He had planned raising them **chronologically
with** His people all the while. Thus, Jesus foretold to His disciples:
"The hour is coming, in the which **ALL** that are in the graves [the
wicked Israelites and wicked Gentiles alike] shall hear his voice [in the
General Resurrection], and shall come forth" (John 5:28b-29a).

It follows that if God resurrected both the wicked of Israel and
the heathen together in the same resurrection "hour" He took also
them **_all_** into Paradise. However, He put the Israelites in <u>their</u> Land,
and the heathen in **their** lands. What lands? Answer: the lands that
corresponded to those they had lived in here on earth before they died.
Paradise, an entirely new world very likely had the same continental
geography and national boundaries that were here on earth.

Therefore, they all awoke at the same time in Paradise, once again
in the lands they remembered. The same nations that surrounded Israel
here on earth surrounded Israel in Paradise as well. Here on earth,
however, the heathen did not understand that the God of Israel is
God of all peoples, even themselves. But now [i.e. after they entered
Paradise] it quickly became known to them that the God of Israel is
the God and Creator of all people and of all things. If they wanted to
learn about the true God they had to go to Jerusalem and inquire of the
kings and priests in Israel:

> And it shall come to pass in the last days [Jesus' generation],
> _that_ the mountain of the LORD'S house [in Jerusalem in

---

[276]   _True_, not _acculturated_ Gentile peoples

Paradise] shall be established in the top of the mountains [over the Gentile nations], and shall be exalted above the hills [tribes; people-groups]; and all nations shall flow unto it. And many people shall go and say, Come ye, and let us go up to the mountain of the LORD, to the house of the God of Jacob; and he will teach us of his ways, and we will walk in his paths: for out of Zion [Jerusalem in Paradise] shall go forth the law [the ways of Jehovah], and the word of the LORD from Jerusalem. And he [the LORD—i.e. Jehovah] shall judge among the nations [Gentile peoples], and shall rebuke many people: and they shall beat their swords into plowshares, and their spears into pruninghooks: nation shall not lift up sword against nation, neither shall they learn war any more. O house of Jacob, come ye, and let us walk in the light of the LORD.—Is. 2:1-5

CONCLUSION

Dear reader, much of this discussion is about "the kingdom of heaven" [i.e. "third heaven"—II Cor. 12:2, 4], the very gospel [i.e. restoration gospel] that Jesus preached to the Jewish nation of His day:

Jesus came into Galilee, preaching the gospel of the kingdom of God, And saying, the time is fulfilled, and the kingdom of God is **AT HAND**: repent ye, and believe the gospel. —Mark 1:14b, 15

Note the words, **"AT HAND."** "At hand," correctly interpreted, means the same thing as "is," or "is come," as seen in the following passages:

Blessed are the poor in spirit, for theirs **IS** the kingdom of heaven . . . Blessed are they which are persecuted for righteousness' sake: for theirs **IS** the kingdom of heaven—Matt. 5:3, 10

But if I cast out devils by the Spirit of God, then the kingdom of God **IS COME** unto you.—Matt. 12:28

Moreover, in terms of the High-Calling salvation rank **"AT HAND"** means **"now" [i.e. Jesus' generation]** as in the following passages:

For he saith, I have heard thee in a time accepted, and in the day of salvation have I succoured thee: behold, **NOW** *is* the accepted time; behold, **NOW** *is* the day of salvation.—II Cor. 6:2

Of which salvation [i.e. High-Calling Salvation] the prophets have inquired and searched diligently, who prophesied of the grace *that should come* unto you [i.e. church members]: Searching what, or what manner of time the Spirit of Christ which was in them did signify, when it testified beforehand the sufferings of Christ, and the glory that should follow. Unto whom it was revealed, that not unto themselves, but unto us they did minister the things, which are **NOW** reported unto you by them [i.e. the apostles] that have preached the gospel unto you with the Holy Ghost sent down from heaven; which things the angels desire to look into.—I Pet. 1:10-12

Finally, according to Mark's Gospel the words, "is fulfilled," and, "at hand," are synonymous:

Now after that John was put in prison, Jesus came into Galilee, preaching the gospel of the kindom of God, And saying, The **TIME IS FULFILLED**, and the kingdom of God is **AT HAND**: repent ye, and believe the gospel.—Mark 1:14-15

By this Scriptural testimony we can say and believe with all confidence that with the coming of Jesus Christ [i.e. in His public ministry among the Jews] God's kingdom, or Paradise-like reality [i.e. the kind of blissful life then going on in "the third heaven"—II Cor. 12:2, 4] *had come!* It had come to ***them*** right there in Galilee and Judea through the works and miracles of the Son of God who then lived in their midst.

It came *to the Jews* each time Jesus healed one of them, or fed them, or taught them the real meaning of godliness, and how to practice faith, hope, and charity among men [see Jesus' "sermon on the mount" in Matt. 5-7]. To all the Jews who came to Him, believing, Paradise was a present and current state. Thus, Jesus taught the Jews to pray: "Our Father which art in heaven, Hallowed be thy name. Thy kingdom come. Thy will be done in earth, as *it is* in heaven [i.e. as it is in Paradise above: "the third heaven"—II Cor. 12:1-4]—Matt. 6:10.

Through Jesus Christ and His miracles and teachings God answered their prayer, and gave His Son the power to do for the Jews here on earth what He was also doing for people in Paradise above. That is, Christ healed "all" their diseases and infirmities.[277] He commanded the demons to leave them alone, casting them out. He gave seeing to the blind, walking to the lame, and speaking to the dumb.[278] In short, God, through Jesus Christ, had brought His kingdom [His paradise] to earth, as it was in heaven!

In short, Christ gave the repentant and obedient Jews [in Galilee and in Judea] a taste of the "Land of Israel" in Paradise that God from the days of Abraham had given unto their righteous and faithful fathers.

Wednesday, Dec. 1, 2010

NOTES

---

[277] Matt. 8:16
[278] Luke 7:21-22

Appendix C

The Lethal Wound that Was Healed

And I saw one of his heads[279] **as it were wounded to death; and his deadly wound was healed**: and all the world[280] wondered after the beast.—Rev. 13:3

<u>What Was the Lethal Wound?</u>

<u>The "deadly wound" was none other than Christ's wound (death), foretold by Isaiah</u>:

> . . . [H]e was **wounded** for our transgressions, *he was* bruised for our iniquities: the chastisement of our peace *was* upon him; and with his stripes we are healed.—Is. 53:5

All the water- and Holy-Spirit-baptized church members living during Jesus' generation, believed the gospel and were true, born-again sons of God: "Behold," John wrote, "what manner of love the Father hath bestowed upon us, that we should be called the <u>sons of God</u>: therefore the world knoweth us not, because it knew him not. Beloved, <u>now are we the sons of God</u>, and it doth not yet appear what we shall be: but we know that, when he shall appear, we shall be like him; for we shall see him as he is" (I John 3:1-2).

---

279   I.e. the 6th head of the seven-headed beast
280   I.e. the Asian cosmos or "world"

Again, these Christians understood and believed that Jesus' death on the cross was *for them*, as Isaiah wrote: ". . . he [Jesus] *was* wounded for **our** transgressions, *he was* bruised for **our** iniquities: the chastisement of **our** peace *was* upon him; and with his stripes **we** are healed. All we like sheep have gone astray; we have turned every one to his own way; and the LORD hath laid on him the iniquity of **us** all" (Is. 53:5-6).

In other words Christ's death [i.e. His **"wound"**] was also the believer's death or wound. The believer owned it, took it into his own body by faith, knowing that God imputed it to him. Thus, that wound killed the believer as much as it did Christ. Paul, therefore, wrote the following:

> Know ye not, that so many of us as were baptized into Jesus Christ were baptized into his **death**? Therefore we are buried with him by baptism into **death** . . . For if we have been planted together in the likeness of his **death** . . . our old man is **crucified with _him_** . . . he [any born-again church member] that **is dead** is freed from sin. Now if **we be dead with Christ**, we believe that we shall also live with him.—Rom. 6:3, 4a, 5a. 6a, 7-8

> Set your affection on things above, not on things on the earth. For **ye are dead**, and your life is hid with Christ in God.—Col. 3:2-3

Being "Healed" of Jesus' Wound

In Rev. 13:3 (see first paragraph, p. 264) we read that the sixth head of the beast was **"healed"** of Christ's "deadly wound." Any Christian *during Jesus' generation*[281] who fell away from the Faith, and who persisted in his apostasy *past the deadline* (the deadline was about Jan. 15, AD 69) could not go back to Christ. Before the deadline he

---

[281] "During Jesus' generation"—Dear reader, please note this caveat carefully. Everything said in APPENDIX C pertains **only** to Christians and apostates in the time of Jesus' adult-time generation (i.e. AD 26-72). Therefore, you have no need whatsoever to be frightened by any of its contents, doctrines, or warnings against committing apostasy and going past a deadline. In fact, true, Biblical apostasy could be committed only by Christians of Jesus' generation, and God's judgment and wrath could fall **_only_** on **_them_**.

could, but after it he couldn't. Is this not what the Hebrews writer meant when he wrote:

> For it is impossible for those who were once enlightened, and have tasted of the heavenly gift, and were made partakers of the Holy Ghost, And have tasted the good word of God, and the powers of the world to come, If they shall fall away *[and remain apostate beyond the deadline]*, to renew them again unto repentance; seeing they crucify to themselves the Son of God afresh, and put him to an open shame.—Heb. 6:4-6

Does the Bible say anywhere whether or not some of the apostates may have returned to the faith before the deadline? Yes. Jesus said in His mini-epistles to the seven churches of Asia [see Rev. 2 & 3] that apostates could "overcome," but only if they did it during the "space" [of time] remaining before the onset of the Great Tribulation (see Rev. 2:21-22). Jude also indicated the possibility of some returning to the Faith within a time limit:

> And of some [some apostates] have compassion, **making a difference** [i.e. when or if successful]: And others save with fear, **pulling them out of the fire**; hating even the garment spotted by the flesh.—Jude 22-23

Here Jude indicated the possibility, if not the probability, that a compassionate Christian skilled in the word of God—[cf. Heb. 5:13-14]—could succeed in saving an apostate. However, it would be like just *barely* saving him. The passage draws the picture of an apostate being pulled back "out of the fire"—i.e. from the Lake of Fire [i.e. the Second Death]—*just in the nick of time*; that is, *just before the Jan. 15, AD 69 deadline!*

("Five Are Fallen")

> And there are seven kings: **five are fallen**, one is, *and* the other is not yet come; and when he cometh, he must continue a short space.—Rev. 17:10

Before the said deadline[282] [i.e. during the "falling away" period][283] multiple thousands of Christians in Asia committed apostasy. John said the seven churches of Asia had already gone through the trauma of five distinct waves of apostasy: "five are fallen," he wrote (Rev. 17:10a). Each of the "waves" involved about 10,000 Christians, and, in Revelation are symbolized by the word "head(s)," as in "a beast . . . having seven **heads** and ten horns" (Rev. 13:1). In sum, this means that by the time Revelation reached the seven churches of Asia [ca. AD 67-68] *50,000 church members had apostatized!*

John wrote that two more waves of apostasy were due to happen:

> And here *is* the mind of wisdom. The seven heads are seven **mountains**,[284] on which the woman sitteth. [285] And there are seven **kings:**[286] five are fallen, and one is, and the other is not yet come.—Rev. 17:10

---

[282]   Remember, the deadline occurred about January 15, AD 69.

[283]   The falling-away period preceded the Great Tribulation period, with no time-gap between them. Thus, the falling-away period [AD 64-68] and the Great Tribulation period [AD 69-72] together lasted for eight and one-half years, the "one-half" year seen in the prophetic wording, "half a time" (Rev. 12:14). The whole period culminated in the Second Coming of Jesus in midsummer of 72.

[284]   In the apocalyptic genre, in which John wrote Revelation, the word "mountains" symbolizes a discreet "government," usually a large one, with many subjects or followers, and in this case an average 10,000 adherents. Any one of the seven heads, therefore, had its own false-doctrinal predication, its own dictatorial-style government, and its own unique and impending judgment from God. Throughout this book, therefore, I have interpreted "seven mountains" to mean seven separate **waves** or **movements** of apostasy.

[285]   The "Woman," a.k.a. "the great whore" (Rev. 17:1); or the "false prophet" (Rev. 13:11; 16:13; 19:20; 20:10); or the Antichrist (I John 2:18) **"sitteth"** on the seven **"mountains."** This means that the Great Whore/False Prophet controlled the **"king"** [chief leader] of each of the **"heads"** of the seven-headed beast.

[286]   In this APPENDIX I have designated the word "kings" to mean the *founders* or the chief *leadership cadres* of the seven apostate movements. The seventh king, or founder of the seventh apostate movement, should be identified as THE "Antichrist," and his followers as "antichrists" (cf. I John 2:18).

("One Is" and The First Martyrdom Episode)

> And there are seven kings: five are fallen, **_one is_**, *and* the other is not yet come; and when he cometh, he must continue a short space.—Rev. 17:10

The "One is" Mountain was the **sixth head** of the beast (if five "heads" had fallen, then it is logical to count the next two as the sixth and seventh heads of the seven-headed beast). This "One-is"-sixth-head of the beast already existed when John was writing Revelation on the prison Isle of Patmos. However, it had not yet persecuted or killed the First-Episode martyrs.

But they began persecuting Christians and killing them **_soon_** after John was released from Patmos and returned to Asia. I say **"soon"** considering that Revelation starts out with the words "things which must **shortly** come to pass" (Rev. 1:1). John wrote:

> And it was given unto him [**sixth** head] to make **WAR**[287] with the [31,500[288]] saints, and to overcome [kill] them. —Rev. 13:7a.

It was immediately after the deadline, January 15, AD 69, that the 3½-year-long Great Tribulation started and the massacre of the First Martyrdom Episode elect brethren of Christ began. When the killing ended 31,500 enduring-to-the-end Christians [Matt. 24:13], or one out of every four of Jesus' elect brethren, had laid down their lives for His "name's sake" (cf. Matt. 10:22; 19:29; and 24:9), thus beginning the fulfillment of the scenario described in the Fourth Seal: "And power

---

[287] **WAR**—The Greek word for "war" here—i.e. πολεμον [polemon]—is used sixteen times in the New Testament, and in each instance the case can be made that it signifies a long-lasting, large-scale war or battle. See *Strong's Concordance*, Greek Dictionary, #4171 and *The New Englishman's Greek Concordance and Lexicon*, p. 732.

[288] These 31,500 martyrs equaled the "great multitude" that no man could number" (see Rev. 7:9). No **man** had been able to count them, but the Holy Spirit revealed their number.

was given unto them over the fourth part of the earth,[289] to kill with the sword, and with hunger, and with death, and with the beasts of the earth" (Rev. 6:8). The massacre went on for over a year[290] or for "an hour, and a day, and a month, and a year" (Rev. 9:15).

("The Other Is Not Yet Come" And The Second Martyrdom Episode)

And there are seven kings: five are fallen, and one is, *and* **the other is not yet come**; and when he cometh, he must continue a short space.—Rev. 17:10

Revelation specifies two episodes of martyrdom of Christians in Asia, understood in the following passage from the fourth and fifth seals of the book with seven seals.[291]

And when he [Jesus] had opened **the fourth seal**, I heard the voice of the fourth beast say, Come and see. And I looked, and behold a pale horse: and his name that sat on him was Death, and Hell [Gk. Hades] followed with him. And **power was given unto them over the fourth part of the earth [i.e. over the fourth part of Christ's elect brethren]**, to kill [them] with sword, and with hunger, and with death, and with the beasts of the earth. And when he had opened **the fifth seal**, I saw under the altar the souls [i.e. 31,500 reincarnated persons comprising the FIRST MARTYRDOM EPISODE] of them that were slain [by the sixth head] for the word of God, and for the testimony which they held: and they cried with a loud voice, saying, How long, O Lord, holy and true, dost thou not judge and avenge our blood on them that dwell on the earth [in Asia]? And white robes were given unto every one of them; and it was said unto them, that they should rest yet for a little season, until their [3,500][292]

---

[289] I.e. Fourth part of the Christians in Asia, "earth" being synonymous with the "dust of the ground" from which God had created their bodies. See Gen. 2:7; Psalm 103:14.

[290] From Jan. 15, AD 69 through March 16, AD 70

[291] "book with seven seals" (Rev. 5:1)

[292] This smaller number of 3,500 martyrs killed in The Second Martyrdom Episode comprised the second of two witnesses against the Antichrist. Each of the two

fellow-servants [SECOND MARTYRDOM EPISODE] also and their brethren, that should be killed as they were, should be fulfilled.—Rev. 6:7-11

At this time [i.e. about June-July of AD 69] the **seventh head** of the seven-headed beast [i.e. the Antichrist] instigated, indoctrinated and controlled by the False Prophet—and the False Prophet by Satan—appeared on the scene in Asia. This was the final head, which [like each of the previous six heads] numbered about 10,000 antichrists. These, added to the 60,000 Christians already fallen, gives us the total of 70,000 antichrists mathematically indicated in Rev. 11:13.

It was these same 70,000 that were "the third part"[293] of the original,[294] 210,000-strong Christians in the seven churches of Asia. Collectively, the 70,000 constituted Revelation's "beast . . . having seven heads and ten horns" mentioned in Rev. 13:1 (cf. 12:3 and 17:7).

The Ten Horns, of course, were the ten, ad hoc Roman magistrates that the emperor had set up in Asia to facilitate and expedite the trials [i.e. kangaroo trials] of the First Martyrdom martyrs and the Second Martyrdom martyrs.[295]

---

instances of martyrdom had its own cadre of witnesses. In the First Martyrdom Episode 31,500 Christians who gave their testimony of Jesus and salvation in the courts of the Ten Horns were killed. The First-Martyrdom witnesses are understood in Matt. 10:28-39 and 16:24-26. Because there were two groups of witnesses, and because these 3,500 were the second witness, the Holy Spirit referred to them as **"the two witnesses"** (see Rev. 11:3).

293   See "the third part"—Rev. 8:7-12 and 9:15.

294   Here the word "original" means the thousands of Christians that had already been living in Asia [i.e. those earlier converted under Paul's Gentile mission] and the multiple-thousands of additional Christians that **fled** to Asia from Italy and Greece westward and from the Palestinian war zone eastward. These had all come together in Asia while John was still on Patmos and before the falling-away of the sixth and seventh heads of the beast.

295   Dear reader, to help you see the bigger picture in Revelation, the 31,500 First Martyrdom martyrs are the same as the woman's "man child" [see Rev. 12:5], and the Second Martyrdom martyrs are called the woman's "remnant" [see Rev. 12:17]. Moreover, the first are also called "a great multitude" [Rev. 7:9], and the second are also called the "two witnesses" [Rev. 11:3].

EXPLANATION AND SUMMARY

> And I saw one of his heads as it were wounded to death; and
> his deadly wound was healed: and all the world wondered after
> the beast.—Rev. 13:3

Dear reader, I hope that you have understood this book's unique description of the Antichrist. Let me recount the things the book says about the Antichrist so that you can compare and contrast them with the teachings of most of today's commentators.

First, this appendix shows that the Antichrist is not some still-to-be-in-the-future Jewish antagonist to Christ and the gospel. Rather, the Antichrist **was** [i.e. note: *past tense*] the Israelite[296] Leader of the final **seventh** head of the seven-headed beast who lived during Jesus' generation nearly two thousand years ago. He had been a bona fide, Spirit-filled, water-baptized member of Christ's body who was "enlightened," had "tasted of the heavenly gift," and was one of the "partakers of the Holy Ghost" (Heb. 6:4). He had not "held fast his profession of faith" (Heb. 10:23), but had turned "the grace of our God into lasciviousness, and [denied] the only Lord God, and our Lord Jesus Christ" (Jude 4b). He had "sinned willfully" (v. 26). He had "trodden under foot the Son of God, and counted the blood **wherewith he was sanctified**, an unholy thing, and had done despite unto the Spirit of grace" (29). He had done all these things before he *outwardly* manifested himself in AD 69 as the "man of sin" and the "son of perdition" (II Thess. 2:3).

Second, every single one of the 70,000 apostates comprising the seven-headed beast suffered the lethal wound and was healed of it by willfully and publicly denying Christ.

The premillennial doctrine that _only one evil man_ [i.e. **_the_** Antichrist] had the "deadly wound" and was "healed" of it has been a serious, misleading concept. Rev. 13:12-18, correctly interpreted, teaches that all 70,000 apostates had and were healed of the "deadly wound" of Christ. The sixth- and seventh-head apostates were

---

[296] I.e. not necessarily a Jew of the tribe of Judah, or Levi, or Benjamin. He could have been from any of the twelve tribes of Israel.

"healed" of the wound first. Then, the Leader of the <u>seventh</u> head of the beast—i.e. the Antichrist, a.k.a. the False Prophet—by doing "wonders" and "miracles" like those of Elijah,[297] "deceived" the 50,000 "harmless" constituents of the first five apostate movements [cf. "five are fallen"—Rev. 17:10] after they exceeded the deadline, or used up all the "space" God gave them to repent but did ***not*** "repent" or "overcome" (Rev. 2:21, 26, and Rev. 16:11). When they remained apostate beyond that deadline [i.e. ca. Jan. 15, AD 69], that is when they were "healed" of Christ's wound, repentance or overcoming having by then become "impossible" (Heb. 6:4-6).

Third, there is the difference of time, setting, nationality, and religion. According to some premillennialists, for example, the Antichrist is[298] a nominal Jewish-Catholic about to appear on the prophetic landscape. Many believe he will be of German descent—a highly intelligent, smooth talking, well-admired European politician, industrialist, philosopher or a dynamic, hypnotic-charismatic churchman [e.g. a newly elected pope or Greek-Orthodox Patriarch?].

Actually, Revelation says that the Antichrist was a bloodline, genealogical descendant of Israel [i.e. not necessarily a Jew; cf. Rev. 7:4-8] that made his début in Asia [today's western Turkey] during the time of Jesus' adult-time generation, or AD 26-72.

Fourth, Premillennial doctrine says that there must be a revival of the Roman Empire inasmuch as (1) the ancient empire has long since dissipated, and (2) Daniel foretold that all end time prophecy was to be fulfilled ***when the Roman Empire exists***. The Roman Empire in Daniel is symbolized by the "fourth beast"—Dan. 7:7, 19, and 23.

But, correctly interpreted, not only Daniel but Jesus and the apostles taught that the entire end time prophetic agenda was fulfilled during Jesus' generation, before it "passed away"—Matt. 24:34; Luke 21:22 & 32. Since that is when the Roman Empire really existed in history it must be that Daniel, Jesus, and the apostles were right.

---

[297] "Miracles like those of Elijah"—The Old Testament prophet Elijah was touted to have called fire down from heaven, although it was God that did it in support of Elijah's mission to apostate, Baal-worshiping Israel. See I Kings 18:36-39; cf. Luke 9:54.

[298] "Is"—Many premillennialists think that the Antichrist is an adult person living today and waiting in the wings to be "revealed" (cf. II Thess. 2:3).

Fifth, premillennialism teaches that when the Bible speaks of "all nations" [e.g. Dan. 3:7; 4:1; 6:25; Matt. 25:32; 28:19] Rev. 11:2, 9; and 19:15, 18] we must understand **_ALL_** the nations that will be on earth when Jesus returns as well as **_ALL_** individuals comprising them.

Wherever end time prophecy is mentioned in the Bible, however, the words "all nations" mean only a limited number of people FROM all nations. For example, the church contained a limited number of Israelites from each of the twelve tribes of Israel (Rev. 7:4-8). Jesus taught that the church would be His "little flock" (Luke 12:32), certainly too small a concept to think that He meant the entirety of the world's people and all the world's nations.

Sixth, popular modern-day eschatology says that Jesus' eternal kingdom will soon be established on this earth, while the Bible teaches that it has existed in the "third heaven" or "Paradise" since the year AD 72, the year of Jesus' Second Coming and the Rapture. The Third Heaven and Paradise, as explained in the New Testament, are the same thing as the "new heaven and a new earth" (Rev. 21:1; cf. Is. 65:17; 66:22; II Pet. 3:13).

Seventh, most eschatologists insist that when Jesus comes again, "every eye shall see him" (Rev. 1:7), and by "every eye" they mean _all people living on earth at His coming, whether sinner or saint._

Jesus, however, taught His disciples that "Yet a little while [i.e. after His death and burial] . . . **the world [i.e. people not His disciples] seeth me no more;** but ye [shall] see me" (John 14:19). Indeed, His disciples _did_ see Him after His death and burial for forty days (Acts 1:3), while the Jews did not see Him at all. The Gospels make no mention of the Jews, or just everyone in general, seeing Jesus during the forty days. Remember, Jesus had told the Jews: "Ye shall not see me henceforth, till ye shall say [later, in Paradise], Blessed _is_ he that cometh in the name of the Lord" (Matt. 23:39).

All who accept Jesus' teaching, therefore, must conclude that the words "every eye" in Rev. 1:7 cannot mean anyone other than His own disciples. One might say that Saul the Pharisee saw Him on the road to Damascus, and that that contradicts what I am saying. However, Luke wrote that Saul beheld only "a light from heaven" (Acts 9:3), a light that blinded him on the instant (Acts 9:8). Neither did any of his fellow journeymen see Jesus: "And the men which journeyed with him stood speechless, hearing a voice, **but seeing no man**" (v. 7).

Furthermore, when Jesus was taken up to Paradise two angels said to the disciples, "Ye men of Galilee, why stand ye gazing up into heaven? this same Jesus, which is taken up from you into heaven, <u>shall so come</u> **in like manner** <u>as ye have seen him go into heaven</u>" (Acts 1:11). If Christ's disciples, and no one else, saw Jesus go up into heaven, then if His return was "in the same manner," all unbiased and intelligent interpreters must conclude with me that only **His elect brethren** saw Him coming in the clouds in midsummer, AD 72.

Eighth, many end time Bible scholars today erroneously teach that the literal earth and all its elements will be burned up, with the unwarranted caveat that *only its **surface*** will be burned up, to purify it of its ages-old *trash, topographical dangers, and man-made impurities and poisons.* God will then, through His mighty power, re-make the earth [cf. resurface it]. This *repaved* earth, they unwarrantedly assert, is what the Bible calls "the new earth."

The Bible says, however, that "*One* generation passeth away, and *another* generation cometh: but the earth [surface or otherwise] abideth forever" (Eccles. 1:4). The psalmist seems to agree, saying, "*Who* [i.e. God] laid the foundations of the earth, *that* it should not be removed for ever" (Psalm 104:5).

There is no true contradiction of Scripture here. The problem is the faulty exegesis these Bible scholars give to the words "the heavens" and "the earth" as used by Peter in II Pet. 3:7 and 10. These expressions are apocalyptical with symbolical meanings, not common, everyday meanings. For example, earlier in chapter three Peter referred to "the world that then was" (v. 6), meaning the antediluvian world of Noah's day. When he said that it "perished" he did not mean that the literal earth perished, but that the ***people*** on the earth perished, a worldwide tragedy that he said in plain language in his first epistle (I Pet. 3:20) and also in II Pet. 3:6:

> For Christ also hath once suffered for sins, the just for the unjust, that he might bring us to God, being put to death in the flesh, but quickened by the Spirit: By which also he went and preached unto the spirits in prison [i.e. the deceased wicked antediluvian population]; Which sometime were disobedient,

when once the longsuffering of God waited in the days of Noah, while the ark was a-preparing, wherein few, that is, eight souls were saved by water.—I Pet. 3:18-20

> For this they [the scoffers—II Pet. 3:3] willingly are ignorant of, that by the word of God the **HEAVENS** [i.e. the righteous antediluvians who by faith were translated into Paradise[299]] were of old, and the **EARTH** [i.e. the billions of wicked, unrepentant antediluvians] standing out of the water and in the water; Whereby the **WORLD** [Gk. cosmos] that then was, being overflowed with water, perished. But the **HEAVENS** [i.e. the high-ranking "false prophets" and "false teachers" in the end time church[300]] and the **EARTH** [i.e. the lower ranking "many antichrists"[301]in the church] which are now, by the same word are kept in store, reserved unto fire against the day of **judgment and perdition of ungodly men**.—II Pet. 3:5-7

The *earth* did not perish (only fleshly, living beings can perish), although its surface indeed was **greatly altered** by the super-rapid rushing, charging, and swirling of unbelievably large dimensions of water that erupted from mighty aquifers and by the rain coming crashing and crushing down upon the earth from the heavens for "forty days and nights" (Gen. 7:11-12)! It should be clear that Peter's topic in chapter three is not to be understood as God's judgment and destruction of the Universe or the Solar System [i.e. "the heavens and the earth"], but rather the "perdition of ungodly men," as plainly stated in II Pet. 3:7. Thus, the "heavens and the earth" mentioned twice in the chapter (vv. 7 and 10) should be exegeted as the **false prophets** and the **"many antichrists"**[302] that perished in the Lake of Fire before Jesus' generation "passed away"—see Rev. 20:14-15 and Matt. 24:34.

As support for this interpretation we should note that nowhere in all Jesus' words do we read of the literal world being burned up. We do read His warning to the unbelieving Jews of being burned up

---

299   "Translated into Paradise"—See under "TWO," pages 222-223.
300   "False prophets" and "false teachers"—Matt. 24:11, 24, and II Pet. 2:1
301   See I John 2:18.
302   See I John 2:18.

in Gehenna fire,[303] and to the end time Christian apostates of being cast into the Lake of Fire.[304] Neither Gehenna nor the Lake of Fire, however, by any stretch of the imagination can be interpreted to mean the literal conflagration of planet Earth.

Neither do we find any support for this interpretation in the Old Testament teachings. Note, for example, the following passage:

> For, behold, the day cometh, that shall burn as an oven; and all the **proud**, yea, and **all that do wickedly**, shall be stubble: and the day that cometh shall burn **them** up, saith the LORD of hosts, that it shall leave them neither root nor branch.—Mal. 4:1

Nowhere in this passage does the whole world burn up. It does not state: "the day cometh in which the whole world shall be burned up, as in an oven." Some Bible scholars read that into the passage, but the passage does NOT say that. Like Peter, Malachi was concerned with the wicked children of Israel being burned up, not the morally-neutral earth. He knew what happened in the wars of his day. The victorious armies burned down whole cities and the houses in them, so that fire killed many inhabitants as well as the sword:

> Thus saith the LORD; For three transgressions of Judah, and for four, I will not turn away *the punishment* thereof; because they have despised the law of the LORD, and have not kept his commandments, and their lies cause them to err, after the which their fathers have walked: **but I will send a fire upon Judah, and it shall devour the palaces of Jerusalem**.—Amos 2:4-5

Note also:

> And in the fifth month, on the seventh *day* of the month, which *is* the nineteenth year of king Nebuchadnezzar king of Babylon, came Nebuzaradan, captain of the guard, a servant of the king of Babylon, unto Jerusalem: And he burnt the house of the LORD, and the king's house, and all the houses of Jerusalem, and every great *man's* house burnt he with fire.—II Kings 25:8-9

---

[303] See e.g. Matt. 5:22, 29, 30; 10:28; 11:23; 23:33, and Luke 16:23.
[304] See Matt. 13:30, 40, 42, 50; Rev. 20:14-15.

In sum, the destruction by fire of ancient Judah and the destruction by fire of the antichrists of Peter's day must be understood in their own contexts and time/place settings. Neither God nor His prophets talked about the shenanigans and mischief of peoples far removed from the geographical prophetic theater [i.e. the Near East and the Mediterranean peoples]. Nothing is said in the Bible, for example, about God being wrathful toward the Chinese, or the Japanese, or the Mongols, or any other Far East peoples. God spoke of no judgment against the people of India, or the South Sea Islanders, or the artic Laplanders, or the primitive people in the western hemisphere such as the Aztec and Inca Indians, or the North American Indian tribes. Prophecy is simply not about such far-away people. This is not to say that God did not love them, or help them, or have compassion on them in their troubles, it's just that they were not on His ***prophetic*** Radar Scope.

God's end time wrath was to fall only on those who had Christ's deadly wound and became [through apostasy] "healed" of it. Only apostate Christians of Jesus' generation may be so accused or described.

NOTES

Appendix D

"The Second Death"

He that hath an ear, let him hear what the Spirit saith unto the churches; He that overcometh shall not be hurt of **the second death**.—Rev. 2:11

Blessed and holy *is* he that hath part in the first resurrection: on such **the second death** hath no power, but they shall be priests of God and of Christ, and shall reign with him a thousand years.—Rev. 20:6

And death and hell were cast into the lake of fire. This is **the second death**.—Rev. 20:14-15

But the fearful, and unbelieving, and the abominable, and murderers, and whoremongers, and sorcerers, and idolaters, and all liars, shall have their part in the lake which burneth with fire and brimstone: which is **the second death**.—Rev. 21:8

Adamic Sin and Adamic Death

From all past ages to the present the vast, great majority of Adam's descendants have been dying only *one death*, having no thought or fear whatsoever of dying again—i.e. a **second death**. Not until John wrote Revelation was the possibility of dying two times revealed (see the above passages).

Adam's sin in the Garden of Eden (he ate fruit from the forbidden tree, or "the tree of knowledge of good and evil"[305]) is the cause of death throughout the world, as Paul explained:

> Wherefore, as by one man [Adam] sin entered into the world, and **death** by [that] sin . . . **death** passed upon all men. —Rom. 5:12

> **Death** reigned from Adam—Rom. 5:14a

> . . . through the offence of one [Adam] many be **dead**— Rom. 5:15

> . . . by the offence of one [Adam] *judgment came* upon all men to **condemnation**—Rom. 5:18

> . . . it is appointed unto men **ONCE TO DIE** . . . after this the judgment.—Heb. 9:27

In sum, dear reader, whether you count yourself a Christian, an Atheist or Agnostic, or any other religion, there is but one death [i.e. Adamic Death] that awaits you and me. We will receive the "appointed-once-to-die" death that we read of in Heb. 9:27. Only *that* death awaits us all.

On the bright side, after we die "once" we all look to be resurrected [i.e. reincarnated] and taken into Paradise, never to die again. The following passage from Revelation pertains to us all:

> And God shall wipe away all tears from their eyes; and **there shall be no more death**, neither sorrow, nor crying, neither shall there be any more pain: for the former things are passed away.—Rev. 21:4

Being Born Again and the High-Calling Salvation Rank

OUR reincarnation in Paradise will be the equivalent of **_OUR_** new birth. That is when **_WE_** will be born again.

---

[305] See Gen. 2:17; 3:6, 17-19.

There are significant differences, however, in our new birth [which won't take place until we die] and that which happened to the Christians living in the Roman Empire during Jesus' generation. First, it happened to *them* while they were still alive. Second, *they* were all Israelites, whereas **we** come from all nations on earth, whether Israelites or not. Third, Christians in Jesus' generation had to first hear the gospel preached[306] and believe, giving up the rest of their lives on earth as bond-slaves to Jesus Christ. Today, no one must hear the gospel first or believe it, or dedicate the rest of his life to Jesus Christ. Finally, if Christians of Christ's generation later fell away from the Faith, they incurred the wrath of God and were cast into the Lake of Fire at His Second Coming, whereas if WE become Christians and later fall away it will not bode us any punishment or wrath from God whatsoever. We do not await Jesus' Second Coming.

Thus, the Second Death pertained only to the Christians that lived during the time of Jesus' generation. When those that apostatized were cast into the Lake of Fire they died AGAIN, the ***SECOND*** death.

> . . . and **THEY** were judged every man according to their works . . . whosoever [of them] was **not found written in the book of life** was cast into the lake of fire. This is the **second death**.—Rev. 20:13-15 (wording rearranged for clarity)

However, Christians then, like everybody else from all generations, still had to die "once" [Heb. 9:27], which was the "Adamic Death" discussed above.

But how did Christians of Jesus' generation die the Adamic Death, since Christ taught that all who believed on Him "had passed from death unto life" (John 5:24)?

Notice what the apostle Paul said happened to the Christians of Christ's generation [NOT to Christians of later generations]:

> Know **YE** not, that so many of **US** as were baptized into Jesus Christ were baptized into his **death?**—Rom. 6:3

---

[306] See I Cor. 1:21.

Paul, in effect, said that at His baptism Jesus died the Adamic death that passed on to all men due to Adamic Sin (Adamic Sin is better known today as Original Sin):

For in that he died, he died unto **SIN** once—Rom. 6:10

We know that the word "sin" in this passage cannot mean any sin that Jesus committed, for, as the Holy Spirit testified of Him: "Who [i.e. Jesus] did no sin"—I Pet. 2:22. Therefore He had to die to some other sin, which, of course, was Original Sin. This shows us that at His natural birth by the virgin Mary, He was born with the stigma and the stain of Adamic Sin, just like anybody else "made of woman" (Gal. 4:4). It also shows us, therefore, that at birth Jesus had Adamic flesh, by which He had inherited and possessed Adamic Sin. This Adamic Sin remained with Jesus up until the time He was baptized, and that is WHY He was baptized:—i.e. to finally rid Himself of Adamic flesh and to be reincarnated with NON-Adamic flesh—i.e. be born again.

We see that Jesus was aware that He had Adamic Sin from the brief conversation He and John had at His baptism:

Then cometh Jesus from Galilee to Jordan unto John, to be baptized of him. But John forbad him, saying, I have need to be Baptized of thee, and comest thou to me? And Jesus answering said unto him, Suffer *it to be so* now: for thus it becometh us to fulfill all righteousness.—Matt. 3:13-15

That is, when baptized ***Jesus was born again*** in Non-Adamic flesh, making Him for the first time ***righteous***, no longer a "carrier" of Adamic Sin. With His resultant righteousness He was made fit to be the Sacrifice for all sin and the Savior of all men, referring both to the sins [plural] of Israel, and also to the sin [Original Sin] that all men inherit from Adam.

. . . [H]e *was* wounded for **our** [Israel's] transgressions, *he was* bruised for **our** [Israel's] iniquities: for the chastisement of **our** [Israel's] peace *was* upon him; and with his stripes **we** [Israel] are healed.—Is. 53:5

. . . for the transgressions [sins] of my people [Israel] was he stricken.—Is. 53:8d

. . . for he shall bear their [Israel's] iniquities.—Is. 53:11c

For God sent not his Son into the world to condemn the world; but that the world [both Israelites and non-Israelites] through him might be saved.—John 3:17

Him [Jesus Christ] hath God exalted with his right hand *to be* a Prince and a Saviour, for to give repentance to **Israel**, and forgiveness of [their] sins.—Acts 5:31

For since by man [Adam] *came* death [Adamic Death], by man [Jesus] *came* also the resurrection of the dead.[307] For as in Adam all [men] die, even so in Christ shall all [men] be made alive.—I Cor. 15:21-22

High Calling Salvation

The salvation of all 1st-century church members (during Jesus' generation) was a special, one-time-only salvation called, among other things,[308] "high calling" salvation (Phil. 3:14). The salvation of the rest of mankind was not High Calling salvation (God did not *call* them) but "restoration" salvation; that is, the restoration of them to pre-Fall innocence. Pre-Fall innocence automatically meant salvation, since Adam, before he sinned, was in no way condemned or subject to death.

Note the following passage by Paul that contains reference to both kinds of salvation:

. . . God is the Saviour of **all men**, specially of **those that believe**.—I Tim. 4:10c

The words "all men" refer to restoration salvation, but the words "those that believe" refer to high-calling salvation, which all church members of Jesus' generation had, and ONLY they.

---

[307] The "dead" here refers to **all** who have died, not just to Israelites.

[308] E.g. "holy calling" (II Tim. 1:19); "heavenly calling" (Heb. 3:1); and "so great salvation" (Heb. 2:3)

The high-calling salvation was SPECIAL in that it gave EVERLASTING LIFE to them that believed and an ETERNAL INHERITANCE IN THE KINGDOM OF GOD. This is the salvation rank—i.e. "the gospel of the kingdom of God"—that the apostles preached in the Great Commission, throughout the Roman Empire of their day. Notice what Peter said to those so "called" and saved:

> For so an entrance shall be ministered unto **YOU** abundantly **into the everlasting kingdom** of our Lord and Saviour Jesus Christ.—II Pet. 1:11

It was this salvation that the rich young man had in mind when he asked Jesus, "[W]hat good thing shall I do, that I may have eternal life?"—Matt. 19:16. Jesus answered:

> [I]f thou wilt be **PERFECT**, go *and* sell that thou hast, and give to the poor, and thou shalt have treasure in heaven: and come *and* follow me (Matt. 19:21).

When that young man "went away sorrowful" (Matt. 19:22), Jesus said to His disciples:

> Verily I say unto you, that a rich man shall hardly enter into the kingdom of heaven. And again I say unto you, It is easier for a camel to go through the eye of a needle, than for a rich man to enter into the kingdom of God.—Matt. 19:23-24

That is one reason why high calling salvation is called "special"; it required total surrender to God! It demanded that a believer abandon his old life and give himself completely up to Jesus Christ and the gospel of the kingdom of God.

Only those that did so believe on Jesus, gave up their old life, took up their cross and followed Jesus, even to the extent of leaving their fathers, mothers, siblings, wives, children, houses, properties, and yes, their own lives also[309]—were "worthy" of "so great [a] salvation" (Rev. 3:4).

---

[309] See Matt. 19:29.

Moreover, the rewards and blessings God gave those He called in high-calling salvation were immeasurably great. No wonder God called it High Calling! Christians who endured in their faith to the end, and carried their cross for Christ no matter how great the cost to them [even martyrdom] rejoiced unspeakably when He came "the second time without sin unto salvation" (Heb. 9:28). Jesus came in the clouds and swept them up into the air, out of all the fiery trials, crying, danger, and suffering that they were experiencing in Asia. He received them into His Father's house (Psalm 23:6), from whom each one received (according to their works):

- everlasting life in a glorified, incorruptible, immortal body (I Cor. 15:51-54);
- a "new name written, which no man knoweth saving he that receiveth *it*" (Rev. 2:17);
- white robes and a crown of life and glory (Rev. 2:10; 19:8; Rev. 2:10; I Pet. 5:4);
- "the morning star" (Rev. 2:28);
- a mansion in glory (John 14:2);
- be made a "pillar" in the temple of God in Paradise (Rev. 3:12);
- "the name of my God, and the name of the city of my God, *which is* new Jerusalem (Rev. 3:12);
- Jesus' "new name" (Rev. 3:12);
- "power over the nations" (2:26);
- a massive land grant in Paradise containing cities full of people, over whom they would rule as kings and priests (Matt. 19:29; Luke 19:17, 19; Rev. 1:6);
- the privilege of eating at the table of the King of kings and Lord of lords (Rev. 19:9, 16);
- privilege of sitting down with the Father in his throne (Rev. 3:21).

The Downside of High-Calling Salvation

As great as High Calling Salvation was, it is no wonder that partakers in it had to give up everything they owned in this world and take up their cross and follow Jesus to the end. In short, the cost of its rewards in Heaven was death in Christ on this earth, as Paul wrote:

> For ye are dead, and your life is hid with Christ in God.
> —Col. 3:3

Another downside was that Christians during Jesus' generation could lose it all! If they did not grow in grace (see II Pet. 1:2; 3:18); if they did not "Study to shew [themselves] approved unto God, a workman that needeth not to be ashamed, rightly dividing the word of truth," or "shun profane *and* vain babblings," (see II Tim. 2:15-16), they stood a good chance to fall away from Christ.

If they became weak in their faith and began to fear what man could do to them in the coming Great Tribulation (see Matt. 10:26, 28, 31; I Pet. 1:7; 4:12), they would surely fall from Christ.

If they failed to put on "the whole armour of God," they would not be able "to withstand in the evil day" (Eph. 6:13).

If they did not "hold fast [their] profession" and began "forsaking the assembling of [themselves] together," they would soon "sin willfully . . . trod under foot the Son of God, count the blood of the covenant . . . an unholy thing, and [do] despite unto the Spirit of grace" (Heb. 10:23, 25, 26, 28).

If they backslid into these faults they would surely fall away from Christ and incur the wrath of God upon themselves. They would become the very enemies of God, upon whom He would take vengeance:

> For Vengeance *belongeth* to [God] and He would recompense them and judge his people.—Heb. 10:30 (adapted)

Yes, they knew that they would be in for a "much sorer punishment" than the ancient Israelites received who had "despised Moses' law," and had "died without mercy" (Heb. 10:29). In Revelation we learn just how much more sorely God would "recompense" them for denying Christ before men. He would:

- "fight against them with the sword of [His] mouth" (Rev. 2:16);
- "kill [them] with death,[310] and "give unto every one of [them] according to [their] works" (Rev. 2:23, adapted);

---

[310] I.e. the "second death"

- "come on [them] as a thief" (Rev. 3:3);
- "blot out [their] names out of the book of life" (Rev. 3:5; cf. 20:15);
- "make them to come and worship before [the] feet of Jesus' elect brethren" whom they had just persecuted and slain in Asia (Rev. 3:9; adapted);
- "take away [their] crown" (Rev. 3:11);
- "spue [them] out of [His] mouth" (Rev. 3:16);
- freeze them in their "filth" and "unjustness" (Rev. 22:11);
- "take away [their] part out of the book of life, and out of the holy city, and from the things [i.e. blessings] which are written in this book [of Revelation]" (Rev. 22:19);
- "cast [them] into the lake of fire . . . **This is the second death**" (Rev. 20:14-15).

NOTES

Appendix E

Revelation Numeric

In the last days of Jesus' generation the church that He built[311] began to be infiltrated by apostate teachers.[312] These false prophets arose due to Nero's sudden policy-downgrade toward Christians after blaming them for the Great Fire of Rome in AD 64. Whereas Nero had been tolerant of Christians, now he became hostile to them and began killing them. No doubt His new policy was to exterminate all Christians in the empire.

Christians fled Rome and headed for Asia where there was still a stable Christian population unmolested by persecution. One of the reasons for the stability was that the Christians stayed to themselves, not all in one place in order to gain political clout in opposition to the pagan majority, but in seven widely separate towns in Asia in order NOT to be a threat, and especially to wait for Jesus' Second Coming and the Rapture. In Revelation John called these "the seven churches of Asia."[313] Thus, in Asia pagans and Christians were able to maintain a friendly stance toward one another.

However, after learning of Nero's determination to exterminate Christians, a great pall of fear struck Christians everywhere, and they became much troubled.[314] Jesus foretold that this would happen,[315] and

---

[311] Matt. 16:18; cf. Matt. 24:34
[312] Matt. 24:5, 11; I Tim. 4:1; II Tim. 4:1-4; II Pet. 2:1
[313] Rev. 1:4, 11
[314] Cf. II Thess. 2:1-2.
[315] Matt. 10:17-18, 28, 31

that His "elect" would find themselves fleeing from one city to another to escape the terror of persecution:

> But when they persecute you in this city, flee ye into another: for verily I say unto you, Ye shall not have gone over the cities of Israel, till the Son of man be come.—Matt. 10:23

> Then let them which be in Judea[316] flee into the mountains:[317] Let him which is on the housetop not come down to take any thing out of his house: Neither let him which is in the field return back to take his clothes . . . For then shall be great tribulation, such as was not since the beginning of the world [i.e. the beginning of the church world] to this time, no, nor ever shall be. And except those days should be shortened, there should no flesh [i.e. no Christian flesh] be saved: but for the elect's sake those days shall be shortened.—Matt. 24:16-18, 21.

The false prophets had a "lie" they were teaching to the Christians in Asia. This lie, Paul foretold, would be effective in causing many Christians in Asia to fall away. The lie said that it would be all right if Christians apostatized. It would save them from persecution, and God would forgive them for it after Nero's wrath toward them went away. Apostasy, the teachers assured, would be their means of peace and safety. But Paul wrote:

> . . . when they [the false prophets] shall say, Peace and safety; then sudden destruction cometh upon them, as travail upon a woman with child; and they shall not escape [i.e. they shall not escape Nero's wrath].—I Thess. 5:3

---

[316] In His word "Judea" Jesus actually meant wherever Christians were at the end time, which happened to be in Asia, home of "the seven churches of Asia." The reasons the Christians there could be called "Judea" were because they were followers of the Jew Jesus Christ; "salvation is of the Jews" (John 4:22); and because they were *symbolically* a "Judea" in exile. Moreover, they were the true "Jerusalem" on earth at that time ever since Jesus declared Jerusalem in Judea to be already "desolate" (Matt. 23:37-38). Thus, Paul wrote that God viewed Christians to be the "Jerusalem which is above . . . which is the mother of us all" [Gal. 4:26].

[317] I.e., the mountainous wilderness in Asia (Rev. 12:6, 14)

Nevertheless, many Christians in Asia fell for this lie to the extent that 70,000 of them abandoned the Christian way and took up either a pagan or a Jewish life style,[318] *temporarily* of course [as the lie went]. This was a lot of apostasy, for 70,000 was a full "third part"[319] of the original Christian population in Asia of 210,000 (see below). The Revelation Math involved here is as follows: 210,000 ÷ 3 = 70,000.

10,000

This number is not specifically mentioned in Revelation, but is another extrapolated number from the figures that *are* specifically given. The number should not be accepted as definite, but as a possibly *"average"* number.

Recall that the beast having seven heads represents the Antichrist, a.k.a. John's collective "many antichrists" (I John 2:18).[320] If the total number of antichrists came to 70,000 [see above], then all seven heads of the beast had a collective 70,000. Therefore, if we divide 70,000 by the number of heads, we see the numeric suggestion or possibility that the "average" membership of each head was 10,000. Note I am not saying that it is *certain* that each head had exactly 10,000 apostates. See FN#284, p. 267.

210,000

Since we understand that 70,000 people constituted one-third of the church population in Asia we can compute the entire Christian membership there before the great falling away took place. It was an astounding army of 210,000 Christians living in Asia! Revelation Math: 3 x 70,000 = 210,000.

---

[318] Cf. "the Jewish way"—Rev. 2:9; 3:9; "the pagan way"—Rev. 2:20.
[319] See "the third part"—Rev. 8:7-12; 9:15; 12:4.
[320] See p. 17, Paragraph 4.

14*0*,000

This number, 14*0*,000, is not a mistake; it is an *extrapolated* number,[321] one that comes out when doing "Revelation Math" with all the numbers John specifically wrote down in Revelation.

To find it we need only use the first two numbers above: i.e. 70,000 and 210,000. The number 14*0*,000 appears when we ask the question: "How many Christians in the seven churches of Asia endured to the end, were raptured, obtained eternal life, and received an inheritance in the kingdom of God?" Clearly, the answer results by subtracting the number of apostates from the original church membership of 210,000 [210,000 - 70,000 = 14*0*,000]!

4,000

Here is another extrapolated number that belongs in the equation of Revelation Math. We see it immediately when we notice the difference between the 14*0*,000 Christians that endured to the end and the 14*4*,000 elect brethren of Christ that were "sealed":

> And I saw another angel ascending from the east, having the seal of the living God: and he cried with a loud voice to the four angels, to whom it was given to hurt the earth and the sea, Saying, Hurt not the earth, neither the sea, nor the trees, till we have sealed the servants of our God in their foreheads. And I heard the number of them which were sealed: *and there were* sealed an hundred *and* forty *and* **FOUR** thousand of all the tribes of the children of Israel.—Rev. 7:2-4.

Four thousand elect are suddenly seen missing when we do the Revelation Math [144,000 - 140,000 = 4,000]. This is only one of the soteriological problems that crop up and stare us in the face as we study Revelation. If we just quit studying, saying such things as, "Revelation is impossible to understand," or, "God didn't really *intend* for people to

---

[321] Revelation contains several extrapolated numbers that result from correctly doing Revelation Math; that is, figuring with the numbers that John specifically wrote down in Revelation.

understand Revelation," we are only half right. That's true in that He never intended anyone *who gave up on Revelation,* to understand it. He <u>did</u> intend it to be understood, however, by anyone who struggles on with Revelation, *believes* it IS supposed to be understood, searches for answers, and ESPECIALLY prays to God to help him understand it.

My study of the 4,000 led me to identify them as:

- "The rest of the dead" (Rev. 20:5);
- The receivers (Matt. 10:40-42);
- The eleventh-hour hires (Matt. 20:6-7, 9);
- The sheep (Matt. 25:32-40);
- The mammon of unrighteousness (Luke 16:9)

14<u>4</u>,000

The 14<u>4</u>,000 in Revelation have nothing to do with the modern doctrine that at Jesus' coming only an elite 144,000 Jehovah's Witnesses will enter [i.e. be raptured into] Heaven to rule over the peoples on earth that were left behind, including, I gather, many Jehovah's Witnesses themselves not of 144,000 [high-calling?] rank. Rather, they ***were*** [past tense] the Christians of Christ's generation called and chosen of God to sit with Christ on His throne at His AD 72 Second Coming:

> To him that overcometh will I [Jesus Christ] grant to sit with me in my throne, even as I also overcame, and am set down with my Father in his throne. He that hath an ear, let him hear what the Spirit saith unto the churches.—Rev. 3:21-22

Not all the 144,000 were church members, only 14**0**,000 were. Following the church age [i.e. AD 29-69], during the Great Tribulation period, God CHOSE 4,000 Israelite mammon—i.e. filthy rich entrepreneurs in Asia—to sustain[322] 105,000 Christian refugees [i.e. the "woman" that "fled into the wilderness"[323]] for an astonishing three and a half years [ca Jan. 15, AD 69 through midsummer of 72]. Jesus' "Parable of the Sheep and Goats," by interpretation, says that these

---

[322] I.e., "nourish," Rev. 12:14
[323] Rev. 12:6a

mammon obtained eternal life and an inheritance in the kingdom of God (see Matt. 25:34, 46).

"Double"

> And I heard another voice from heaven, saying, Come out of her,[324] my people, that ye be not partakers of her sins, and that ye receive not of her plagues. For her sins have reached unto heaven, and God hath remembered her iniquities. Reward her even as she rewarded you, and **double** unto her **double** according to her works: in the cup which she hath filled fill to her **double**.—Rev. 18:4-6

In this section let us recall that there were two episodes of Christian martyrdom during the Great Tribulation: (1) The First Martyrdom Episode, ca Jan. 15—June 15, AD 69[325]; and (2) The Second Martyrdom Episode.[326] "A little season" of about three years elapsed between them (June 15, AD 69 through June 15, 72). It is this "double" numeric that reveals to us exactly how many Christians died in The First Martyrdom Episode and how many in The Second Martyrdom Episode. See the two following numerics.

Doubling "The Fourth Part," or 35,000

> And I looked, and behold a pale horse: and his name that sat on him was Death, and Hell followed with him. And power was given unto them over **the fourth part** of the earth [i.e. over the fourth part of the *post-apostasy* church membership in Asia], to kill with the sword, and with hunger, and with death, and with the beasts of the earth.—Rev. 6:8

Before the apostasy the total church membership was 210,000 (see above). After it only 140,000 Christians remained in the churches. The "fourth part" of 140,000 is 35,000 [140,000 ÷ 4 = 35,000].

---

[324] Come out of "Babylon," Rev. 18:2.
[325] For this five month period, see Rev. 9:5, 10.
[326] These two episodes are clearly understood in Rev. 6:9-11.

The passage above says that God gave "Death" [i.e. Antichrist—cf. Rev. 20:14] the power to kill 35,000 Christians in Asia. Using the double-the-punishment numeric we know that 70,000 antichrists paid for their murder of the 35,000 Christians. The 70,000 can be found in two ways: (1) by doubling the 35,000 figure, and (2) by using the Revelation Math provided in Rev. 11:13 [10 x 7,000 = 70,000].

3,500 and 31,500 and 63,000

The 3,500 figure is the number of Christians Antichrist killed in Asia in The Second Martyrdom Episode just 3½ days before Jesus' appearing (Rev. 11:11). In the Judgment God, doubling 3,500 [2 x 3,500 = 7,000], killed twice as many antichrists in "a great earthquake" on the day of Jesus' appearing (Rev. 11:13).

Doubling the 31,500 Christian martyrs gives us the 63,000 antichrists God judged [killed] by having them cast into the Lake of Fire at Jesus' Second Coming (Rev. 20:14-15). Adding 3,500 and 31,500 gives us the total of 35,000 Christians that laid down their lives for their faith in Christ (Matt. 10:39). Doubling the 35,000 gives us the 70,000 Antichrist-citizenship of "the city" or of Babylon that God judged in one day and one hour of that day—i.e. on the day of Jesus' appearing [2 x 35,000 = 70,000]. Also, see Rev. 11:13 for more Revelation Math resulting in the 70,000 figure [10 x 7,000 = 70,000]. Don't forget another way to see the 70,000. Also, don't forget that one third of the original, pre-apostasy church membership was 70,000 [210,000 ÷ 3 = 70,000].[327]

12,000

Of the tribe of Juda *were* sealed twelve thousand. Of the tribe of Reuben *were* sealed twelve thousand. Of the tribe of Gad *were* sealed twelve thousand. Of the tribe of Aser *were* sealed twelve thousand. Of the tribe of Nepthalim *were* sealed twelve thousand. Of the tribe of Manasses *were* sealed twelve thousand. Of the tribe of Simeon *were* sealed twelve thousand. Of the tribe of Levi *were* sealed twelve thousand. Of the tribe of

---

[327] See also pp. 289-290.

Issachar *were* sealed twelve thousand. Of the tribe of Zabulon *were* sealed twelve thousand. Of the tribe of Joseph *were* sealed twelve thousand. Of the tribe of Benjamin *were* sealed twelve thousand.—Rev. 7:4-8

Here, again, we see the numeric 144,000. The Math is simple: multiply 12 x 12 = 14**4**,000.[328] Remember, dear reader that not all 144,000 were church members, only 14**0**,000 were. For the explanation of the additional 4,000 see p. 76 (bottom half) and p. 77. See also FN#38, p. 84, and p. 188.

105,000

This is the number of Christians that fled into the wilderness, and that Jesus symbolized as "a woman clothed with the sun, and the moon under her feet, and upon her head a crown of twelve stars" (Rev. 12:1), and referred to as "the woman" in the follow-up verses 4, 6, and 13-17.

On about Jan. 15, AD 69 the "woman"—i.e. composite Christian refugees from the seven churches of Asia—fled into the wilderness [Rev. 12:6, 14]. She numbered only 105,000 because out of the original 140,000 post-apostate elect Christians from those churches the "first beast,"[329] in a blitzkrieg "war with the saints,"[330] massacred 31,500 of her, reducing her to 108,500 (140,000 - 31,500 = 108,500). These martyred saints constituted the **First Martyrdom Episode** that we have frequently exegeted from Rev. 6:9-11.

During the blitzkrieg the First Beast also *captured* and *imprisoned* 3,500 more of the woman's number. These constituted the "two witnesses,"[331] that throughout the Great Tribulation gave their miraculous[332] "testimony"[333] for Jesus before the Ten Horns for three and one-half years [Rev. 11:2-3]. In midsummer of AD 72 the Ten Horns sentenced the Two Witnesses—i.e. the **Second Martyrdom**

---

[328] See 14**4**,000, pp. 290-291.

[329] See Rev. 13:3, cf. v. 12.

[330] Rev. 13:7

[331] Rev. 11:3

[332] Miraculous—Cf. Luke 21:14-15 with Rev. 11:3-7.

[333] See Matt. 10:19-22, Mark 13:11-13, and Luke 21:13.

Episode[334]—to be slain in the same manner as those of the First Martyrdom Episode. Thus, the number of the "woman" that fled into the wilderness was 105,000, as seen in the following "Revelation Math" summary: 140,000—31,500 = 108,500 - 3,500 = 105,000.

666

This numeric is found in the following passage:

> Here is wisdom. Let him that hath understanding count the number of the beast [i.e. the "beast having seven heads"—Rev. 13:1]: for it is the number of a man; and his number *is* Six hundred threescore *and* six [or 666].—Rev. 13:18

[See Appendix A for a full explanation of this number.]

---

[334] Also frequently exegeted from Rev. 6:9-11. In Luke 21:12-16 this Second Martyrdom Episode was foretold by Jesus!

Bibliography

BIBLES

Concordant Literal New Testament, © copyright 1976; Second Printing 1978 by the Concordant Publishing Concern, 15570 West Knochaven Road, Canyon Country, CA 91351, U.S.A.

Holy Bible, The, Old and New Testaments in the King James Version; Regency Publishing House; copyright © 1976 by Thomas Nelson, Inc., Nashville, Tennessee

New American Standard Bible, The; copyright © 1960, 1962, 1963, 1968, 1971, 1972, 1973, 1975, 1977 by The Lockman Foundation, Holman Bible Publishers, Nashville, TN 37234, U.S.A.

New World Translation of the Holy Scriptures, by the New World Bible Translation Committee; revised 1971 C.E.; copyright © 1961 by Watch Tower Bible & Tract Society of Pennsylvania

The Book for Teens, special ed. for the *New Living Translation*, copyright © 1996 by Tyndale Charitable Trust; Tyndale House Publishers, Inc., Wheaton, Illinois 60189

The Message//Remix: The Bible in Contemporary Language; copyright © 2003 by Eugene H. Peterson; published by Alive Communications, Inc., 7680 Goddard St., Suite 200, Colorado Springs, CO

The NIV Study Bible, Gen. Ed. Kenneth Barker; copyright © 1995 by The Zondervan Corporation Zondervan Publishing House, Grand Rapids, Mi 49530, USA

BIBLE COMMENTARIES

Clarke's Commentary, by Adam Clarke, LL.D., F.S.A. &c. copyright © ca. 1955-1960 by Abingdon Press, New York and Nashville

Expositor's Bible Commentary, The: with the NIV translation of the Holy Bible, vol. 12, by Alan F. Johnson, Th.M., Th.D.; Gen. Ed. Frank E. Gaebelein; copyright © 1981 by The Zondervan Corporation, Grand Rapids, Michigan

Revelation, the Final Analysis, by William H. Hogue, BA, MAT; non-published, copyright© 2001 by William H. Hogue, Jeffersonville, IN

Word Biblical Commentary by David E. Aune; Gen. Editors David A Hubbard and Glenn W. Barker; Publisher, Word Books, Dallas, TX; copyright © 1997 by Word, Incorporated

BIBLE DICTIONARIES

Halley's Bible Handbook, An Abbreviated Bible Commentary, Twenty-Third Edition, copyright © 1959 by Henry H. Halley; Zondervan Publishing House, Grand Rapids, Michigan 49506;

Harper's Bible Dictionary, Gen. Ed. Paul J. Achtemeier; copyright © 1985 by The Society of Biblical Literature; Harper & Row, Publishers, San Francisco. CA

Holman Illustrated Bible Dictionary, copyright © 2003 by Holman Bible Publishers; Gen. Ed. Trent C. Butler; Holman Reference, Nashville, Tennessee

Unger's Bible Dictionary, by Merrill F. Unger; Moody Press; copyright © 1957 by The Moody Bible Institute of Chicago

ENCYCLOPEDIAS

New Encyclopaedia Britannica, The, 15th Edition, © 1990, Chicago

Funk & Wagnalls New Encyclopedia, ©1972; Funk & Wagnalls, Inc., New York

World Book Encyclopedia, © 1979 U.S.A.; World Book-Childcraft International, Inc., a subsidiary of The Scott & Fetzer Company, Chicago

GREEK AND HEBREW HELPS

Analytical Greek Lexicon, The; copyright © by Zondervan; 1st printing 1967, 2nd printing 1967, 3rd printing 1968; Zondervan Publishing House, Grand Rapids, MI

Interlinear Bible, Hebrew-Greek-English, With Strong's Concordance Numbers Above Each Word, The; Second Edition copyright © 1986 by Jay P. Green, Sr.; Gen. Ed. & Translator; Hendrickson Publishers, Peabody, Massachusetts 01961-3473

Interlinear Literal Translation of the Greek New Testament, The; copyright © 1956 by George Ricker Berry, Ph.D.; Zondervan Publishing House, Grand Rapids 2, MI;

Kingdom Interlinear Translation of the Greek Scriptures, The; copyright © 1985 by Watch Tower Bible and Tract Society of Pennsylvania and International Bible Students Association; Publishers: Watchtower Bible and Tract Society, Brooklyn, New York, U.S.A.

Biblical Hebrew Step-by-Step, Second Edition, copyright © 1957, 1978, 1980 by Menahem Mansoor; Baker Book House, Grand Rapids, Michigan

Let's Study Greek, Revised Edition by Clarence B. Hale; copyright © 1959 by The Moody Bible Institute of Chicago

New Englishman's Greek Concordance and Lexicon, copyright ©1982 by Jay P. Green, Sr.; Hendrickson Publishers, Peabody, Massachusetts 01961-3473

New Strong's Exhaustive Concordance of the Bible, with Main Concordance, Appendix to the Main Concordance, Topical Index to the Bible, Dictionary of the Hebrew Bible, and Dictionary of the Greek Testament, The; copyright by James Strong, LL.D., S.T.D.; © 1990 by Thomas Nelson Publishers, Nashville, London, Vancouver

Vine's Expository Dictionary of Old and New Testament Word, by W. E. Vine; copyright © 1981 by Fleming H. Revell Company, World Bible Publishers, Iowa Falls, Iowa

HISTORIES

History of Rome, by Michael Grant; Charles Scribner's Sons, New York; copyright © 1978 by Michael Grant

Keepers of the Keys, by Nicolas Cheetham; Copyright © 1982 by Sir Nicolas Cheetham; pub. Charles Scribner's Sons, 1983

Life and Works of Flavius Josephus, The, translated by William Whiston, A.M.; copyright © 1957; the John C. Winston Company, Philadelphia, Toronto

Nero, the End of a Dynasty by Miriam T. Griffin; copyright © 1984 by Miriam T. Griffin, Yale University Press, New Haven and London;

The Twelve Caesars, An Illustrated Edition, by Gaius Suetonius Tranquillus; copyright © 1984; Penguin Books Inc., 40 West 23rd Street, New York, New York 10010, U.S.A.; Translation copyright © Robert Graves, 1957; Introduction, editorial matter and revisions to the translation, copyright © 1979 by Michael Grant

Twelve Caesars, The by Michael Grant; Charles Scribner's Sons, New York; copyright © 1975 by Michael Grant Publications Ltd.

INTERNET

http://chemistry.about.com/cs/howthingswork/f/blbodyelements.htm (See *The Second Coming of Jesus—Think Again, FN#101, pp. 101-102.*)

http://en.wikipedia.org/ The_Root_of_All_Evil%3F—p. 7 of 9, 2/5/2009 (See *The Second Coming of Jesus—Think Again, FN#133, p. 152.*)

MISCELLANEOUS

The Real White Pages, Greater Louisville telephone directory); © AT&T *Advertising Solutions, 2010, pp. 282, 285, & 291*

NON-FICTION

Ante-Nicene Fathers, The, vol. I, by editors the Rev. Alexander Roberts, D.D. and James Donaldson, LL.D; copyright © 1987 by American Reprint of the Edinburgh Edition, revised and Chronologically arranged, with brief prefaces and Occasional notes, by A. Cleveland Coxe, D.D. (Wm. B. Eerdmans Publishing Company, Grand Rapids, Michigan)

Why I Am Not a Christian and Other Essays on Religion and Related Subjects, by Bertrand Russell; edited by Paul Edwards; copyright © 1957 by George Allen & Unwin Ltd., A Touchstone Book, published by Simon and Schuster, Inc., Simon and Schuster Building, Rockefeller Center, 1230 Avenue of the Americas, New York, New York 10020

Worlds, Part One of Revelation—an Interpretation for 2001 & Beyond, by William H. Hogue, BA, MAT; self-published, copyright © 2002 by William H. Hogue, Jeffersonville, IN

NOTES

About the Author

As an avid student of the Bible since age 13, and with God's leave and grace, William H. Hogue has interpreted the Second Coming of Jesus, the Rapture of the Church—and many other important, life-changing New Testament doctrines—in a whole new light. That is, they are in agreement with Jesus' and His apostles' teaching that they were primarily meant for their own time and generation. William, his wife, his four children, and eight grandchildren live in and around metropolitan Louisville, Kentucky. From his alma mater the University of Louisville William has bachelor degrees in English and Humanities (1964), and a master's degree in the Art of Teaching (MAT, 1971).